Investigating Ramps and Pathways With Young Children (Ages 3–8)

Investigating Ramps and Pathways With Young Children (Ages 3–8)

EDITED BY

Beth Dykstra Van Meeteren
With Allison J. Barness, Shelly L. Counsell,
Mary Donegan-Ritter, Lawrence Escalada,
Linda May Fitzgerald, Sherri Peterson,
Brandy Smith, Jill Uhlenberg,
and Sarah Vander Zanden

STEM for Our Youngest Learners Series

TEACHERS COLLEGE PRESS

TEACHERS COLLEGE | COLUMBIA UNIVERSITY
NEW YORK AND LONDON

Published by Teachers College Press,® 1234 Amsterdam Avenue, New York, NY 10027

Copyright © 2023 by Teachers College, Columbia University

Front cover photo by Sean O'Neal.
Graphics by Hannah Van Meeteren

Library of Congress Cataloging-in-Publication Data is available at loc.gov

ISBN 978-0-8077-6764-1 (paper)
ISBN 978-0-8077-6765-8 (hardcover)
ISBN 978-0-8077-8137-1 (ebook)

Printed on acid-free paper
Manufactured in the United States of America

To the creative and innovative children, staff, and faculty at the Freeburg Early Childhood Program, and especially to Dr. Rheta DeVries, who guided us all with her question: "What is there in this experience for children to figure out?"

Contents

List of Figures

Acknowledgments

Many educators, families, and children across the state of Iowa have contributed to the writing of this book. We thank the children of the Freeburg Early Childhood Program from 2001 through 2007, who taught us the capabilities of young children in STEM (science, technology, engineering, and math) thinking and learning, and Sharon Doolittle for starting the ball rolling in our research in Ramps and Pathways. We thank the teachers at Freeburg for sharing their ideas and thinking in this book.

We thank the Iowa Governor's STEM Advisory Council and their STEM Hub managers for connecting us with Iowa educators by investing in our state's youth at a critical time of their learning: early childhood. Their STEM Scale-Up Program funded research-based professional learning in Ramps and Pathways, along with a classroom kit for over 400 Iowa educators. You will find many of their stories and photos in this book. We thank Hannah Van Meeteren for preparing the graphics to illustrate our ideas.

We are grateful to Peggy Ashbrook for the use of her photos and for sharing her experiences with Ramps and Pathways with young children.

We thank Brandy Twedt and her kindergartners for sharing their experiences with integrative STEM and literacy through Ramps and Pathways. A special thank you goes to Dr. Lisa Chizek and the innovative administration and early childhood educators at North Tama County Community School District in Iowa. The results of their honesty and creative thinking when piloting and improving Ramps and Pathways experiences and materials for us are playing out in early childhood classrooms throughout Iowa and, with the publishing of this book, beyond.

We also thank our partnerships with the University of Northern Iowa's (UNI) Child Development Center and faculty within the College of Education at UNI, with the Campus Advisory Board, and with the State Advisory Board of the Iowa Regents' Center for Early Developmental Education (IRCEDE). We are grateful to Dr. Lawrence Escalada for sharing his expertise in physics; to Marcy M. Seavey, the University of Northern Iowa's STEM coordinator, for her leadership; to Yin Yee, whose work kept us organized; and to Dr. Lisa Riedle, department head of Applied Engineering and Technical Management, whose students and faculty manufacture our educational products to make them available for educators to purchase.

Finally, we thank the inspiration behind over 30 years of innovative early childhood education: the first director of the IRCEDE, Dr. Judith Finkelstein, and subsequent directors Dr. Anne Federlein, the late Dr. Rheta DeVries, and Dr. Betty Zan. This work would not exist without their foundational contributions and wisdom.

Introduction

Welcome to the joyful learning and teaching that occur within integrative STEM (science, technology, engineering, and math) and literacy experiences! If you are familiar with other books in this series, you may notice that this table of contents is similar to those of the other books in the series, with some exceptions in *Investigating STEM With Infants and Toddlers (Birth–3)*, the first title in our series. This is by design, as we wanted educators to be able to pick any title in this series as a starting point for thinking about how to integrate STEM and literacy in the early childhood classroom. However, within each title in the series, we weave in examples and information specific to the STEM experience featured in that book. We have also updated research and information as we have written every book.

As we write these books, we try to demonstrate for the reader ways to immerse children in the act of inquiry using the Inquiry Teaching Model as a guide. Inviting learners to choose an inquiry according to what most interests or intrigues them is one of those ways. Therefore, you can pick the area of focus that most appeals to you and start with that book. You do not have to proceed through the book series in a linear way, nor do you have to read each chapter within a book in order, because we find that linear lesson plans tend to constrain learning. Scientists, technicians, and engineers will tell you that they go back and forth more often than they go straight ahead down one path of inquiry. We hope that our book series will allow you to do that, too.

CHAPTER 1

STEM on Their Own Terms

Grown-up engineering, which is as old as civilization, maintains the youth, vigor and imagination of a child. This is why, when presented to children on their own terms, the excitement of engineering is immediately apparent and fully comprehendible.

—Henry Petroski, 2003

WHO WE ARE

We are former and current preschool through Grade 2 (PK–2) educators who remain dedicated to supporting others in the field through expanding ideas about children, their needs, their development, their interests, and their thinking about the world. We are continually trying out new materials with young children because we believe that early learning in STEM matters (Spaepen et al., 2017). We have taught other adults about what we have learned from children in higher education settings, professional learning trainings, conference presentations, classroom coaching or mentoring, and writing. Because we have been where you are in the classroom, we designed this book to offer new insights about your work. Some of the ideas you read here may be familiar to you, and some may be new. We view learning as a process. We support your learning, but we also expect to learn ourselves in the writing of this book.

WHO WE HOPE YOU ARE

If you are working with young children ages 3–8, we hope you will find this book helpful. As preschool and primary-grade teachers, librarians, STEM instructional coaches, and administrators, your teacher education programs may have heavily focused on either child development (early childhood) or science content (elementary education, middle school, or high school science education). Credentialed in education or not, as an early childhood professional you may fall along a broad continuum of training or preparation, from high school through college or mainly from experience. *Investigating Ramps and Pathways With Young Children* seeks to assist you in taking a developmental approach to STEM learning and teaching. We understand the importance of accepting and valuing young children's approximations of science and engineering practices with the goal of better understanding conventional science and engineering practices in later years. Our intention in this book is to support you and to honor your important work as an educator of young children.

WHO WE ARE WRITING ABOUT

We are passionate about the full range of diversity among young learners, preschool through 2nd grade, including children with disabilities. Over time, we have become passionate about STEM as well, and we have noticed the lack of daily STEM experiences for young children. Just as we have watched these children become readers through daily immersions in literacy experiences, we have watched them become creative problem-solvers in classrooms where they are able to encounter daily immersions in STEM experiences. Children flourish in classrooms that offer both of these experiences every day. They thrive when these experiences are intentionally designed from the perspective of children's development and interest in phenomena, and how children come to understand science content through the practices of science and engineering. Instead of relying on short, preplanned, and packaged STEM lessons or activities to teach children about STEM, we encourage educators to give power to the children to experience STEM on their own terms, using phenomena with which they are already engaged, but which adults often overlook or may even dismiss as "mere play." Our approach is compatible with the universal design for learning (UDL) framework, developed by the Council for Exceptional Children (CEC) and the Center for Applied Special Technology (CAST), a nonprofit education research center that also encourages flexible, individualized learning. Empowering all children as science learners recognizes their uniqueness and, in so doing, increases educators' awareness needed to minimize barriers in order to maximize everyone's learning. Henceforth, all reference to young children and learners entails the full range of diversity among children.

In this chapter we work to pull back the curtain to reveal STEM in the young learners' world, where it is exciting and meaningful to them. We will attend to two critical behaviors in early STEM: inquiry and engineering. Finally, we will describe four elements of the early childhood classroom environment: (1) the physical environment, (2) the intellectual environment, (3) the social–emotional environment, and (4) the promotional environment. Attention given to these elements is essential not only for STEM learning, but for all learning.

When we closely observe young children at play, we can notice how engaged they are in the movement of objects. Jamell's vignette (see Textbox 1.1) describes a young learner who reveals his interest in the phenomena of force and motion through his actions on the playground structure's slide during recess.

TEXTBOX 1.1. STEM ON JAMELL'S TERMS

As children rushed to the playground structure for morning recess with their teacher, Jamell had his sights set on one particular feature that he enjoys, the slide. Jamell climbed to the top and prepared for a quick ride down. He was somewhat surprised and disappointed at how he slid. Yesterday, he had gone much faster. Climbing back to the top, he tried again with the same results. Noticing some wood chips in the mulch, he scooped up a handful and decided to send them down one at a time. He observed the first chip slide and then began to twist, tumble, and slide the rest of the way down. Jamell let another chunk go and observed the same motion. He decided to let a handful go all at once and watched as some chips slid faster than others. Jamell took another ride down the slide and found that he was sliding faster than he did before. Jamell's observant teacher watched as he picked up more handfuls of mulch and climbed back up. Jamell released a whole handful and watched them mostly slide all the way to the bottom. He took another fast ride down the slide and gleefully picked up another handful of mulch to repeat the process over and over until he heard the whistle to go back in. On his way up to the door, with excitement he told his teacher, "I know how to make myself go fast on the slide!" "I noticed that! Tell me more!" replied his teacher. Jamell went on to tell her that when he released the wood mulch on the slide first, he slid down faster. "So you noticed that when the wood chips went down faster, you went down faster." Jamell nodded and said, "You have to send the wood chips down first." Jamell's declaration to his teacher revealed his interest in a phenomenon that is familiar to many children on the playground: the feeling of physically moving down the slide or ramp and observing how other objects move down a ramp. His actions demonstrated a trial-and-error form of exploration. Jamell's observant teacher had an opportunity to follow Jamell's and other children's interest in force and motion and began to ponder how to bring this interest into the classroom to investigate it more closely. Jamell's teacher had the gift of noticing and identifying her children's interest in the world and how it works, and in this case, curiosity about how objects move on a ramp.

In the late 1990s, Dr. Rheta DeVries, eminent early childhood researcher and a director of the Iowa Regents' Center for Early Developmental Education (IRCEDE), established the Teacher Practitioner Council for early childhood educators across the state of Iowa. These teachers self-selected to be part of the council and had the support of their administrators to implement innovative practices in their preschool, kindergarten, 1st-grade, and 2nd-grade classrooms. Several times a year, the teachers traveled to the IRCEDE on the campus of the University of Northern Iowa to participate in book discussions; to learn how to create a classroom environment that fosters children's intellectual, social–emotional, and personality development; and to explore physical knowledge experiences for children that allowed them to construct an understanding of the world and how it works (DeVries & Zan, 2012). Kamii and DeVries (1993) defined physical knowledge activities as experiences that enable children to act on objects and observe the object's movement or change. One of the book's chapters focused on inclines and provided examples of teachers and children placing objects on wide boards positioned to be inclines and observing how a variety of objects moved down the incline. However, children quickly lost interest in the experience. Kamii and DeVries shared a teacher's concern that "the activity was too artificial, too much like a test, and too divorced from natural play" (1993, p. 131). The idea of using a troughed incline was introduced as a way to sustain children's interest.

At one gathering of the Teacher Practitioner Council, preschool teacher Sharon Doolittle shared how she had placed rain gutters, a version of a troughed incline, on the children's playground near a structure surrounded by pea gravel. Sharon observed how the children leaned a gutter against the structure, repeatedly released scoopfuls of pea gravel at the top of the gutter, and watched it trickle down. Sharon had the brilliant idea of bringing her children's interest into the classroom by adding wooden track (made of lengths of cove molding purchased at a local home improvement store) and marbles to her set of unit blocks. She watched with excitement as the children began creating ramps to move the marbles.

Rheta and her team of researchers—Drs. Christina Sales, Linda Fitzgerald, Betty Zan, Carolyn Hildebrandt, and Rebecca Edmiaston—purchased enough track to allow the teachers to engage in what we call *teacher play*. In teacher play, teachers explore and work with open-ended materials to consider experiences they may offer to children.

Rheta stressed that to be worthy of children's time, an experience must meet four criteria:

1. *Producible:* A child is able to independently produce an action to make something happen.
2. *Immediate:* The result of a child's action is immediate.
3. *Observable:* The result of the child's action can be observed by the child.
4. *Variable:* There is something for the child to vary to determine whether the variation changes the result.

Teacher play revealed these experiences in force and motion met all four criteria.

1. A child could independently **produce** an action to set a marble in motion.
2. The result of a child's action to get the marble to move was **immediate.**
3. The result of the moving marble was visibly and audibly **observable** by the child.
4. The child could **vary** the steepness of the ramp to get different results, or the child could **vary** the object to move on the ramp.

Once the teachers agreed that all four criteria were met, they brainstormed relationships the children could construct in this experience. Examples of relationships discussed included the following:

- The shape of an object affects how it moves or doesn't move on a ramp.
- The shape of an object affects how it moves once it leaves the end of a ramp.
- The material an object is made of affects how it sounds as it moves on a ramp.
- The steeper the ramp, the farther the marble rolls.
- The steeper the ramp, the faster the marble rolls.
- The lower the ramp, the slower the marble rolls.

The teachers took track back to their classrooms to introduce to their children the experience of what was to become known as Ramps and Pathways. The children eagerly embraced the materials and went to work (see Textbox 1.2). Before long, engineering the simple design of a linear track was not challenging enough for many of the children, so they increased their own design challenges. Over time, they began to design systems that enabled a marble to turn a corner, or drop down onto a lower track to continue on its path. Noticing a fast-moving marble sometimes overcomes a gap between two tracks, their systems began to feature jumps. They began building systems with hills and valleys, and features that reversed the direction of the marble. All of these design challenges and more are conceived by curious and creative young children engaged in Ramps and Pathways play all over the world. The IRCEDE's work with Ramps and Pathways has been requested by educators and enjoyed by children in Korea, Mexico, Brazil, Thailand, Russia, China, Colombia, and Japan.

TEXTBOX 1.2. TRACK, UNIT BLOCKS, AND A MARBLE

Charlie picked up a small container of colorful marbles and carried them to the block center. As he walked, he could hear the marbles rattle and feel the weight of the container shifting as the marbles rolled from one side of the container to the other. Kneeling on the carpet by the unit block shelf and wooden track, he selected a 2-foot track and placed it in front of him. Peering into the container of marbles, he reached in and picked up each marble one at a time and placed them on the track. He noticed that the marbles were spread out on the track, but in a row. Charlie used a finger to push the blue marble on one end of the track closer to the red marble next in line. The blue marble clicked as it struck the red. Charlie observed how the collision of the two marbles resulted in the red marble rolling on to strike the next marble, which struck the next marble, which struck the next marble, and so on. Charlie picked up the track with the marbles on it, placing a hand on each end to keep the marbles from rolling off. He raised the right end of the track and created an incline, resulting in all the marbles rolling to the left end. He raised the left end and observed the marbles rolling back to the right. Charlie spent the next few minutes alternating the heights of each end and observing how the marbles rolled each time to the lower end. He could make the marbles roll slowly by lifting one end just a little, and roll quickly by lifting one end higher.

Tanajah and Will joined Charlie in the center. Charlie said excitedly, "Look at what I can do!" and described what was happening as he demonstrated what he was doing. "I can make all of them roll really fast, and I can make all of them roll real slow. I like how they keep knocking into each other." Tanajah and Will each picked up a track and joined his exploration. Charlie had satisfied his curiosity about how marbles move as he changed the position of his hands and turned his attention to how he could use blocks to position the track into a ramp. Charlie stacked two blocks and leaned a track against them. He released the marbles one by one on the top of the ramp and observed how they slowed down as they rolled onto the carpeted floor and came to a stop. Charlie decided to place another track at the bottom of his ramp to make a pathway that would not slow the speed of the marbles. Tanajah and Will became interested in what Charlie was making happen and asked if he needed more track added to make a longer pathway. Together, they built a system in one line with enough track to make a marble roll across the classroom. With each addition of track, they found they needed to reexamine the previous connections to ensure they aligned to allow the marble to roll from one track to the next.

Charlie and his peers were engaged in the phenomenon of force and motion using Ramps and Pathways materials. They were curious to learn what they could make happen with unit blocks, track, and marbles, and they posed their own problems to solve. They were enjoying STEM on their own terms. They were engaged in inquiry.

INQUIRY

An Internet search for the term *inquiry* yields a remarkable 135 million hits. The online Merriam-Webster dictionary definition reads:

1. A request for information;
2. A systematic investigation often of a matter of public interest;
3. An examination of facts or principles: Research. (Merriam-Webster, n.d.)

Even as adults we continue the process of learning new ideas or connections every day. We do this through the development of preconceptions, or early understandings of a concept or a relationship. Through experience, we modify those preconceptions to a new level, sometimes repeating the modification process over time, and sometimes reaching a full and accurate understanding of that concept. This does not always occur, however, even in adulthood.

When we engaged in teacher play with Ramps and Pathways materials, we began to describe what we were noticing using words we had learned in our own schooling in science. When we observed large, heavy marbles roll farther, we said they had more momentum. When Lawrence Escalada, a professor of physics at the University of Northern Iowa, agreed to work with us and questioned us on what we meant by momentum, we soon found our understanding of the concept of momentum was incomplete. Larry explained that momentum is defined as the mass of an object multiplied by its velocity. Velocity. There was a word we hadn't used in a long time. To keep it simple, Larry suggested we not use the word *velocity* (as direction was not important at this time) but instead use the word *speed*. So, momentum equals mass of an object multiplied by its speed. Then we found we had a misconception about mass.

We had believed that mass and weight were the same thing, but this is not accurate. A marble's mass can be defined as the amount of matter (or stuff) it has. The amount of stuff (matter) a marble has in it is the same regardless where it is in the entire universe. If we took the marble to the Moon, it would still have the same amount of stuff (matter) in it. But its weight would not be the same. The marble's weight can be defined as a force (or push or pull) acting on it due to the celestial body (e.g., Earth or Moon) it is on. This force is gravity (another word we use, but as adults, we still have challenges explaining it). The marble's weight is different on the Moon from its weight on Earth because a different celestial body is pulling on it. The mass of an object can also be considered the amount of resistance it has in changing its motion. This resistance is called inertia. For example, the more mass (matter or stuff) that a marble has, the harder it is to get it to move or to get it to stop.

So what does this all mean? It means that just like our young learners, our own conceptual understanding of phenomena is still evolving as adults. It means that using words that sound "sciency" doesn't translate to conceptual understanding. In general terms, we can consider momentum as how much stuff (or matter) is moving and how fast it is moving. Thus, a heavy marble (that has more stuff to make it heavy) that is moving at the same speed as a lighter marble (that has less stuff) has more momentum than the lighter marble. This also means that when a child explains, "The heavy marbles are harder to stop," this verbal explanation is enough. When a child explains, "The lighter marbles are easier to stop," this verbal explanation is enough. When a child explains, "The marble needs more speed to make it up the next ramp," this verbal explanation is enough. We do not and should not ask children to use words in their explanations such as *momentum*, *inertia*, *gravity*, and *velocity*, even though they are terms relevant to experiences within Ramps and Pathways. Children who have been taught these words and use them without being able to explain what they mean are not developing more intelligence than children who can explain what they are observing in their own words. We believe the opposite is true. *Momentum, inertia, gravity, velocity,* and even *acceleration* are formal science words used to describe complex phenomena for which many of us as adults are still working to construct an understanding. They are not appropriate for children at this age. We do not want to coach children to recite such words when given a prompt; we want them to construct an understanding of phenomena and explain their ideas about what they observe using words that are familiar to them.

Psychologist Jean Piaget studied young children to understand how they learned about the world around them. His work was a foundation for much of what we know today about education. Piaget (1971) characterized the process of learning as constructing knowledge because he believed that humans control that process internally. He described three kinds of knowledge that exist. The first kind of knowledge he termed *physical knowledge*, which is the set of properties of objects that we experience through our senses—their texture, size, shape, and so on. The second kind of knowledge Piaget described is *logical–mathematical knowledge*, which is based on the relationships that exist between two or more objects (or people). Dr. Rheta DeVries, a student of Piaget, used to describe these two kinds of knowledge as two sides of the same coin because they are closely related. Once we have physical knowledge about something, we can begin to explore the relationships of those characteristics by flipping back and forth between our physical knowledge and logical–mathematical knowledge constructions. Piaget's third kind of knowledge is *cultural* or *social knowledge*, such as the name we give an object. This knowledge is passed from one person to another. Calling marbles, baseballs, and basketballs *spheres* is cultural knowledge, with different words used in other languages. This kind of knowledge is passed from person to person rather than being constructed internally. We give children the names of things, providing the cultural knowledge, so that we can communicate with each other about those objects.

As an example of the relationship between physical knowledge and logical-mathematical knowledge, we can examine what we know about a marble, what it is and what it does. We use our senses to construct the physical knowledge of a marble: smooth, round, made of glass, three-dimensional. Our logical–mathematical knowledge allows us to see what happens when we put the marble on an incline. If the ramp is steep, the marble will roll a long distance once it leaves the bottom end of the ramp. If the incline is lowered, it will roll a shorter distance. Piaget told us that these preconceptions or constructions about the properties of an object and how it moves are the result of experience. The more experiences we have with the materials, the more we understand the relationships and the more accurate our conceptions become as we make sense of the world of force and motion.

Of course, other people can tell us the information, but young children tend to hear this information skeptically. They want and need experience to construct that knowledge, that is, to believe it. Even adults will not always believe information provided by someone else. For example, a "wet paint" sign may not prevent us touching a newly painted object. For very young children, the whole world is subject to engagement and exploration so they can construct these two kinds of knowledge. The more physical knowledge we construct, the more

relationships we can uncover or develop and understand. This is inquiry.

Many people work through an inquiry approach. Doctors have a base of knowledge. When they discover a problem or symptom with a patient, they gather information and make a diagnosis. If that symptom is unusual or outside their knowledge base, they perform tests and gather data to solve the problem. That's inquiry. Educators work through inquiry, many without realizing it. We observe children and identify problems with their learning; try strategies, gathering data as we go; and work to solve the learning problem. Again, that's inquiry.

The question is, What does inquiry look like in young children?

What We Mean by Inquiry Learning and Teaching

Warden (2021) noted four approaches to inquiry learning and teaching. She described them as follows:

1. *Free inquiry:* Children are empowered to select the inquiry and the adult supports the process.
2. *Guided inquiry:* Adults select the inquiry and children explore in their own ways.
3. *Controlled inquiry:* Adults choose the inquiry and provide the resources to solve the problems.
4. *Structured inquiry:* Children follow the lead of the adult as they all do the same inquiry. (p. 4)

Our approach favors the first and the second types. That is, we strongly believe that children should be the first line in deciding what to explore. Whenever possible, materials should be chosen based on children's interests that educators have observed.

Educators should be aware that guided inquiry, with adults selecting the topic to be explored, may result in children choosing not to engage with the materials presented to them. Educators who know their children well will notice when materials spark curiosity and they will pursue those interests with the children. Educators will also notice when children lose interest quickly and seek other activities. This is a sign that adults have not selected materials that engage the children, or that the children may have been pressured to follow the adult's lead.

When adults select both the materials and the problems to be solved, as in controlled or structured inquiry, older children who have developed the ability to resist impulses often will comply to please the adults. Children who are struggling to develop inhibitory control and cannot yet resist impulses reveal their disinterest by turning their attention to something else they find interesting, or by acting out. Some adults may read this as a short attention span and/or misbehavior. However, we have found that it is less of a problem of attention spans and misbehavior and more of an indication that the materials and problems were not meaningful or interesting to children.

Some educators suggest that inquiry is a cycle, or that learning can be described as a trajectory where all children engage in activities in the same set of steps or even in the same sequence. Free inquiry describes a set of actions or strategies that engage children in learning based on their interests. This means that among different children, actions or materials used may look similar. This can happen. More likely, actions and explorations will vary from one child to the next because they are interested in different things. For inquiry to be successful, adults must accept this seemingly messy approach while children are learning.

Inquiry Teaching Model

Many of those 135 million Internet hits about inquiry are focused on the system for educators to manage inquiry in their classrooms or educational settings. In other words, the models describe how to teach through an inquiry approach. Most of these models are geared toward learners substantially older than 8 years of age. Instead, we use the Inquiry Teaching Model (ITM) developed by the staff of the Iowa Regents' Center for Early Developmental Education (IRCEDE) at the University of Northern Iowa and described in the book *STEM Learning With Young Children* (Counsell et al., 2016), which is based on our experiences with early childhood educators of children from preschool through 2nd grade (PK–2).

The ITM is nonlinear. That is, the process varies depending on the child, the educator, and the

materials they are exploring, as indicated by the arrows in Figure 1.1.

The ITM describes what the educators do. While older children and adults learning through inquiry can manage their actions and seek out materials on their own, young learners are just getting started on managing their actions and are responsive to open-ended materials available to them. The most basic role of the educator is to provide interesting materials. Dr. Rheta DeVries was noted for her approach: "What is there in this activity for children to figure out? If there isn't much to figure out, then it may not be worthy of children's time" (DeVries, personal communication, 2001). Young learners deserve interesting and thought-provoking materials. Without those materials, managing behaviors becomes difficult, frustrating both children and educators.

Dr. Judith Finkelstein, founder of the Iowa Regents' Center for Early Developmental Education, also remarked about the need for high-quality experiences for young children. Her mantra addressed the relationship between curriculum and guidance or discipline in the early childhood classroom: "The best guidance is a good curriculum" (Finkelstein, personal communication, 1989). When children are engaged with interesting materials offered for

Figure 1.1. Inquiry Teaching Model

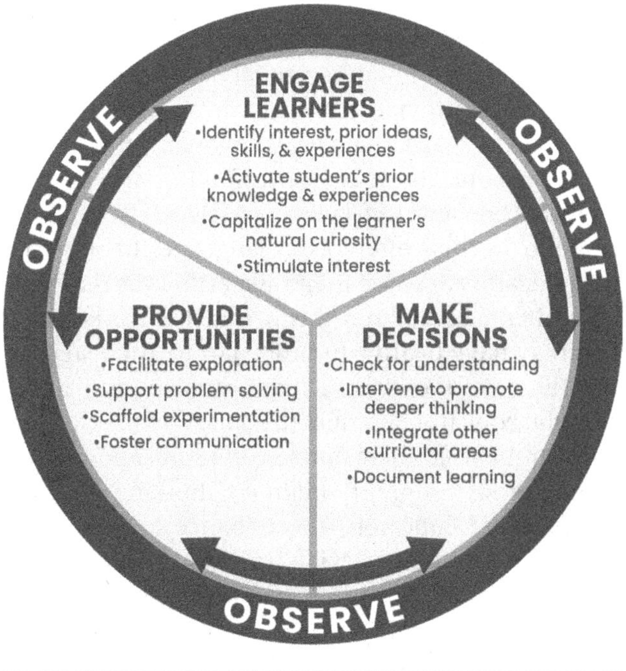

Adapted from Counsell et al. (2016).

extended time periods, the need for educator intervention to manage behavior is reduced.

We provide a description of the components of the ITM here. We also include examples of educators' actions and comments throughout this book in order to support your understanding of how this model works. We even suggest that adults who spend time "messing about" with materials (Hawkins, 1965), as did the teachers in the Teacher Practitioner Council, are actually engaging in the same processes that young children do as they explore materials.

Observe. The role of observation is vitally important in inquiry. Observations lead and support the other parts of the process. In addition, observations are vital in all forms of assessment, as well as in reporting learning to parents, administrators, or others.

Engage Learners. Educators can provide materials that invite exploration and encourage learning. When teachers place materials within children's view in an appealing manner, the children will explore them. Educator observation will support understanding the limits of engagement, so educators can provide new materials or ask questions that stimulate additional explorations. Observations can direct us to understanding what questions young children may have.

Provide Opportunities. Providing materials and observing the children's actions allow educators opportunities to build vocabulary. The same observations will provide information about children's struggles to reach their goals, allowing the educator to expand on ideas and scaffold or support explorations. Using self-talk or parallel talk supports children in their attempts at language. In self-talk, the educators describe their own actions as they perform them. Sometimes this is called a think-aloud. You may have heard educators narrate their steps to identify a word or solve a math problem. In parallel talk, the educator describes the child's actions as they happen. Beyond their simple communication, these strategies also support children's thinking and understanding. Educators also enhance opportunities to learn when they provide comments or ask open-ended questions to support children's explorations.

Make Decisions. Children's engagement or lack of it, noted through observation, supports the educator in deciding whether to add or delete materials, whether to suggest observing another child's approach, or whether to simply watch without interfering. When a child becomes frustrated, the educator must decide how much to intercede. We hold specific beliefs about allowing children to problem-solve on their own without telling them what to do. There are strategies, however, that can support the children in their own problem solving rather than just telling them the answers to their questions.

Teaching through inquiry means teaching all children with intention. As you read through the ITM, you can see within each section where educators are intentionally working to support children's learning through engaging with curriculum and materials and through decision-making about how to proceed. Their actions support the children's construction of both physical knowledge and logical–mathematical knowledge, and when appropriate, educators provide cultural knowledge through their interactions with the children.

In all the ways previously noted, the ITM exemplifies the kinds of instructional practices utilized within UDL settings and, thereby, promotes the full range of learners' access to STEM teaching and learning needed to maximize learning outcomes (Center for Applied Special Technology, 2011). The three UDL principles—(1) multiple means of representation, (2) multiple means of action and expression, and (3) multiple means of engagement—taken together, create flexible paths to learning for children that are also central to the ITM. Guided and informed by an educator's careful observations of children, inclusive educators use multiple means of representation and expression to support learners' engagement, provide opportunities, and make informed decisions. Educators can use visual supports such as photos, drawings, pictures, and diagrams of ramp structures to help stimulate children's interest and activate prior knowledge and experiences; foster communication as they discuss various STEM ideas and concepts with children; and check for children's understanding. Children with language delays or dual language learners can likewise use multiple means of expression using photos and their own drawings. Educators can provide labels for new items, cocreate a graphic organizer, provide encouragement for explorations, and ask questions that guide the children's focus on what happens. The open-ended, three-dimensional materials used during Ramps and Pathways investigations are highly engaging and appealing to all learners. Children's ramp structures provide a visual and tactile representation that they can readily point to and use to demonstrate what they know and have figured out. During investigations, a nonverbal child can be paired with a verbal peer and together they can express their ideas and share their accomplishments (Donegan-Ritter & Fitzgerald, 2017). Altogether, the three UDL principles further enhance and enrich educators' effective implementation of the ITM, which in turn increases access for a wide range of children and encourages participation in STEM investigations within inclusive settings.

This book embraces the integrative nature of STEM and proposes a framework to include STEM learning every day in ways that do not interrupt but enhance learning in literacy, mathematics, science, and social studies. Within this framework, young learners have a daily invitation to engage with force and motion. Children are supported in finding out answers to their questions about objects and movement in their world (science), and they develop agency as an active player within the designed world (engineering and technology) that also demands an understanding of spatial relationships (mathematics). Excited by what they can make happen, children become more invested in learning the tools of literacy and mathematics to collaborate and communicate with their peers and their community (social studies). STEM on their own terms is how integration becomes successful (Krajcik & Czerniak, 2014; Mitchell et al., 2009; Portsmore & Milto, 2018; Tank et al., 2018; Venville et al., 1998).

Investigating Ramps and Pathways With Young Children is not meant to replace your science curriculum, but it will greatly enhance it. It is not filled with recipes for STEM lessons, but instead serves as a guide to assist teachers in creating a learning environment sensitive to their young learners' unique strengths and interests in the context of Ramps and Pathways experiences. It is written for teachers and adults who work to address age- or grade-level standards but also desire to nurture creativity and stimulate the intellectual curiosity of the preschool, kindergarten, 1st-grade, or 2nd-grade children in

their care through a universal design for learning where all children can engage in STEM.

ENGINEERING

The National Research Council (NRC, 2009) challenged K–12 education to shift away from the siloed teaching of science, technology, engineering, and mathematics. Teaching these subjects separately discourages more than encourages child interest in science and mathematics. Instead, the NRC advocated for children to experience STEM in an integrative context by capitalizing on their natural interest in engineering. You can have lessons on science alone, and on mathematics alone, but when you have lessons that involve engineering, you also have science, mathematics, and technology. Engineering is not a stand-alone subject. Engineering is viewed as the glue that holds science, technology, and mathematics together, and thus it serves as an effective driver of STEM learning (Thornburg, 2009).

Early childhood teachers can envision their children engaging in science and mathematics but may question whether they can add engineering to their students' learning. Children need no formal introduction to engineering, as their play often involves engineering. Henry Petroski (2003), renowned civil engineer, called attention to the importance of recognizing and valuing young children's approximations of engineering behavior. He stated that the act of design is ingrained in children's imagination, in their choices, and in their play activities involving objects. They are engaging in engineering as they move sand with dump trucks in the sandbox, build structures out of unit blocks, alter recipes in preparing food snacks, or move objects along ramps and pathways. Brophy and Evangelou (2007) reaffirmed Petroski's ideas about the genesis of engineering in their analysis of children's actions as they engaged in informal unit block play. Nothing fastens unit blocks together, requiring builders to "work with the shapes, weights, texture (friction) and position of the blocks to develop the structural integrity of their creations" (p. 8). In their observations of young children at work, they found that the children continually displayed creative problem solving, sensitivity to others' perspectives, and development of new knowledge as they persevered toward their own goal, all in the act of informal play. Most interesting, Brophy and Evangelou witnessed children's working knowledge of details of physical properties in their world "to invent increasingly complex and interesting designs and designs that satisfy the governing properties of the world" (p. 8). Brophy and Evangelou described children's approximations of engineering behavior as precursors to engineering, or developmental engineering.

When children are engaged in developmental engineering, they grapple with foundational concepts within mathematics, science, and engineering. They do not learn to follow an engineering design process to complete an activity in one lesson; instead, they are immersed in experiences over time and develop engineering habits of mind: systems thinking, creativity, optimism, collaboration, communication, and attention to ethical considerations (Katehi et al., 2009). These habits of mind align beautifully with the 21st Century Skills (Partnership for 21st Century Skills, 2009), which will serve them well in future learning in formal school and ultimately in their future careers. When we learn to recognize developmental engineering in children's play and support it, constructing an understanding of science and mathematics becomes an essential quest for the child.

Types of Problems in Developmental Engineering

In developmental engineering, children operate within three types of problems that differ in frequency: one macro, several meso, and many micro problems (see Figure 1.2) or, in other words, one grand, several medium, and many small problems. Developmental engineering starts with an invitation to take on one grand, open-ended problem such as, How can I make a marble move in an interesting way? Under this grand problem, children think up several of their own design challenges, which may include to make a marble move faster or slower, turn a corner, or reverse direction. As children produce their designs, their progress will be interrupted by many, many problems or failures that are often physical in nature. These frequent problems of physics nudge children into making a change or improvement in their design ideas, and the engineering continues until they are confronted by another round of problems of physics. Perhaps the marble

Figure 1.2. Developmental Engineering's Three Types of Problems

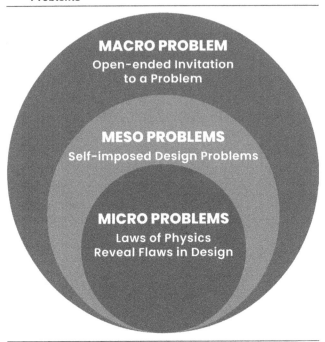

ricochets too wildly off a barrier placed in its path to knock it onto the next track, or the marble does not go fast enough to overcome an incline.

As children grapple with these smaller problems, they may take one of four actions: (1) they may succeed in finding a solution and continue with their design; (2) they may decide portions of their design are possible with very few adjustments; (3) they may decide their design is not physically possible, scrap it, and think up a totally new design; or (4) they may become frustrated and walk away. In all our years of combined experiences with young children, we have rarely seen children walk away when they were able to pose their own challenges.

Children learn a great deal of science through their own design challenges. As young learners grapple with the physics of how the speed of a marble can make it more difficult to change its direction, they deepen their ever-increasing working knowledge of physics in force and motion phenomena. With every intersection of meso design problems and micro physics problems, a child's understanding of science concepts within force and motion deepens and leads to a creative and improved design. Practicing engineers use their understanding of science and math to efficiently design technology. In contrast, children's interest in designing and engineering their own technology leads to deeper understandings of science and mathematics concepts. Children are not learning just *about* engineering; they are engaging *in* engineering thinking and developing engineering habits of mind.

Constraints in Early STEM

A simple definition of engineering is "design under constraint" (Wulf, 1998). In Charlie's vignette at the beginning of this chapter (see Textbox 1.2), Charlie is engaged in engineering on his own terms. He is in the beginning stages of designing a system to produce a specific movement of marbles under three sets of constraints: (1) the constraints of the materials at hand, (2) the constraints of the laws of physics and mathematics, and (3) the constraints of opportunity to engage in design.

Constraints of Materials. The materials for Ramps and Pathways experiences are simple: objects to move, track, and supports to hold track in place. Charlie's teacher has placed containers of same-sized but different-colored marbles to move, and 1-, 2-, and 3-foot lengths of track near the unit blocks that can serve as supports for the track. As Charlie handles the marbles on the track, the physical properties of the marbles beg for his notice: the roundness of the marbles that allows them to roll, the clicking sound resulting from the collision of the glass marbles, and the channel in the middle of the wooden track that keeps the marbles in a row rather than in a mixed group. For young learners, simple materials such as small objects to move, track, and blocks to use as supports are a rich context for investigating properties of materials and engineering their movement.

Constraints of Physics. The physics involving force and motion are far from simple, and are abstract and complex for young learners like Charlie. As referenced earlier in this chapter, educators themselves grapple with concepts and definitions of vocabulary within force and motion, such as momentum, inertia, gravity, velocity, and acceleration. When we engaged in teacher play with physics professor Lawrence Escalada, we found we were using the vocabulary incorrectly. This level of complexity in force and motion is addressed in college physics and

will not be addressed in this book, nor is it required understanding for teachers to engage in STEM learning with young children. Yet Larry emphasized that the foundation for this level of complexity starts with early childhood educators engaging in force and motion experiences with their children and encouraging children to describe what they are noticing in their own words. The physics of force and motion that young learners and their teachers can investigate include the following:

- The shape of an object affects how it moves.
- The direction of an object can be changed if you block its path.
- You can speed up an object's movement by making an incline steeper.
- You can slow down an object's movement by making a gentler slope.
- A heavy object is harder to stop than a lighter one.
- It is harder to change the direction of a heavy marble than that of a lighter marble.

Constraints of Opportunities. The depth of children's understanding of concepts is determined by the amount, variety, and quality of their experiences with ramps and pathways over time. Charlie is fortunate to have the opportunity to explore these properties and laws of physics. Someone has given him access to open-ended materials to investigate force and motion. No one is interrupting the design problem Charlie has posed to himself. No one is demanding that he instead work to solve someone else's design problem. Charlie is allowed time and multiple attempts to pursue his goals of moving a marble in a straight line the length of the classroom by reducing the friction of the pathway. Most importantly, Charlie was not told how to solve the problem, but was allowed to develop his own process to figure it out. Within this process, Charlie's conceptual understanding of how the properties of materials affect how they can be moved within the physical world deepens with every iteration of his problem solving.

As we pointed out above, practicing engineers use their conceptual understanding of science and mathematics to efficiently engineer. Young engineers use their practice of engineering to learn concepts in science and mathematics that, in turn, enhance their efficiency in engineering.

lead by example -Ask ??

PREPARING AN ENVIRONMENT FOR STEM

Children are fascinated with the world, curious about how it works, and born with the habit of mind to continuously investigate it. They raise and explore their own questions through rudimentary experiments without being burdened with adult instructions. And yet, they ask adults even more questions that are important to them. They ask a lot! Harvard professor of child psychology Paul Harris (2012) stated that a child between ages 2 and 5 asks 40,000 questions. At first, children ask for names of objects. By around age 2 and a half, they request explanations in addition to facts. By age 4, the lion's share of requests is for explanations. This quickly changes when the child enters formal schooling in kindergarten. The number of questions a child asks begins to drop drastically. Harris reported that this is cross-cultural and theorized that one of the reasons this may happen is due to the comfort factor: Children are more comfortable asking questions at home. However, child psychologist Alison Gopnik (2012) suggested another reason that is more troubling. Gopnik believed that schools begin teaching too much, too soon. As a result, we cut off children's exploration and stifle their creativity, curiosity, and inquiry habits of mind instead of nurturing them. We need to do better by our future innovators. Children have their own questions about how to effectively move objects. Charlie, Tanajah, and Will worked for a long time to figure out how to connect a smooth pathway that enabled a marble to travel a long distance. Because their teacher chose not to preteach the role of inclines in making things easier to move and how to reduce friction, Charlie, Tanajah, and Will were able to come to a conceptual understanding of how to create an incline that is steep enough to give a marble enough speed to roll a long distance, how the smoothness of the track did not interfere with the speed of the marble as much as the carpet did, and how the connections between each track needed to be aligned to allow the marble to roll from one track to another.

Model Curiosity

Children take cues from their adult educators. Research has shown that when educators actively encourage exploration by asking open-ended questions or pointing out unique features—or by just being attentive and encouraging with a smile, eye contact, and interjections—children show more inquisitiveness. The less curious the educators, the less curious their children (Hackmann & Engel, 2002; Henderson & Moore, 1980). When educators themselves model curiosity and act on it, they have a powerful effect on their children's agency in inquiry (Engel, 2011). When a curious child asks their educator a question, the best response is to model curiosity by responding, "I hadn't thought about that! How could we find that out?"

To the detriment of our nation's ability to lead in innovation, curiosity is considered a luxury rather than an essential component of formal school settings in the United States. Teachers of young children are under immense pressure to follow legislated mandates of curriculum standards and learning objectives and are compelled to ensure that children respond with the appropriate answers to what is measured on standardized tests. As a result, young children spend their school days enacting routines that involve identifying letters and their sounds, reading words correctly at a fast pace, answering questions with one right answer, and memorizing math facts. Under the pressure of standardized testing, teachers use these routines to meet goals for child mastery of skills outside of a purposeful context, rather than developing habits of inquiry (Engel, 2011). Choosing to teach narrow skills over nurturing habits of inquiry happens most often in schools serving children from low-income families. This widens the achievement gap even further (Engel & Randall, 2009) and diminishes intrinsic interest in learning.

When teachers make a decision to support children's inquiry, many are led to believe they can do so only by following a teacher's guide with fidelity. Compliance with a traditional teacher's guide does not bode well for engaging children or for nurturing innovation. In one study (Engel & Randall, 2009), teachers were video-recorded helping 9-year-old children complete a science activity. All the teachers were shown the materials and the activity, and were given a sheet that included instructions with a series of questions. Half of the teachers were told by the researcher, "Please help this student learn more about science." Then, as the researcher left the teacher with the student she added, "Have fun learning about science!" The other half of the teachers were told by the researcher, "Please help this student fill out the worksheet." Then, as the researcher left the teacher with the student she added, "Have fun doing the worksheet!" Everything else was identical. There was a significant difference in the teachers' pedagogy between the two groups. The teachers who had been encouraged to help the student "learn about science" were responsive to the child's actions, even when the child strayed from the task to do something different with the materials. These teachers would encourage the child's innovative actions by responding, "Oh, what's that you're doing?" Or, "How interesting. What's it doing?" They assisted the pursuit of the child's own questions and, as a result, nurtured the child's habits of inquiry. The teachers who had been encouraged to complete the worksheet said things like, "Oh, wait a minute. That's not on the instructions." When the children were innovative and began to pursue an answer to their own question, the teacher redirected them to the task of following the directions to complete the science worksheet. Rather than nurturing habits of inquiry, the instructional focus was nurturing the habit of following directions (Engel & Randall, 2009). The study illustrates how the instructional goals of teachers can positively or negatively impact their young learners' opportunity to engage in inquiry in science and engineering practices. It also illustrates how inquiry is snuffed out when teachers are required to follow a teaching manual with fidelity even when they know their children are not grasping meaning from the scripted lesson. How we engage with our young learners and allow teachers to teach significantly impacts the development of children's curiosity and innovative thinking.

In *Investigating Ramps and Pathways With Young Children*, we invite educators of young children to rediscover their own interest in how the world of objects works. This begins by igniting their own curiosity through teacher play. In teacher play, educators explore the same materials they will offer to their young learners to determine relationships among materials and phenomena, and learn what children have the possibility of figuring out using the materials. This results in understanding what their young learners need in order to successfully engage in STEM learning through science and engineering practices.

Ignite Curiosity Through Teacher Play

When teachers engage in teacher play by exploring the materials they will offer to their children, they have the opportunity to reflect on their pedagogy as they investigate. They consider advantages and disadvantages of providing specific materials as they notice variables within the materials and ponder when and how to offer them. The vignette in Textbox 1.3 illustrates two teachers beginning to engage with materials for Ramps and Pathways.

TEXTBOX 1.3. TEACHER PLAY WITH MATERIALS

Teacher 1: Look at all these objects we can give children to try to move on the tracks.
Teacher 2: I noticed they aren't all round. Lots of them won't work at all because they won't roll.
Teacher 1: Yes, but I think the children can think about how those things move. For example, the cube slides.
Teacher 2: And the popsicle stick slides. So does the flat stone. But take a look at the spool. When I send it down with the holed end first, it slides, and when I send it down with the holes to the side, it rolls.
Teacher 1: I love how it depends upon the position of the spool! I wonder what other things move differently depending on how they are set on the track.
Teacher 2: I think the egg will move differently. Let's try it.

As teachers engage in teacher play, they come to understand how children's experiences in Ramps and Pathways can meet and go beyond many of the Next Generation Science Standards (NGSS Lead States, 2013a) and preschool standards. While engaged in their own play, teachers contemplate various forms of questions or suggestions to offer their children to deepen thinking and nurture habits of inquiry and engineering. We encourage educators to take the time to explore Ramps and Pathways materials: handling and building structures to move a variety of objects; investigating how the properties of those objects affect how they move; and configuring track to build a system to move a marble in complex and entertaining ways. We challenge educators to be present in the moment of their own investigating processes; to notice patterns and regularities; and to experience joyful surprise when the expected, or even the unexpected, occurs.

Preparing Four Aspects of the Environment for STEM Learning

When educators become more curious themselves about force and motion phenomena, they are more aware of how much space they will need and the kinds of materials to gather. They may be nervous about how their young learners will respond to the materials. Will they use them safely? Will any of the children still want to mouth standard-sized marbles? What can they learn from them? Considering four aspects of the educational environment will help educators successfully engage their children in STEM learning with Ramps and Pathways: (1) intellectual, (2) physical, (3) social–emotional, and (4) promotional (see Figure 1.3).

Intellectual Environment. According to Lilian Katz (2015), intellectual goals are "those that address the life of the mind in its fullest sense (e.g., reasoning, predicting, analyzing, questioning, etc.) including a range of aesthetic and moral sensibilities" (p. 1). Using only grade-level–specific content standards to plan and implement STEM experiences limits opportunities for children to investigate phenomena to their satisfaction. To create a rich intellectual environment, teachers focus on creating an educational environment that empowers children to explore objects and physical phenomena and pursue their own questions and problems. Doing so will develop children's habits in taking initiative in their learning, actively exploring, and observing closely in order to recognize, define, and describe phenomena (Kamii & DeVries, 1993). An intellectual environment is one in which content standards become meaningful for children, not just for adults to use for accountability purposes. It is an environment that enables children to engage in science and engineering practices every day, in addition to the time block set aside for science.

Figure 1.3. Four Aspects of a High-Quality Early Childhood Environment

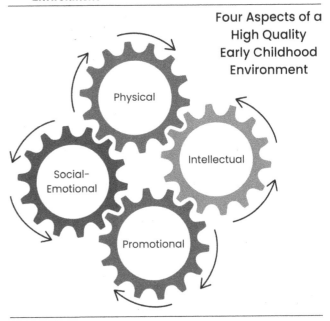

Physical Environment. Retail businesses invest a great deal of time and expense in designing the physical environment of their stores. Consumer researchers have found that lighting, music, floor space, decoration, scent, and colors all play a role in drawing in and keeping shoppers in the store. Researchers in education have likewise found that the physical environment plays a role in learning. The layout of the classroom itself communicates to children whether their role in learning will be active or passive. Loris Malaguzzi (Gandini, 2011), founder of Reggio Emilia's educational philosophy, recognized how influential the physical environment could be in igniting children's creativity in learning and expression. He viewed the parents and caregivers of children as a child's first teacher, the classroom teacher as a child's second teacher, and a thoughtfully laid out physical environment as a third teacher. The layout of the classroom and availability and placement of materials can pull children into an active role of learning by provoking children's questions, actions, and thinking (Piaget & Duckworth, 1973). A thoughtfully structured environment is flexible and responsive to the needs of both the educators and the children. Instead of the teacher directing all of the operations within the classroom, the teacher co-operates the classroom with the children.

This means the teacher is sensitive to the children's needs and interests, and involves children in shared decision-making on how the classroom operates. The furniture is movable to accommodate the needs of children's investigations. STEM learning is accessible to all possible learners when teachers design the environment using the principles of the Universal Design for Learning framework established by the Center for Applied Special Technology (CAST, 2011). Materials are presented in an appealing manner and readily accessible to all children, and include objects that are easy to grasp. A variety of seating arrangements encourages collaboration as well as moments of self-selected solitude.

Social–Emotional Environment. The quality of science and engineering activities and curriculum hinges upon the social–emotional atmosphere developed through the educator–child relationship. When an educator dictates the activities for the day and makes all the decisions about the operation of the classroom, it limits children's ability to make their own decisions (Piaget & Duckworth, 1973). Children become dependent on the teacher, are more passive in their thinking, and have less need to learn ways of communicating their ideas effectively. This is not an environment that fosters creativity or invites inquiry. In contrast, Piaget (1932/1965) recommended that in order for children to become the confident, active, and creative problem-solvers needed in inquiry, educators must provide them with opportunities to exercise their moral and intellectual autonomy, or the ability to take different perspectives into consideration and make decisions based on their own thinking. These opportunities involve giving children agency to make choices and decisions, a voice in classroom rulemaking, and a structure to engage in conflict resolution when personalities clash. When educators provide these opportunities, they support the children in considering other children's points of view, engaging in decision-making, and being accountable for their decisions. When educators invest time and work to establish a community of learners founded on mutual trust and respect, an environment that nurtures inquiry and creativity becomes a reality (Geiken et al., 2009). If some children are still mouthing objects, a teacher can make an executive decision to include only objects that do not fit into

a choke tube. Other safety concerns can be easily addressed in class meetings, resulting in a cocreated list of expectations for working safely. Teachers have shared how they model the danger of carrying large lengths of track horizontally, and how easy it is to knock into furniture or into other children. Their children made the decision to carry the track vertically to keep everyone safe. To avoid the danger of stepping onto loose marbles, the class may add an expectation to always have a "catcher" at the end of the system. Some teachers wait to cocreate a set of rules until the need arises. Others know that their children are likely to unknowingly endanger themselves or others, and therefore introduce the materials by discussing safety issues and starting the cocreation of rules at the beginning.

Ramps and Pathways is a science and engineering experience that exercises children's executive functions (EFs). These functions include working memory, inhibitory control, and cognitive flexibility (Miyake et al., 2000). Children who have a well-developing working memory are beginning to relate what came earlier to what came later, do mental math, and engage in reasoning by holding bits of information in their head and perceiving how those bits relate. Children with a well-developing inhibitory control are beginning to be able to ignore distractions to stay focused on work and suppress their first inclination to blurt out something, go ahead of someone else standing in line, or strike in anger; rather, they respond with a more appropriate action. They are able to make themselves wait for something they want and persevere to complete a tedious task. Children with well-developing cognitive flexibility are beginning to view things or situations from different perspectives. They can switch from sorting objects by one rule to sorting the same objects by another. The successful development of these skills will impact "an individual's happiness and success throughout life" (Diamond, 2016, p. 11) as well as reduce social disparities in achievement.

Children are not born with these skills, but they are born with the potential to develop them. Fostering the growth of children's EFs is less about practicing them and more about creating an environment that allows executive function skills to develop (Mattera et al., 2021). Classroom environments that enhance EF development in young children do not require them to sit still for long periods of time and obediently complete seatwork in silence. Classroom environments that allow movement and choice reduce stress in the classroom, foster social bonding, and cultivate joy, pride, and self-confidence. Such classrooms are the contexts that nurture EFs (Diamond & Lee, 2011). Science and engineering experiences such as Ramps and Pathways are such a context. We will illustrate how children develop EFs in the context of Ramps and Pathways at the end of Chapter 2.

Promotional Environment. Just as the physical environment provides a cue to the role of the child in the classroom, what is promoted by displays on walls and shelf space communicates what is valued and important. When all that is featured on the classroom's walls or shelving are commercially produced posters, districtwide goals, or teacher-created charts and graphics, it sends a message to the children that what they produce doesn't much matter. Promoting the process of children's learning by posting and featuring unique artifacts created by children not only at the end of learning, but also during the learning process, invites child reflection and serves to deepen and extend learning. These artifacts promote the valuable evidence of child engagement and the unique and personal learning of the community of children and their educators who live and learn within those walls. Opportunities to display these child-created artifacts are highly valued by children, creating a desire to learn the tools of literacy and mathematics to accurately communicate their thinking to an audience. In Chapter 4, ideas will be offered for creating and displaying models and artifacts of Ramps and Pathways experiences in ways that augment literacy learning.

SUMMARY

Ramps and Pathways experiences are a context in which children develop engineering and science concepts by engaging in the practices of science and engineering over time on their own terms. As children engage in developmental engineering and design and build their own systems to move marbles in interesting ways, they exercise and develop executive function skills that will benefit them in all academic domains. With advanced planning, educators can ensure that the children across a full range of differing abilities and characteristics can meaningfully participate in inquiry experiences.

Educators who invest time in exploring Ramps and Pathways materials and experiences themselves prior to introducing them to their children will develop insights that will support children in conducting successful investigations. Thinking from the perspectives of their children will inform their own decisions about time, space, materials, opportunity, and support. Educators who carefully consider the intellectual, physical, social–emotional, and promotional aspects of their classrooms are able to create an educational atmosphere that is conducive to developing science and engineering habits of mind, as well as inspiring a desire within their children to learn the tools of mathematics and literacy. Educators can view other children's use of materials as inspiration and re-create similar experiences that are tailor-made for their own children. They can do this best when they form strong partnerships with their administrators, fellow educators, families, and community.

CHAPTER 2

School Partnerships That Support High-Quality STEM

It's far more fulfilling to listen for and respond to the multiple rhythms that children bring into the classroom than to see children as essentially interchangeable and unknowable. Children need connections to learn—and so do teachers.

—Carol Ann Tomlinson and Amy Germundson, 2007

American public schools are a reflection of a nation that is diversifying at a rapid pace. When administrators and teachers embrace the diverse cultures of children, families, and communities, they create a universally designed educational environment that is inclusive, meaningful, and effective for everyone. This chapter begins with the editor's reflection on the partnerships that empowered her to value investigations and pedagogy that is child-centered with her 1st-graders, and how this framework of learning and teaching is akin to "teaching as jazz." We examine the importance of forging school partnerships among classroom teachers, special education teachers, STEM coaches, and administrators to envision developmentally healthy preschool through 2nd-grade classroom environments that embrace inquiry and nurture STEM learning. In Chapter 6, we describe how the family and community are vital partners in early STEM. We recommend that teachers, instructional coaches, principals, and other administrators read Chapters 2 and 3 together and have regular conversations about

- how to determine if a STEM experience is appropriate for PK–2 children;
- ways to provide high-quality STEM experiences every day;
- the impact that high-quality STEM experiences can have on the development of executive functions; and
- what high-quality integrative STEM and literacy can look like in PK–2 classrooms.

Schools are most effective for young learners when they are sensitive to and partner with children's families and communities. These partnerships will be discussed in greater detail in Chapter 6.

TUNING THE INSTRUMENT

I began teaching 1st grade in a rural Iowa public school during the 1980s. I was fortunate to land in a district where teachers challenged themselves and one another to be innovative in our pedagogy. In my 18 years at Laurens-Marathon Community School District, we were led by two principals, Lee Robinson and Dan Braunschweig, whom psychologist Adam Grant would describe as leaders with "confident humility" (Bilyeu, 2020). Lee and Dan both respected the education and expertise of the elementary teachers they led and, in Dan's words, "got out of the way" to enable the teachers to continuously sharpen and expand their pedagogical tools and knowledge that would enhance student learning. He regularly stated, "If it's good for kids, let's do it."

From day one, fellow teacher Sandy Aronson set the bar for what it took to understand the complexity of teaching in early childhood, and to understand that licensure is not the end but the beginning of a teacher's education. My colleagues Sue Kroesche and Jan Johnson urged me to let my 6-year-olds write under the big idea of "How do these marks help me communicate with others?" They mentored me in how to observe the process of writing with 6-year-olds, something that was highly un-usual at the time. They helped me understand how to value children's approximations in their spell-ing and writing, as these approximations revealed where children were conceptually in their under-standing of our technology of the written word. This knowledge allowed me to custom-tailor the next lesson or experience to bring them to a more nuanced understanding of the world of print. My hunger to know more grew with many after-school discussions with fellow teachers Jeri, Judy, Bonnie, Audrey Ann, Karen, Sandy, Les, Diane, Pat, Jo Ann, Sue, Sylvia, Carol, and the Jans.

I cut my teeth on the groundbreaking work of Donald Graves, Lucy Calkins, and Brian Cambourne. I watched with fascination the simi-larities and differences in how each of my young learners embraced the big idea of writing to ex-press themselves first for their own enjoyment, and later for an audience. I came to understand how a child's prior knowledge and experiences uniquely influenced how they engaged in the writing pro-cess. Every student had something new to teach me about learning and teaching. Without realizing it, I began my career immersed in perpetual action re-search in student-led learning.

The last 6 years of my career as a 1st-grade teacher were in the Freeburg Early Childhood Program, an experimental school in Waterloo, Iowa, led by the eminent early childhood re-searcher Dr. Rheta DeVries. Rheta challenged me to apply my student-centered approach to literacy learning to science learning with the big ideas of "What is in the world?" "How does it work?" and "What can I make happen when I interact with it?" Once again, I watched with fascination the simi-larities and differences in how my young learners responded to phenomena. I came to understand how a child's prior knowledge and experiences uniquely influenced how they engaged in the prac-tices of science and engineering. My young learn-ers eagerly engaged with the STEM experiences I provided. As a result, they developed science and engineering dispositions in how they viewed and approached the world. These dispositions were ob-servable in their agency to design solutions to the problems they posed and encountered, not only in STEM, but in reading, writing, mathematics, and social studies.

Over time and with experience, I learned to better anticipate the responses and interests of 6-year-olds as I addressed learning standards. Every year, the children led me to go beyond the standards with unique twists and turns as we investigated phenomena together. Every year had similarities and repeated experiences, but each year was dis-tinct from the previous years, and each repeated experience was fresh and different because of the unique curiosities, interests, and experiences of the children who came to learn and live with me in our classroom.

Teaching as Jazz

Carol Ann Tomlinson and Amy Germundson (2007) wrote an article on differentiated instruction, and described this way of learning and teaching using the analogy of jazz:

> Like jazz musicians, great teachers blend sounds from different traditions, hear and echo students' rhythms, and improvise on a dime. . . . Like jazz, great teaching calls for blending different cultural styles with educational techniques and theories. It requires recognizing that there are independent rhythms in the classroom. Most of all, great teach-ing demands improvisation in how teachers invite an array of young lives into the music with us. Dif-ferent teachers create jazz in different ways in the classroom. But excellent teachers always create it. (pp. 24–25)

We invite you to explore teaching as jazz as you plan experiences that invite your young learn-ers to investigate STEM experiences in Ramps and Pathways. When using a UDL framework, as described in Chapter 1, it is helpful to first view your standards as the melody line (Tomlinson & Germundson, 2007). To ensure that all learn-ers have full access, you will then create a flexible physical and intellectual learning environment that invites improvisation to allow for a range of ex-pressions in learning so all children can play and learn. In jazz, we value the contributions that are made by instruments that support the melody line but may harmonize more than repeat the melody. Eventually each instrument takes the melody lead. Children's work in STEM through inquiry within a

UDL setting reflects that harmony and supportive approach to learning.

Universal Design for Learning: Music for All Learners

In our state, we are beginning to see children sorted into specific classrooms. Transitional kindergartens are appearing to support children between preschool and kindergarten who are not ready for kindergarten. We have seen a school add an additional classroom for children between preschool and transitional kindergarten who were not yet ready for transitional kindergarten. Creative teachers work hard to include all children at their own place in development. One such teacher shared how experience with Ramps and Pathways was a powerful context for some of her children who struggled with speech:

> I have several kiddos with speech issues. Ramps and Pathways has really brought out productive conversations that we have not heard from them yet this year. They are excited to tell us about what they are creating and how they went about creating it. I will encourage our speech pathologist to spend some time with her students in the Ramps and Pathways area.

The kind of mechanism used to group and sort young children into classroom placements according to "presumed" development is not what the Council for Exceptional Children (CEC) and the Center for Applied Special Technology (CAST) envisioned as a Universal Design for Learning (UDL). These sorted or even segregated learning arrangements are static rather than flexible and a far cry from inclusion. While the UDL framework recognizes that research findings reveal that the way people learn is as unique as their fingerprints, the sorting framework described above groups children according to generalizations (and at its worst, subsequent stereotypes) that fail to appreciate learners' individualization. As such, the very placements that were created to support teaching and learning are, in the end, actual barriers preventing maximum learning that could otherwise be achieved within inclusive UDL settings. The UDL approach challenges teachers to consider, and then eliminate, classroom barriers that may prevent any child from reaching learning goals. However, legislated institutional barriers that now track children into self-contained rather than diverse, inclusive settings cannot be eliminated by teachers or building administrators.

In this book, we focus on children's interests in force and motion phenomena to develop science and engineering dispositions as they explore the movements of objects within our world. In the process, children ponder the properties of objects and how they can capitalize on those projects to engineer a system to move that object.

Improvising on the Melody of Standards

The Head Start Early Learning Outcomes Framework (ELOF) was written for children of ages birth to 5 years. The ELOF challenges educators to design learning experiences in the classroom to support children's development across five domains: Approaches to Learning; Social and Emotional Development; Language and Literacy; Cognition; and Perceptual, Motor, and Physical Development. The Next Generation Science Standards (NGSS) were written for the grade band of kindergarten through 2nd grade. The NGSS challenge kindergarten, 1st-grade, and 2nd-grade teachers to approach science learning and teaching in a manner drastically different from traditional science instruction: by engaging their children in eight practices of science and engineering over time so they will conceptually understand science and engineering content. This understanding may not be at adult levels, but rather demonstrate a practical understanding of what happens when materials are manipulated. Children engage in the practices of science to investigate the properties of objects and materials, and how those properties affect movement. Children engage in the practices of engineering to contribute to the designed world by building systems to move objects in creative and interesting ways. In the process of design, they enhance their understanding of the physics of force and motion. The practices of science and engineering can easily be adapted for young learners in preschool (Ramanathan et al., 2022), and for the remainder of this book, we will refer to the NGSS as encompassing preschool through Grade 2, or PK–2.

Science and engineering practices are what children do to make sense of phenomena and are as essential to STEM learning as phonics and comprehension are essential to learning to read. In fact, giving children opportunities to engage in science and engineering practices on a daily basis enhances their approaches to learning to read, write, use mathematics, and interact within the social world (Akerson & Donnelly, 2010; Metz, 2008; National Center for Quality Teaching and Learning, 2022) by giving them authentic reasons to use and make sense of the tools of literacy and mathematics.

How to Get to Carnegie Hall?

Musicians grow when they are encouraged to practice, practice, practice playing their instrument every day. Practicing scales to improve their understanding of how their body and their instrument work together is meaningful only when they are also given an opportunity to play music they enjoy every day. Thinking like scientists and engineers in science lessons improves children's understanding of what scientists and engineers do. However, unless children are immersed daily in the "music" of science practices and engineering, we cannot influence the architecture of their brains to form the habits and dispositions of accomplished scientists and engineers. To do this, teachers must provide a universally designed learning environment that allows children to engage in science and engineering practices every day. Developing such an environment requires strong partnerships.

GETTING THE BAND TOGETHER

If you are a teacher who is nervous and uncertain about including STEM in your classroom, or an administrator who wants to invite your PK–2 teachers to engage their children in early STEM but is uncertain on how to begin or how that might look, you are not alone. Many PK–2 teachers are comfortable with the idea of growing readers, but far less comfortable with the idea of growing scientists and engineers. A 2018 study found only 13% of elementary teachers are confident in teaching physical science and only 3% are confident in teaching engineering (Banilower et al., 2018). A third of PK–2 educators are reluctant to include STEM in their classrooms, and some question whether STEM is even appropriate for the early years (Park et al., 2017; Wan et al., 2020). Despite this reluctance, an overwhelming number of early educators believed STEM to be important for cognitive development and future careers. However, only a third of them felt comfortable teaching STEM content (Park et al., 2017). The fact that you are reading this book indicates your interest and potential commitment to early STEM. To help you succeed, let's consider partnerships that will assist you.

The Impact of Educator Preparation Programs on Perspectives on Early STEM

The educators supporting children's STEM learning in early education come from a wide variety of teacher preparation programs: early childhood, elementary, special education, middle and high school, middle and high school science education, and teacher librarian. The variance among the different types of teacher preparation programs can muddy the waters when considering STEM content and instructional approaches. Ultimately, best practices include creating and maintaining rich learning environments for our youngest learners (Buchanan et al., 1998; File & Gullo, 2002; Vartuli, 1999). Those of us with elementary-oriented teacher preparation (K–5) who find ourselves teaching in grades K–2 may do so with a lack of understanding of how children develop within and across domains, the typical features of child development, and the appropriate benchmarks at different ages. Those of us with an early childhood-oriented teacher preparation (birth through Grade 3) who find ourselves teaching 1st or 2nd grade may do so without a great deal of content knowledge. When these differences exist in educator preparation programs, they may result in an either/or scenario: K–2 children either have a teacher who understands how K–2 children learn but lacks expertise in science, or they have a teacher who understands science but lacks expertise in how K–2 children learn (Bornfreund, 2012).

Teacher training for special educators in PK–2 classrooms varies greatly from one state to another. Blanton and Pugach (2011) described three types of special education teacher preparation training: discrete programs where general education and special education are separate with little collaboration; integrated programs in which general education and special education programs are coordinated with some overlap in curriculum; and merged teacher training programs where all of those enrolled are trained to be dually certified in general and special education. In Iowa, differences in PK and K–2 licensure further delineate the training that teachers receive. Teachers who have early childhood licensure in Iowa can choose between unified licensure that authorizes them to teach in inclusive settings with children from birth to 3rd grade, or a PK–K licensure that qualifies them to teach children in preschool and kindergarten. In addition to the licensure for inclusive PK–3 classrooms, there is a separate licensure for PK special education. In elementary teacher preparation programs in Iowa, general education and special education are separate, as is licensure, with some colleges and universities operating with a discrete model and others with a more integrated model. In early childhood teacher preparation programs, preservice teachers are likely to have experiences in classrooms where children receiving special education services are fully included with their peers in a school-based or community preschool classroom. In K–2 classrooms, this is less likely, with many districts continuing to operate self-contained special education classrooms or pull out services for children eligible for special education. Specially designed instruction is likely to be very carefully monitored by school administrators and special education consultants and coaches, and children may be out of the general education classroom during math and literacy blocks.

The problem becomes even more complex when we consider administrators' educational preparation programs. When principals are knowledgeable about early childhood theories, they have a strong foundation for understanding child development and the implications for supporting children's learning (Mooney, 2013). However, a significant number of principals overseeing PK–2 teachers lack this foundation. Their own pedagogical expertise as teachers was developed with children in middle and high school. Few administrator preparation programs spend adequate time on early childhood education theory and developmentally appropriate practice (Abel et al., 2016). Consequently, administrators responsible for leading PK–2 classrooms may not be aware that kindergarten, 1st grade, and 2nd grade are, by definition, part of early childhood (Brown et al., 2014),

and instead may think of kindergarten, 1st grade, and 2nd grade simply as lower elementary and not significantly different from upper elementary. As a result, there is a trend toward a more academic pedagogy that is out of step with child development. There is a significant increase in the number of preschool and kindergarten children who are required to attend to teacher-directed instruction in letter sounds and sight words—in direct contradiction to the research in early childhood development and best practices (Abel et al., 2016). The fallout of academic preschools is coming to light with a study examining the long-term ramifications of academic or poor-quality preschools (Durkin et al., 2022). Dale Farran (2022), one of the researchers in this study, blogged about her concern about academic preschools and proposed an iceberg model of early developmental competencies. Currently, schools are focused on the tip of the iceberg, or things that are easy to test and quantifiably measure, like letters, letter sounds, and numbers. Schools are ignoring or detaching what lies underneath the tip of the iceberg: the child's need for a broad vocabulary, interest in language, curiosity, persistence, attentiveness, incidental learning, drive to learn, predictability, memory, and self-control. None of these can be easily measured, but they are essential for long-term development (Farran, 2022). All these competencies are nurtured when administrators and their teachers provide high-quality STEM experiences for the children every day.

Forging Partnerships for High-Quality Early STEM Learning

PK–2 STEM learning is powerful when administrators recognize both the challenges and the advantages of having PK–2 faculty who come from diverse teacher preparation backgrounds. A wise administrator creates a work environment where the professional knowledge and expertise of degreed teachers is respected, valued, and put to good use. These administrators form partnerships with their teachers with early childhood expertise, teachers with expertise in content, and teachers with expertise in UDL to collaboratively work to improve their pedagogy. Within this environment, teachers and administrators are encouraged to draw upon each other's strengths and expertise; to value other perspectives, including those of their young learners; and to be creative and innovative in their teaching to meet the unique and diverse needs of the children in their classrooms. Teachers are trusted to use their professional judgment to make decisions in their classrooms. This collective confidence predicts higher levels of child learning (Goddard et al., 2015). When elementary school principals, preschool directors, coordinators, and instructional coaches provide space and flexibility for their teachers to define STEM and explore effective ways to investigate concepts in STEM with their young learners, PK–2 children experience high-quality early STEM learning (McClure et al., 2017). In turn, this will positively impact student achievement in middle school and high school math, as well as futures in STEM careers (Navy et al., 2020; Watson et al., 2022).

The leadership style of administrators is crucial. Multiple studies point to leadership of administrators as the major factor in effectively implementing STEM in the classroom (e.g., Margot & Kettler, 2019; Park et al., 2017; Wan et al., 2020). We've had the pleasure of working with administrators who have successfully created such an educational work environment. We have found that educators in such environments are motivated to continuously develop and refine their pedagogical skills based on a collective understanding of child development, STEM content knowledge, and an understanding of inquiry-based learning and teaching. The educators are able to organize experiences that allow children to build new ideas systematically and incrementally, starting from their curiosity and initial conceptions. Their children are engaged in science and engineering practices born out of a genuine need to address questions or problems the children have identified (Reiser et al., 2017). This healthy and creative environment for innovative STEM teaching in turn generates a creative and healthy early childhood learning environment from preschool through 2nd grade that will grow our next crop of innovators. This begins with finding spaces and time for daily STEM learning.

Looking for STEM From the Perspective of Young Learners

In many preschools, science is viewed as less important than language and literacy (Pendergast et al., 2017). Preschool educators may engage in formal

science instruction for only 4.5% of classroom time (Tu, 2006). Science is also avoided by many of us in preschool settings, as we may feel anxious about our ability to teach science (Greenfield et al., 2009), or we underestimate the foundational knowledge our children may already have (Pendergast et al., 2017). We may also underestimate just how close to science learning and teaching we already are. High-quality preschool educators understand the value of playful learning and have spaces (centers) throughout the classrooms. These centers allow children opportunities to create figures with clay, build with blocks, explore water and sand, and so forth, all experiences that spark the intellectual life of the child. Such experiences have the potential to nudge children toward dispositions that engage in reasoning, predicting, analyzing, and questioning (Katz, 2015), all dispositions necessary for STEM learning and STEM careers. By seeing the potential for science and engineering in existing centers, we can connect phenomena to our children's prior experiences, point out unexpected and surprising events, and listen to children's explanations (Andersson & Gullberg, 2014). The result is a high-quality science learning environment that results in stronger learning than is achieved with didactive and explicit science instruction (Hong & Diamond, 2012). The Ramps and Pathways experiences introduced in this book can easily be welcomed into preschool classrooms accustomed to having centers.

High-quality kindergartens, 1st grades, and 2nd grades (K–2) had similar centers until the era of accountability emerged early in 2002 with the arrival of the No Child Left Behind Act. Rather than focus on the intellectual development of young children, the focus shifted to academic instruction concerned mostly with the mastery of literacy skills. Accountability came in the form of standardized tests. Before long, centers that developed the intellectual life of the child were removed from kindergarten, 1st-grade, and 2nd-grade classrooms and replaced with curricula that coordinated with how standardized tests measured academic knowledge of literacy skills. Instructional time devoted to subjects that were not explicitly tested—like social studies, the arts, and science—was reduced. We are now witnessing this same kind of erosion of intellectual life in our preschools.

Science in PK–2 public school classrooms is becoming increasingly rare. The 2018 National Survey of Science and Mathematics found that on average in K–2 classrooms, 80 minutes of daily instructional time is dedicated to large- and small-group reading instruction. Just like the scant 4% of time devoted to science in preschool, the amount of instructional time devoted to science (if it happens at all) in K–2 classrooms is less than 20 minutes. These 20 minutes are typically at the end of the day and frequently are eliminated when there is a schedule change or early dismissal. Within these minutes of science instruction, less than 5 minutes are dedicated to engaging children in the practices of science and engineering (Banilower et al., 2018). This small window of time for science learning often results in decisions to deliver teacher-directed lessons that are predictable and designed to prevent children from experiencing failure that will take time to address (Trautmann et al., 2004). Altogether, the removal of centers, the diminished instructional time for science in favor of literacy, teacher and school accountability based on standardized tests, and pressure to deliver scripted curriculum and teacher-directed lessons designed to increase test results (teaching to the test) become insurmountable barriers that in actuality undermine UDL.

A result of this intense focus on reading and writing is that entire mornings in K–2 classrooms are devoted to literacy learning. The example in Figure 2.1 shows that a K–2 child's morning may begin with large-group literacy instruction, which flows into teacher-led small-group reading instruction, moves to independent literacy practice activities, and ends with a writing workshop. The afternoon is dedicated to mathematics; special classes such as physical education, art, or music; and, if there is time, science or social studies at the end of the day (see Figure 2.1).

Integrative STEM and Literacy

The National Research Council (NRC, 2007) cautioned us about the dangers of siloed teaching of science, technology, engineering, and mathematics that stands in opposition to the UDL, and yet non-inclusive siloed teaching of subjects is alive and well, beginning with kindergarten. However, administrators who partner with their PK–2 teachers are building an understanding of how literacy and STEM learning facilitate each other's development. For example, we work with a school whose PK–2 teachers include STEM experiences for their young learners every day, in addition to high-quality reading instruction. In kindergarten, 1st-grade, and 2nd-grade classrooms, educators dedicate an entire morning to literacy and integrative STEM learning. This begins with large-group literacy instruction, which flows into a series of educator-led small-group reading instruction lessons, independent literacy practice activities, and independent STEM investigations. Children who are not involved in the educator-led small-group instruction work at a series of independent literacy experiences and STEM experiences until their group is called. The morning ends with a writing workshop where children often choose to write about what they are investigating.

Figure 2.1. Typical Use of Instructional Time in K–2 Classrooms

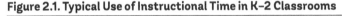

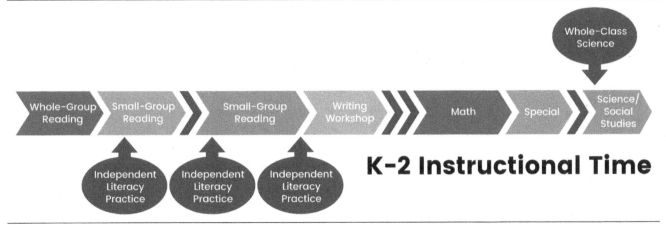

The afternoon may be dedicated to mathematics and special classes and a small block of time for science. What is often different about science instructional time at the end of the day in these classrooms is that the children rarely allow this time to be skipped, because they are eager to discuss and build on their questions and investigations of the morning (see Figure 2.2). Teachers provide multiple means of representation by activating children's prior knowledge and presenting content and information in different ways. Using visuals, displaying cocreated charts of science and engineering practices, and captioning photos and videos are a few examples of how teachers use a variety of ways to present information so that all learners can understand and access the content.

Teachers have noticed discussions are richer, and children are able to articulate their ideas and thinking with confidence. Just as they are developing lifelong habits of reading, they are developing lifelong habits of thinking as a scientist and engineer.

The flexible coexistence of independent literacy and inquiry practices has not reduced, but rather enhanced, children's development as readers. In a case study comparing 1st-graders in a typical literacy-rich classroom with 1st-graders in an integrative STEM and literacy classroom, the children in the integrative environment did as well or better on standardized literacy assessments (Van Meeteren, 2016).

Including independent STEM experiences in Ramps and Pathways alongside independent literacy practice creates a learning environment where children use and practice the tools of literacy to communicate and document their questions and ideas within exploratory inquiry. The context of building ramp and pathway systems is a rich opportunity to model, use, and expand vocabulary in a purposeful way (Hong & Diamond, 2012; Neuman & Wright, 2014). In Figure 2.3 we provide examples of words that fall under six categories. Children have the opportunity to use their own words that describe the properties of an object they attempt to move, as well as adjectives and verbs that explain the motion of those objects. As children work together to construct a system and engage in spatial thinking, they search for words to explain a track or ramp's position. When children and their teacher discuss the success and failure of systems, they can use words that describe the system's condition, as well as words that express the emotion the system evokes. The active nature of Ramps and Pathways is an opportunity to notice and name behaviors of engineers. Finally, we have heard some children use words that describe features of a system that their peers begin to pick up.

Children are motivated to document their thoughts in their science notebooks, grappling with phoneme–grapheme relationships and spelling patterns in the process. They write with audience in mind as they work to describe their efforts for peers and caregivers. In Ramps and Pathways, they explore and develop spatial relationships, a mathematical concept that is essential to STEM careers but is often overlooked in early childhood curriculum. Our framework for early STEM with Ramps

Figure 2.2. Instructional Time in an Integrative STEM and Literacy K–2 Classroom

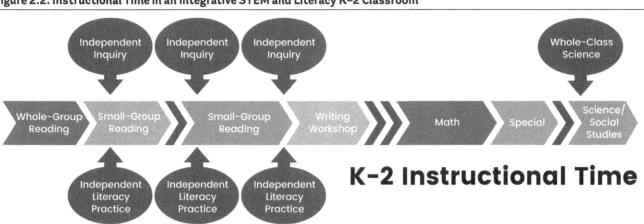

Figure 2.3. Vocabulary in Ramps and Pathways

Property	Motion	Position	Condition	Action	Feature
metal	fast	on top	stable	design	connection
plastic	slow	beneath	sturdy	persevere	corner
glass	wobble	beside	solid	plan	tight corner
wooden	tumble	below	unstable	test	wide corner
hollow	quick	behind	delicate	revise	drop
solid	bounce	above	consistent	troubleshoot	jump
flat	ricochet	over	unfinished	predict	switchback
heavy	jump	under	complete	rebuild	fulcrum
light	roll	around	interesting	consult	hill
length	slide	beyond	innovative	advise	valley
width	bump	outside	fascinating	problem-solve	overlap
symmetrical	knock	inside	tempting	argue	overlap
asymmetrical	block	farther	complex	agree	component
sphere	start	in front of	simple	disagree	
cube	stop	in back of	challenging	challenge	
cylinder	teeter	lower		redesign	
soft	balance	higher		overhaul	
hard	tilt			remodel	

and Pathways may not perfectly align with grade-level NGSS disciplinary core ideas, but it will always align with the practices of science and engineering. When every child experiences inquiry and engineering every day, over time the acts of inquiry and engineering become ingrained in how they think and problem-solve. In other words, it becomes part of who they are and how they engage with the world and what is in it. Educators can capitalize on children's developing science and engineering habits of mind to engage in deeper discussions involving questions, claims, and evidence for grade-level NGSS performance standards and beyond.

Some educators may be reluctant to allow their children to have access to materials if they cannot be there to supervise. We have found that by following four criteria, we can select STEM experiences for young learners that require little educator supervision in order to be successful.

Criteria for Selecting High-Quality Independent STEM Experiences

To successfully shift into providing independent open-ended STEM experiences that support the development of independent behaviors in inquiry, we recommend using four criteria (DeVries & Sales, 2011):

1. *Producible:* The child must be able to produce "what happens" with their own actions.
2. *Immediate:* "What happens" must occur as soon as the child produces their action.
3. *Observable:* The child must be able to see, hear, feel, smell, or taste something that is a result of their action.
4. *Variable:* The child must be able to vary their action or the material used to observe what happens.

The application of these four criteria helps teachers to select and create open-ended experiences that are flexible and child-centered, and that capitalize on individual prior knowledge and experiences in ways that are inclusive and accessible to everyone.

Ramps and Pathways experiences meet these criteria and are a meaningful context for young learners to engage in the practices of science and engineering. These experiences can help build conceptual understanding not only about force and motion but also about what it is to think like scientists to learn about force and motion, and how one can engineer a marble in an interesting way. The vignette in Textbox 2.1 illustrates these four criteria within a Ramps and Pathways experience. Some children have been successful in designing a system that results in moving a marble to roll up and over a hill, or a series of hills. The children and their educator have decided to use only spheres of the same size, but made of different materials: glass, metal, and wood. The overarching or macro problem the children and educator have given themselves is, "How can we get a marble to go up and over hills?" Children have the opportunity to make mental relationships between the properties of a material and how they can control its movement.

TEXTBOX 2.1. MEETING THE FOUR CRITERIA THROUGH A RAMPS AND PATHWAYS EXPERIENCE

Stacy watched as some of her peers began to build working systems to get a marble to roll down one ramp, then back up another, and then back down. She was eager to build, and set to work using unit blocks to build a support to lean a track against to make her first ramp. She built the first support tall to make a steep ramp. Stacy connected the second track at its end and built another support at its far end to make another ramp for the marble to roll up, and connected a third track for the marble to make its descent. To test her system, Stacy **produced** the action of releasing a marble at the top of the first ramp. The result of her action was **immediate**, allowing Stacy to **observe** it roll down the first ramp, slow down as it ascended the second, then reverse its direction and roll back down. Stacy **varied** her design by elevating the first ramp to get the marble to roll fast enough to allow it to go up the second ramp.

In this vignette, Stacy was engaging in an early approximation of a scientific investigation that explored her implicit question of "How can I control the speed of a marble to get it to roll up and over a hill?" She experienced control of her investigation, as she was able to produce actions on her own and immediately see a result of her action. She could take her time observing this result, and she experienced even more control in her decision to choose a variation of her action and learn if the result was different and how it was different. Investigations involving physical science are perfect for young learners, as the results of their actions are immediate. In life science, one has to be patient for days if not weeks for a seed to grow. Patience is difficult for young learners. Physical science allows children to be active in their investigations. Children who are easily excitable, with lots of wiggles, begin tempering their movements and outbursts when they become intrigued by what they observe. Children's active exploration with the laws of physics provides them the movement and excitement they need, with just the right amount of challenge to slow down and closely observe. They exercise their working memory as they compare variations of their actions, and they often engage in flexible thinking by viewing materials in new and varied ways. These experiences are the perfect context in which to grow a child's executive functions.

STEM EXPERIENCES AND THE DEVELOPMENT OF EXECUTIVE FUNCTIONS

If administrators are feeling overwhelmed with behavior referrals, they will love reading and discussing this section with their teachers. All too often, teachers and administrators meet to address behavioral concerns of children in PK–2. At its worst, this results in expulsion. A 2005 national study brought to light an alarming trend in American education: Prekindergarten children were being expelled from state-funded preschools at a rate that was three times higher than that for children in K–12 public schools (Gilliam, 2005). Studies that followed found expulsions to disproportionately affect boys and children of color (U.S. Department of Education, Office of Civil Rights, 2016) and were frequent in both public and private preschools (Giordano et al., 2020; Hooper & Schweiker, 2020; Silver & Zinsser, 2020), despite a widespread understanding that children learn best when there are strong teacher–child relationships, positive behavioral supports, and strong family engagement components in place.

Instead of expulsion, teachers and administrators can support healthy development of children's mental and emotional health by providing an educational environment that nurtures the development of executive functions (EFs). High-quality STEM experiences such as Ramps and Pathways support the development of EFs (inhibitory control, working memory, and cognitive flexibility) and do so at a critical time in brain development. EFs are housed in the brain's prefrontal cortex, which grows the most rapidly in early childhood. This part of the brain manages processes such as reasoning, logic, problem solving, planning, memory, focus and attention, developing and carrying out goals, stopping impulses, and developing personality—all processes exercised in STEM thinking and learning.

A recent synthesis of research on improving EFs pointed to the role of educational environments that provide opportunities for children to engage in experiences in which they are interested and about which they care deeply (Diamond & Ling, 2020). They become emotionally invested when the experience matters to them, and they feel compelled to push through challenges toward eventual success. Other factors in the growth of EFs include giving children choice in how the experience is completed, as well as opportunities to form strong personal bonds with other children who are enjoying the same experience (Diamond & Ling, 2020). In high-quality STEM experiences, children gain feelings of pride and self-confidence and view challenges as positive and gratifying experiences. The open-ended nature of STEM experiences such as Ramps and Pathways calls upon children's exercise of all three EFs; if offered daily, the benefits generalize and transfer to other domains and activities (Diamond et al., 2007).

Inhibitory Control

Inhibitory control refers to both behavioral and attention control. When children are truly interested in a STEM experience, they will resist impulsive behaviors and temper emotions to allow themselves to keep working within that experience. They can ignore auditory and visual distractions to pay attention to the problem or question at hand. Children who are in the beginning stages of developing inhibitory control are not naughty. Dan Gartrell (2004) urged educators to reframe this perceived misbehavior as mistaken behavior. The objective is to teach children to solve problems rather than to punish children for having problems they cannot solve. Creating learning experiences that tap

into children's interest intrinsically motivates them to resist distractions, helping them to regulate their own behavior, attention, and emotions. Teaching children to solve problems rather than punishing them as naughty, off-task, or disobedient is one of the most effective ways to oppose and disrupt suspension and expulsion policies that are among the most extreme barriers to full inclusion and UDL. These are the children in most need of the opportunity to engage in Ramps and Pathways experiences, which have the potential to help them develop inhibitory control.

Teacher-directed instruction and scripted curricula as described in Chapter 1 rely heavily on the compliance of the learner and demand that the child have inhibitory control. The lesson is preplanned, the length of the lesson predetermined; there is usually one opportunity to engage in the active portion of the lesson, and the criteria of success have already been established, with no flexibility, individualization, or differentiation, thereby running counter to UDL. The children's job is to comply to complete the lesson, and hopefully enjoy their activity in it. This is difficult for young children, especially when they are learning to control impulses. If a child is enjoying the activity but time runs out and they cannot complete it to their satisfaction, they must have the inhibitory control to resist the urge to keep going or resist the urge to act out in frustration.

Educators can nurture development of inhibitory control by allowing children to have choices in Ramps and Pathways experiences and the opportunity to be independent in their exploration. This means educators need to trust that children want to learn and will learn without an adult hovering over them. Educators can wade into these waters slowly by gathering as a group to explore materials children will have the opportunity to explore on their own. Handling some of the materials prompts discussion of how to use them safely, how to care for them, and where to place them when they are not in use. Empowering children by sharing the decision-making in how a Ramps and Pathways experience is organized or conducted increases their commitment to the experience. They feel a sense of control and ownership in their playful learning and take their work seriously. As children learn how to regulate their own behavior in daily STEM experiences, they develop inhibitory control, and teachers will notice a change in children's approaches to learning in other domains and activities (Diamond et al., 2007). Over time, educators will observe fewer incidences of blurting out, cutting in line, or striking out in anger.

Ramps and Pathways materials are open-ended and will ignite children's ideas. The teacher may have an idea of what might interest the children and arrange the materials on a shelf to invite them to experience a specific challenge, but a child may choose to do something different from what the teacher expected. In one example, a 2nd-grade teacher glanced up from her work with children in small-group reading to find Kijuan and Kalaziah building two tall structures out of unit blocks in the space children had designated for building Ramps and Pathways structures (see Figure 2.4).

Rather than redirecting the children, the teacher waited until the small-group lesson was finished, then walked to where the children were working. As she got closer, she realized they had built a ramp and pathways system using only single unit blocks

and unit block wedges. They released a marble at the top to allow the teacher to see it in action. The two had positioned enough space between the two structures to allow the marble to roll down a wedge, drop down to the wedge beneath and roll up, then reverse its direction to roll down and drop to the wedge beneath, and so on until the marble had changed its direction 31 times before finally exiting at the bottom on the structure. Stunned, the teacher asked them to show her how it was constructed, drawing their attention to not only what they had done but how they had done it. The two knelt next to the structure and, using loose blocks and wedges, demonstrated how they had figured out a pattern of how to lay the blocks and wedges (see Figure 2.5). Once they had the pattern figured out, they simply repeated it as high as they could reach.

When asked about problems they encountered, the children said they had made small adjustments by sliding the ramps farther into the middle or pulling them out. The result was a masterpiece that was not only beautiful but satisfying in the click, click, click of the marble rolling from one wedge onto the next. The space between the two structures allowed viewers a close-up of the system at work (see Figure 2.6). A video of this system at work can be accessed by scanning the QR code in Figure 2.6.

Figure 2.4. Two Tall Structures

Figure 2.5. Block and Wedge System

Figure 2.6. Working Wedge and Block System (With Video)

The teacher, who was elementary-trained, reflected on the experience and said that in her traditional pedagogy, she might have admonished them for not using the track with blocks to build a system. She would have stopped this creative and innovative design, which was not even a wisp of an idea in her own head. She was grateful to have resisted her first impulse to redirect the children; in other words, she was pleased that she herself was developing executive function skills of inhibitory control in her pedagogy, or manner of teaching. Had she followed her first impulse, she would have stifled an opportunity to nurture the development of a child's brain that is curious, imaginative, creative, and highly capable of problem solving.

Working Memory

Working memory involves holding information in one's mind and mentally working with that information to translate instructions into plans of action, reorder a to-do list, consider alternatives, or relate one piece of information to another. In the example of the block and wedge system, the two children held information about how to position ramps to receive and reverse the action of marbles, and mentally worked with that information along with their knowledge of how the speed of a marble affects a system's success. Those of us who are elementary-trained must hold information in our minds about what it means to engage in the practices of science and engineering as we observe children working with Ramps and Pathways, and then work with that information to make decisions about how to enhance and support children's inquiry and ideas for design. We must exercise our working memory within our pedagogy to continue to develop as STEM educators.

Cognitive Flexibility

Cognitive flexibility refers to the ability to change perspectives, view something from different perspectives, or "think outside the box." Cognitive flexibility allows us to adjust to unexpected changes or take advantage of unexpected opportunities. This is perhaps the executive function that young children with disabilities may need the most but may be the least likely to experience. Outdated assumptions, attitudes, and beliefs about children with cognitive delays may lead teachers to question and doubt whether children who struggle cognitively can brainstorm, take multiple perspectives, problem-solve, and negotiate multiple variables, factors, and considerations during investigations. All of these are the very kinds of opportunities and experiences critical to developing and improving cognition. Kalaziah and Kijuan's choice to use the different materials to serve as ramps is a good example of thinking outside the box. Their educator's decision to not interfere with their exploration is a good example of the educator's cognitive flexibility. If we have been steeped in direct instruction or scripted teaching, it will call upon our own cognitive flexibility to trust that our children want to learn and will learn in open-ended Ramps and Pathways experiences. If administrators are of the belief that a quiet classroom is a well-managed classroom for learning, it will call upon their cognitive flexibility to trust that children and teachers learn in a classroom that has a healthy buzz of active learning. They will be able to envision how every PK–2 classroom can be a makerspace that is rich in learning in all domains.

SUMMARY

High-quality early childhood STEM environments with a universal design for learning are established when teachers and administrators partner to share their expertise in child development, in STEM content knowledge, and in how children best learn in the years of early childhood (i.e., birth to age 8). Administrators and teachers can identify high-quality STEM experiences by using the four criteria of producible, immediate, observable, and variable. Experiences in Ramps and Pathways fit these criteria well, and when offered alongside independent literacy experiences during small-group instruction, they can fuel deeper discussions in whole-class science instruction and enhance the development of skills and behaviors in literacy. As teachers and administrators work together to implement high-quality STEM experiences every day, they provide children with the opportunity to develop executive functions and may mitigate the stress of behavior referrals. Highly effective administrators advocate for early childhood learning by translating educational policy into practice with a deep understanding of child development and early childhood pedagogy. In this collaborative climate, teachers and administrators can advocate for best practices and promote positive school climate while building supportive relationships that connect young children to high-quality STEM learning.

CHAPTER 3

Weaving Ramps and Pathways Experiences Through the Standards for Meaningful Learning

Together, [the Next Generation Science Standards and the Framework for K–12 Science Education] present a vision of science and engineering learning designed to bring these subjects alive for all students, emphasizing the satisfaction of pursuing compelling questions and the joy of discovery and invention. Achieving this vision in all science classrooms will be a major undertaking and will require changes to many aspects of science education.

—National Research Council, 2015, p. 9

TEXTBOX 3.1. SPACE FOR RAMPS AND PATHWAYS IN A 2ND-GRADE CLASSROOM

Diane swung a bookcase around to create a larger space for her 2nd-graders to do investigations within Ramps and Pathways. She had just introduced the space to her students in the morning, and their enthusiasm in creating systems of ramps and pathways took her by surprise. They insisted they needed more space to work and gave her a list of materials they wanted added to the space: a balance scale, ball bearings, and a container to hold all the different kinds of objects they were going to move: "Something like my fishing tackle box," suggested Anton. As she adjusted the workspace to accommodate a place for unit blocks she had borrowed from the kindergarten rooms, she worried about the looks of concern she had seen on the 3rd-grade teachers' faces as they passed by the noise of her excited students. She began to doubt the support of her administrator, who had just lectured the primary team on elevating standardized test scores in literacy.

If engineering is "design under constraint," Diane is most certainly engaged in a complex engineering design problem in her goal of creating science and engineering lessons that "bring these subjects alive for all students, emphasizing the satisfaction of pursuing compelling questions and the

joy of discovery and invention" (NRC, 2015, p. 9). Children reveling in the joy of discovery and invention are not quiet or solemn. At first glance, Diane's active classroom can appear to be chaotic when compared with traditional expectations of children sitting at desks completing paper-and-pencil tasks in silence or reading from a book (see Textbox 3.1).

A person's knowledge and dispositions in STEM are influenced by teachers and their pedagogy from the earliest years of schooling and onward (Campbell et al., 2018). Community and administrative support for creative and innovative teaching leads to creative and innovative children at a critical time in their educational lives, early childhood. In this time of accountability, we recommend that teachers and their administrators read this chapter together and have a healthy discussion on the importance of early integrative STEM, and how high-quality early integrative STEM experiences have the power to lift learning in all domains. Ramps and Pathways is not a curriculum, but illustrates a framework for early STEM that optimizes children's everyday learning by steeping them in experiences that nurture adaptability, problem solving, creativity, critical thinking, and design thinking, all components that are essential to STEM learning (Bybee, 2013; Prinsley & Baranyai, 2015). Packaged curriculum can tick all the boxes in standards, but any curriculum can be greatly enhanced when Ramps and Pathways within the STEM framework is added, as it addresses many standards in ways curriculum does not, especially in developing habits of inquiry and engineering and in crosscutting concepts. This chapter will illustrate how the framework does this.

THE WARP AND THE WEFT OF LEARNING AND TEACHING

As you read this chapter, you are likely wearing or snuggling under an article made of a woven fabric. Looms are used to weave fabric, using vertical and horizontal threads or yarns. The first step in preparing to weave is stringing the loom with the vertical threads, or the warp. Each thread of the warp is held in tension, parallel to the next one, on the frame of the loom. The threads of the warp are useless without the horizontal yarns, or the weft. A simple and straightforward method of weaving is moving the weft over and under, over and under, over and under the threads of the warp. If one yarn is different from the rest, or if the yarn skips a thread in the warp, the difference clearly stands apart from the rest of the fabric and is considered a flaw. Seamstresses cut around these flaws to sew a garment that is marketable. This standard method of weaving will result in a fabric that is useful, but hardly creative and innovative.

We can think of standards as the warp—the vertical threads on a weaving loom. Just as the threads of the warp are held in tension on the frame of the loom, learning standards are held in tension in American education. There are those who believe the goal of standards is to establish a standardized curriculum that meets almost every child's needs in learning in every classroom *if* that curriculum is implemented by the teacher "with fidelity." To ensure fidelity, credentialed teachers are required to follow company-designed and scheduled, scripted lessons.

Norm-referenced standardized tests rank and sort children using numerical measures by comparing one child's performance with that of other children of the same age or grade. Designed to distribute scores across a wide continuum, these tests are constructed so that most learners score in the statistically "average" range, with fewer children receiving scores above and below the average and even fewer at the two extremes. Children whose scores fall below the norm group may be flagged for flawed or insufficient learning. Curricular decisions informed by this deficit framework become the justification for minimizing or completely eliminating children's access to the mainstream (or gifted) curriculum and lessons. Instead, children deemed as "low" performers are placed with an even more teacher-directed, scripted curriculum and skill-drilled instruction. As discussed in Chapter 1, standardized assessments and curricula can become barriers to ensuring the UDL framework within diverse, inclusive settings. Even when the curriculum ticks off every box in the standards, it hardly produces an educational environment that nurtures curiosity, creativity, and innovation. There is an alternative.

A master weaver sits at the loom, the strings of the warp waiting for his interpretation. He examines the diverse assortment of fibers within his grasp, each fiber with its own unique properties. Selecting one of the yarns and examining it in his fingers, he ponders how this fiber will respond to the warp; where this fiber should enter and exit; how tightly or how loosely to pull it; and how its placement next to a different fiber elevates the use of both. Which fibers will enhance another's appearance when woven in and out together and then apart? Which fibers are more striking when woven alone? And when should a fiber be woven back with the others? The decisions of the master weaver result in a tapestry rich with texture and color, each unique fiber touching the next in a way that elevates the distinctive property of the other. We can admire the beauty of the collective whole (see Figure 3.1).

Likewise, the master educator examines the tension of the learning standards that must be addressed. Just as the master weaver considers the qualities of each fiber and how the fibers will respond to the warp, the master educator considers the unique histories, interests, and cultures of each child in the classroom and considers how children will respond individually to the same set of standards. The educator ponders how the diverse experiences of the children might influence where, when, and how they engage with specific standards, and what experiences are necessary for them to have before they engage with a specific standard. The educator considers how much choice to apportion to children within a classroom experience that takes them beyond a standard, and when to pull them back in. Educators who create and maintain an inclusive learning environment according to the UDL frame-work continuously contemplate how novice or limited understandings of one child can be expanded upon, supported, and strengthened by engaging with another child who has had the luxury of more experiences (a peer mediator). The children can, in turn, deepen and enrich one another's learning as they weave in and out of the standards. The master educator's ability to weave the diverse gifts, interests, experiences, and needs of their children into the standards teases out each child's unique, creative, critical, and innovative ways of thinking, bringing richness and texture to the learning within the UDL classroom (see Figure 3.2).

The learning of concrete skills of letters, sounds, and numbers that are finite, definable, and quantifiable (Farran, 2022) within this classroom may result in children's test scores that are in the middle or even higher than the statistical "average" in the short term. However, the deeper, more important underlying skills of a broad vocabulary, interest in language, curiosity, persistence, attentiveness, incidental learning, drive to learn, predictability, memory, and self-control are not all easy to quantify. They are detached from the concrete skills and put aside despite their importance to long-term development and learning (Farran, 2022). The more the materials and activities are rich, creative, and innovative, the

Figure 3.1. Master Weaver

Photo by Parham Moieni on Unsplash.

Figure 3.2. Weaving Children's Innovative Thinking Into the Standards

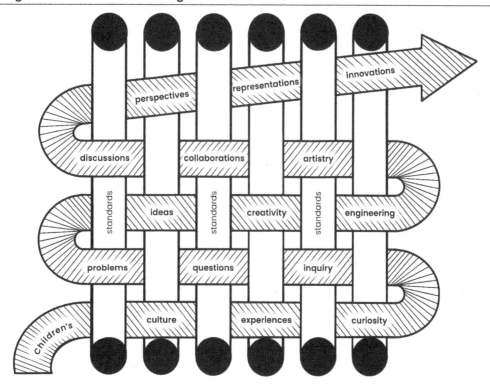

greater the likelihood that all learners will be fully engaged and challenged, and that all learning needs will be met. This kind of dynamic, inclusive learning can be captured in a variety of ways. It can be viewed and understood in photographs of children in the process of learning with descriptive captions composed by the educator or child. The process of learning can be celebrated and promoted on the classroom walls and shelving with displays of child-generated artifacts and models that explain their thinking. Questions the children are pursuing, co-created on chart paper along with forms of ongoing data collection to find answers to those questions, tell the story of how their thinking is evolving.

Children who have the good fortune to learn with these professional educators and supportive administrators do not have to move to another room to be in a makerspace to experience STEM. Their classroom *is* a makerspace and, by design, makerspaces are one of the most effective examples of the UDL in action. The children experience STEM every day. Children's celebrated creative and innovative contributions in their classroom are of much greater value than any distribution of arbitrary test scores. Creativity and imagination are essential if we are to nurture the next generation of innovators.

STEM capabilities are best nurtured through real-world experiences and projects that are authentic to children (Hefty, 2015; Redmond et al., 2011). This is especially true with young learners. Given a set of materials to create a pathway and an object to run along it, young children can engage far longer than the "short attention span" conventional wisdom attributes to them, including children with disabilities. Professional educators who understand child development and how children learn recognize the value of young learners' authentic engagement with ramps and pathways. They weave this engagement into standards in ways that allow each child to continuously grow in their understanding of ramps and pathways as they develop STEM capabilities and dispositions.

In our work with PK–2 educators, we celebrate with them when they experience rich learning and growth occurring in their children, as well as in themselves, when they implement Ramps and Pathways experiences. A 2nd-grade teacher shared her surprise at how powerful a student-led Ramps and Pathways center can be:

As a 2nd-grade teacher, at first I was thinking, "Is this for me???" After providing my students with the materials, I had a complete shift in my thinking. I witnessed all of the wonderful connections and learning happening in my room. I went from "When will I ever find time for this?" to it becoming a part of each day!

Other teachers described how Ramps and Pathways experiences made positive impacts in ways that surprised them. Laura, a preschool teacher, reported, "I was amazed at the vocabulary they used. I heard turn it, tip it, put it up, and point it. One student said, 'Put one side up and one side down and then roll the marble.' They were amazing." Research shows that using spatial language within spatial experiences enhances the development in young children of the spatial thinking that is essential in STEM professions (Kersh et al., 2008; Wheatley, 1990). Joann pointed out the integrative nature of Ramps and Pathways:

Inquiry-based science is so easily adapted and allows students to participate in learning at their level. I have found that students who experience the hands on and problem solving not only retain the concept better but begin to make further concept connections outside of the science activity. Students connect the purpose of math skills and written language in authentic learning.

Ramps and Pathways experiences provide a flexible, inclusive, and nonpressure context that motivates all children to actively participate and communicate what they experience. Working with ramps and pathways enables children with language delays to use multiple means of expression to demonstrate what they know and understand. Children can also draw pictures or use photos to help them communicate new ideas, concepts, and relationships they have constructed during Ramps and Pathways experiences.

Though the standards are the warp that guides learning and teaching, it is critical to expect and plan for child-led experiences that go beyond the grade-level standards and bring vibrant texture and color to STEM learning. Respecting the curiosity of children by following their interests is how creativity and innovation blossom for all children. It is what makes teaching joyful for master educators.

WEAVING RAMPS AND PATHWAYS EXPERIENCES THROUGH THE NGSS

A common set of early childhood standards in science education is the Next Generation Science Standards (NGSS Lead States, 2013a), which are based on the National Research Council's (2012) *Framework for K–12 Science Education*. Prior to the development of the Next Generation Science Standards (NGSS), early childhood science curriculum often employed a teacher-directed approach to teach children facts about science. Learning was assessed on the ability to recall memorized facts. Memorizing science content does not represent the true natures of science and engineering and does little to ignite a passion for STEM learning. To better reflect the true natures of science and engineering, every NGSS standard reflects a three-dimensional vision: (1) Children need to engage in **practices of science and engineering** that mirror the work of professional scientists and engineers. They do this to (2) conceptually understand **core ideas** in the four domains of physical science; earth and space science; life science; and engineering, technology, and applications of science. Over time and through many experiences, children (3) make sense of **crosscutting concepts**, which are themes or tools that hold true in science phenomena across the four domains of science. In other words, children learn and understand science and engineering by *doing* science and engineering. The beauty of this three-dimensional approach to learning is that it challenges teachers to embrace child-centered pedagogy—an approach long championed by advocates for high-quality early childhood education—and it reignites K–2 educators' passion for learning and teaching. Brittany Schwenker, an early childhood special education teacher, described how the open-ended Ramps and Pathways experiences breathed life into the standards that applied in her school. For parent–teacher night, she created a documentation board of photos of her children at work, with examples of how the Iowa Early Learning Standards (IELS; Iowa Department of Education, 2018) were being addressed in regard to approaches to learning, literacy and communication, social–emotional development, mathematics, science, and motor development (see Figure 3.3). As an example of the

Figure 3.3. Promoting the Integration of Standards in Ramps and Pathways

productivity of UDL principles, she documented how children whose challenges might lead to lowered expectations in other classrooms demonstrated meeting age-appropriate standards with the support of inquiry experiences with Ramps and Pathways.

In Chapter 2 we stated that highly effective early childhood educators have pedagogy that is based on an understanding of both child development and STEM content knowledge. The NGSS nudges elementary-trained teachers of K–2 children to shift from teacher-centered instruction to child-centered learning. The NGSS nudges early childhood–trained teachers of K–2 children to become better acquainted with content knowledge important to address at their grade level. Finally, it assists administrators who may need more background in early childhood and elementary pedagogy to support their teachers in adjusting to child-centered STEM content, and to advocate for their educators' creative and innovative teaching that leads to creative and innovative children who excel in concrete skills because of STEM experiences that nurture the essential underlying skills (Farran, 2022).

Ramps and Pathways is not a stand-alone curriculum, but part of a framework that enables STEM learning to occur every day in the early childhood classroom, supporting science learning and enhancing learning in all domains. In the remainder of this chapter, we will crosswalk Ramps and Pathways experiences (the weft) with the standards (the warp) to illustrate how they weave together. We define a developmental approach to the NGSS science and engineering practices and NGSS crosscutting concepts that includes preschool, kindergarten, 1st grade, and 2nd grade. We end with examples of how Ramps and Pathways experiences can support standards specific to each age-group.

WEAVING THROUGH THE NGSS SCIENCE AND ENGINEERING PRACTICES

The Framework for K–12 Science Education (NRC, 2011) identified eight science and engineering practices, designed to mirror the practices of professional scientists and engineers, that are important for children to experience and implement. Appendix F of the NGSS breaks these practices out into a matrix that details the capabilities included in each practice that students should acquire by the end of four grade bands: K–2, 3–5, 6–8, and 9–12 (NGSS Lead States, 2013b). Through our work with PK–2 educators, we have found that the NGSS science and engineering practices for K–2 support preschool as well as K–2 children. PK–2 Ramps and Pathways experiences enable children to engage in all eight practices under the condition of approximation (Cambourne, 1988). This means that educators accept children's attempts to engage in the practices, congratulate them, then guide them gently toward an eventual conventional use of science and engineering practices with experiences over time. Below, we list the eight science and engineering practices as defined by the NGSS. The authors of the NGSS advised that the practices do not operate in isolation but are interconnected. They "tend to unfold sequentially, and even overlap" (NGSS Lead States, 2013b, p. 3). Because the definitions of these practices are often difficult to translate into an early childhood setting, we include a description of what they may look like, feel like, and sound like in PK–2 classrooms within the context of Ramps and Pathways. We include examples of children's approximations of these practices when engaging in Ramps and Pathways experiences. The examples are not exhaustive. You can expect your PK–2 children to demonstrate even more approximations of science and engineering practices.

1. Asking Questions and Defining Problems

Asking questions and defining problems in K–2 builds on prior experiences and progresses to simple descriptive questions that can be tested. (NGSS, Appendix F)

What This Looks Like, Feels Like, and Sounds Like in PK–2 Ramps and Pathways Experiences. Over time and through multiple opportunities, K–2 children ask questions that can be investigated using their own observations to describe and explain how the natural and human-designed world works. In a supportive classroom environment, children develop agency to identify questions and problems in their own world, and they have access to materials and time to design, build, test, redesign, build, and test, repeatedly, to answer their questions and solve problems in which they are interested. While practicing engineers use their understanding of science to solve problems, young engineers focus on engineering their constructions to make something interesting happen, and in the process they learn science. They encounter problems of physics that they must address before they can solve their engineering problem. This begins with a macro or overarching open-ended problem to solve, such as "How can I move a marble in an interesting way?" (see Figure 3.4). Children then choose their own meso- or medium-sized problem, such as "I can make a marble jump over these cars." Initial questions and problems children pose themselves may be quite broad and perhaps even impossible to answer or solve, but it is vital that children be allowed to initiate and explore their own questions and ideas for solutions to their problems; this is especially true for children who demonstrate developmental delays. Adults telling a child that their idea won't work and redirecting them before they even try does little to build the child's confidence and abilities as a problem-solver. The child can respond in one of two ways: (1) the child learns their ideas are not very good and gives up their ideas to take the teacher's direction, or (2) the child still believes their idea will work if the teacher would only let them try, but gives up and follows the teacher's direction. It is best to provide all children time and opportunity to implement their ideas as often as they need until they become satisfied their ideas are not workable. There is as much rich learning in figuring out what doesn't work as there is in figuring out what does work.

As children work to solve their own meso problem, such as "I'm going to make a system to get a marble to jump over the cars," they encounter many micro or smaller questions of physics, such as "What size of block works best?" or "How many blocks high can I make it before it falls over?"

There is synergy within science and engineering practices. In children's playful attempts to engineer a structure, understanding or a working knowledge of science concepts and properties of materials becomes essential to them. As they master this understanding, they bring their new level of understanding to their design. The deeper their understanding of science concepts, the more intricate and successful their design becomes. The more intricate their design, the more often they encounter problems of physics that increase their understanding or working knowledge of science concepts.

Asking questions and posing problems begin informally and may look very different among the children in a classroom. An educator may hear a child verbally express a question, or they may infer what a child's question is by observing their actions. For example, a child placing blocks at the end of a ramp may be working to solve the problem "How can I keep the marble from rolling under the table?"

Figure 3.4. Synergy of Engineering and Science

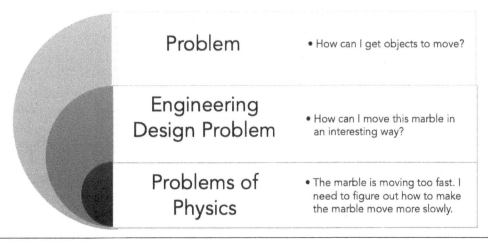

The synergy of engineering and science in students' playful learning

Problem	• How can I get objects to move?
Engineering Design Problem	• How can I move this marble in an interesting way?
Problems of Physics	• The marble is moving too fast. I need to figure out how to make the marble move more slowly.

A child lining up a wall of unit blocks at the end of a ramp may be asking the question "How many blocks will stay standing if I send this heavy ball bearing down the ramp?"

For some teachers and for many adults, playful learning where children are allowed to ask their own questions and pose their own problems may seem frivolous and unworthy of instructional time. Over a century ago, John Dewey (1916/2001) warned us not to confuse work and play in education with work and play in economic terms:

> The defining characteristic of play is not amusement nor aimlessness. It is the fact that the aim is thought of as more activity in the same line, without defining continuity of action in reference to results produced. Activities as they grow more complicated gain added meaning by greater attention to specific results achieved. Thus they pass gradually into work. Both are equally free and intrinsically motivated, apart from false economic conditions which tend to make play into idle excitement for the well to do, and work into uncongenial labor for the poor. (p. 214)

However, early childhood educators who understand intellectual development and child development recognize the power and importance of playful learning. When educators provide their children with access to materials and time to design and problem-solve, design and problem-solve, again and again (in Dewey's terms, "more activity in the same line"), their children develop agency to identify problems in their own world and construct an increasingly deep understanding of science concepts. Over time, young children eventually learn to ask and improve their own questions that can be tested (in Dewey's terms, "pass gradually into work . . . free and intrinsically motivated"), which ultimately leads to rich descriptions and explanations of how the natural and designed world works. Examples of questions and problems children pose themselves in Ramps and Pathways include the following:

- How far can I get this marble to roll?
- What happens when I roll two marbles down two ramps at the same time? Which one will win?
- How can I change the direction of the marble?

- Where do I need to put the can to catch the marble after it drops off the ramp?
- What is easier to control? A large marble or a small one?
- How can I get a marble to go over a hill?
- How can I slow the marble down so it stops rolling off the system?

2. Developing and Using Models

Modeling in K–2 builds on prior experiences and progresses to include using and developing models (i.e., diagram, drawing, physical replica, diorama, dramatization, or storyboard) that represent concrete events or design solutions. (NGSS, Appendix F)

What This Looks Like, Feels Like, and Sounds Like in PK–2 Ramps and Pathways Experiences. Young children can create and use models as tools to share their ideas and explanations when their educators accept and support their approximations of models by congratulating them on what they are doing well and guiding them gently toward models that increase in complexity and accuracy over time. Educators can introduce the idea of models by demonstrating how to create models such as observational drawings with or without labels, diagrams such as concept webs, physical replicas made from plasticine clay or loose parts, dramatizations, or storyboards. Altogether, accepting different models aligns with the key UDL principle of using multiple means of representation to promote and support children's thinking. In our work with children, we have observed three types of models used in Ramps and Pathways: mental models, drawings, and models of a feature in a system (corner, jump, drop, etc.) to demonstrate how the feature can be built effectively.

Mental Models. After multiple experiences designing and developing systems of ramps and pathways, children are able to verbally predict the path of a marble on a ramp system before they try it. We have observed other children walk slowly around their system, and carefully make small adjustments before testing the system. This shows they have created a mental model of the action of the marble that indicates spatial reasoning, which is important for achievement in mathematics, as well as evidence of their mental construction of physics. As children explain their problems or successes in their ramp designs, they may begin to document their ideas through drawing and writing. Practicing scientists and engineers often use models as tools to represent their ideas and explanations.

Drawings. Some early engineering curricula argue that because professional engineers draw plans of their designs before building, young children should be required to draw their plan before building. Drawing a model or plan of a system before building may be difficult for young children, as they do not yet have a strong working understanding of the laws of physics and how those laws govern designs. If drawing a plan is required before building, some children's completion of these drawings may be less about planning an efficient build and more about pleasing the teacher. Rather than requiring a drawing, some educators simply invite children to draw. One teacher extended this invitation by placing clipboards, paper, and markers near the Ramps and Pathways area. Several preschoolers accepted this invitation and began drawing approximations of models of their ramp structures (see Figure 3.5).

Peggy Ashbrook is a columnist of *The Early Years* in the National Science Teaching Association's journal *Science and Children*, and author of several books on early science. Peggy collaborates with us and serves as a consultant for educators interested in Ramps and Pathways. Over the years we have had many discussions about the role of drawing plans in Ramps and Pathways experiences, and Peggy has taken this on through action research, a form of investigation designed for use by educators to improve their own professional practices to better understand why, when, and how children learn (Parsons & Brown, 2002). Peggy shared several photos culled from her work with Ramps and Pathways. The first two figures were produced in a preschool enrichment session where children had several weeks of building ramps and pathways. Peggy asked them to draw the design first. Figure 3.6 shows a spatially recognizable system drawn by a 4½-year-old. Peggy reported that he built his system just like the drawing but with fewer supports. Figure 3.7 shows the prebuilding drawing of a 3-year-old child in the same program. Peggy shared that while the drawing was of a structure he could not build, this child kept the plan right next to him. His structure was loose and not productive.

We have found that children tend to be more interested in drawing a model of what they built after the build is completed. One child drew a model of

Figure 3.6. 4½-Year-Old Experienced Builder's Plans

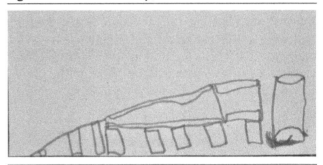

Figure 3.5. Inviting Children to Draw a Model

Figure 3.7. 3-Year-Old Experienced Builder's Plans

his design constructed by leaning a track against a cubelike chair at a pitch steep enough to start the movement of a jingle bell down the pathway. The child laid some material at the bottom of the ramp to slow down the movement of the bell and added a catcher to keep the bell from rolling too far away (see Figure 3.8). As the child explained the drawing, the teacher modeled how to label it by writing down the words of the child's description and drawing an arrow to the portion of the structure being described.

This is the little cube chair.
There's the bell.
There's the ramp.
And there is the little thing that slows it down.
And that is the catcher.

Figure 3.9 was produced by a 1st- or 2nd-grader in an after-school enrichment program led by Peggy and was completed after a build. Children may want to add their own words to their drawings. This drawing does not reveal specifics of the system other than the arrow indicating the direction of the marble, and the use of one ramp and additional track for pathways. The drawing is akin to an illustration to support a story, similar to a storyboard. The child's words included a title and two sentences:

The Ramps
The marbles went fast.
We made ramps

Figure 3.8. Supporting a Child's Use of Models

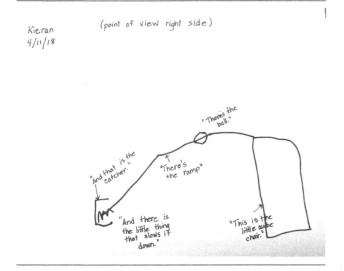

Figure 3.9. Drawing to Illustrate a Story

Figure 3.10. Drawing of a Ramp Comparison

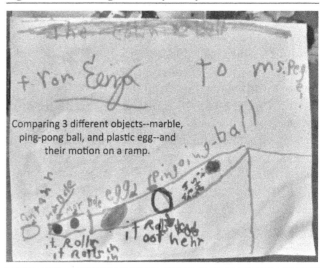

Figure 3.10 is another example of a drawing made by a 1st- or 2nd-grader in Peggy's program. This child captured what was explored in an investigation to compare three different objects and their motion on a ramp. From left to right, the child labeled the container (cintanr) and the blue and the red marbles (morBole). She reported that "it Rolls in." Moving on, she drew and labeled the egg and the ping-pong ball (pingoing-ball) and reported that when it hit the connection between two pieces of track, it rolled off here (it rolls oof hehr) and indicated the direction with an arrow.

Peggy shared another extremely detailed drawing (Figure 3.11). This child provided two points of

Figure 3.11. Two Perspectives of a Ramp and Pathway System

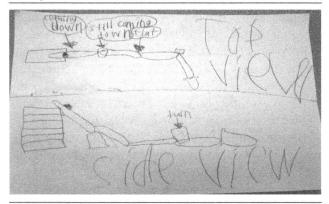

Figure 3.12. Model of a Jump Feature

Figure 3.13. Using a Wedge as a Launch

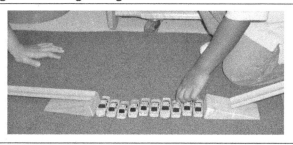

Figure 3.14. A Model of a Problem

view—top and side views. The top view revealed where the system turned a corner. The side view revealed the elevation of the ramp to be six blocks high. Peggy shared with us that the child's parents were in science-related professions. We speculated that her prior experiences with perspective at home with her parents may have led to such detailed drawings.

Models of Features. Another example of models in Ramps and Pathways is producing a model of a specific feature in a system to explain what is necessary for the feature to work. When some 1st-graders became excited after viewing a video of a motorcycle jumping over a row of cars, the rest of the class became somewhat obsessed with designing builds to make a marble jump over a row of toy cars. During class meetings, they would share what they were finding to be effective in designs. Shamia brought track, blocks, and cars to the class meetings to create a small model of her design (see Figure 3.12), explaining her thoughts on the amount of speed a marble would need going up a ramp to make it over the cars. As she explained, other 1st-graders asked her questions or gave advice based on their own experiences. Shamia was having success using a track to serve as a ramp to launch the marble. Clyde had another idea, and presented his model of using a unit block wedge to launch the marble (see Figure 3.13).

Children may use a model to extrapolate their thinking. For example, a group of 2nd-graders worked unsuccessfully to get a marble to travel through a corkscrew-type track with four tight loops. No matter how hard they tried, they found the marble would drop after the second loop. Through discussion, they came to the conclusion that the marble did not have

enough speed to make it through more than two loops. They tried making the first ramp steeper, but found this resulted in losing control of the marble before it could enter the loop. They felt what was needed was a longer first track at a specific pitch to give the marble time to roll up to the speed they needed and still enter the loops successfully. To explain this to their teacher, they built a smaller model of the corkscrew design (see Figure 3.14). They used this model to demonstrate how the marble had enough speed to make it through two loops. They believed that if they had been able to cut a hole in the ceiling of the classroom so a longer track could stick through, they might have been able to have a ramp long enough for the marble to gain enough speed to make it through more loops.

3. Planning and Carrying Out Investigations

Planning and carrying out investigations to answer questions or test solutions to problems in K–2 builds on prior experiences and progresses to simple investigations, based on fair tests, which provide data to support explanations or design solutions. (NGSS, Appendix F)

What This Looks Like, Feels Like, and Sounds Like in PK–2 Ramps and Pathways Experiences. The description of this practice is daunting. It is helpful to focus on the word *progresses*. This means children will engage in many approximations of simple investigations before their investigation behaviors become conventional.

Developing competency in planning and carrying out investigations begins with observation. Children are already curious about what is in the world, how it works, and how they can interact with it. They use their five senses to explore and observe materials. Their senses give them feedback to generate ideas about a material they are holding. They go beyond the five senses and make good use of their sense of weight, balance, and space to observe and engage in trial-and-error behavior—the beginnings of investigative behavior.

It will take experience over the years for PK–2 children to develop the skills to plan and complete an entire investigation on their own, even a simple investigation based on a fair test. The ability to observe is key in their development. If children's observational skills are not developed enough to spot an unfair test, the idea of a fair test is not very meaningful. Teachers who honor the children's approximations of investigative behavior by noticing and naming the behaviors of observation and trial and error can gently nudge children to more conventional investigative behaviors over time.

Investigations do not happen unless there are questions for which to find answers and problems for which to find solutions. In traditional instruction, the teacher asks the questions and poses the problems. The questions a teacher asks are critical in determining what the children feel compelled to do: investigate or provide a correct answer. A teacher's questions can reveal the rigor of a teacher's instructional goal and expectations for the students or even a teacher's comfort in interpreting how to address a set of science and engineering standards. For example, the NGSS kindergarten standards suggest children may "formulate answers to questions such as: 'What happens if you push or pull an object harder?'" (NGSS Lead States, 2013a, p. 3) and provide a performance expectation to "plan and conduct an investigation to compare the effects of different strengths or different directions of pushes and pulls on the motion of an object" and "analyze data to determine if a design solution works as intended to change the speed or direction of an object with a push or a pull" (p. 4). Reading these statements often leads teachers to focus narrowly on *push* and *pull* in children's investigations. Questions can become merely a mechanism for getting the children to guess at the information the teacher wants them to learn, or even to parrot back an answer the teacher is looking for (see Textbox 3.2).

TEXTBOX 3.2. QUESTIONS THAT CONSTRAIN

Teacher: What happens to the marble after I let it go at the top of this ramp?

Brendan: It goes down.

Whitney: It went way far! It went fast!

Teacher: Yes. It goes down. Why does it go down?

Whitney: Gravy. Gravy makes everything fall down.

Brendan: Can we get it to go farther?

Teacher: Gravity makes everything fall down. Not gravy, but gravity. Is this a push or a pull?

Brendan: Nobody pushing it!

Teacher: Yes, no one is pushing it. Gravity is moving it. Is gravity pushing or pulling it?

Brendan: Gravity pushes everything down! When I jump, gravity pushes me back down.

Teacher: Gravity brings you back down, but does it push you . . . or . . . does it. . . . (Waits for a child to complete the sentence.)

Whitney: Pull!

Teacher: Yes! It pulls you down! Gravity pulls you down and it is pulling the marble down.

Brendan: I don't see nothin' pulling anything. It just goes down.

Teacher: You can't SEE gravity pulling it down. It is an invisible force.

Tyler: Yay! Magic!

Whitney: My uncle's in the Air Force.

In this example, the teacher was using a version of the Socratic method. However, her questions were tempered to get the children to answer with a word she wanted them to learn. When she didn't get the response she wanted, she used a follow-up question that narrowed the guesses. Her question, "Why does it go down?," seemed to be beyond the child's reach. The teacher asked five questions before she got the answer she wanted. When she did get the answer of gravity, that answer was still a great mystery to the children. Asking young children questions involving "why" tend to frustrate both the teacher and the child. "Why" is not always easily explained or understood.

The child's question that was ignored by the teacher, "Can we get it [per textbox p. 44] to go farther?," is accessible to young children and invites them to engage in active inquiry. Questions that involve "How" are more often tangible and interesting to the children. While the question of how to get the marble to go farther doesn't lead to an investigation that includes the words *push* or *pull*, it does lend well to engaging children in science and engineering practices of planning and carrying out investigations, analyzing and interpreting data, asking questions and defining problems, and developing and using models (see Textbox 3.3). Within these practices over time, children develop science and engineering habits of mind where they feel compelled to observe, have questions, gather information, have more questions or a different question, and adjust the investigation to gather more information (Shouse et al., 2007). Children grapple with NGSS core ideas in engineering problems, solutions, and their optimization, and with core ideas in forces and interactions. Children's curiosity in how to move objects will spur design systems that have objects collide and lead to them stating, "That marble pushed the other to make it move."

TEXTBOX 3.3. QUESTIONS THAT GO FAR

Teacher: I noticed you are interested in investigating how far you can get a marble to go. How might we do that?

Nathan: I need lots of room 'cause mine's going to go far!

Teacher: Lots of room. How could we do that in our room?

Tempest: We can stay in this part of the room. There's more room here.

Teacher: That might work. Let's try it and see. I wonder what else you might need.

Nathan: I need lots of blocks! I'm going to make my ramp really steep!

Teacher: You want your track steep? Show me what you mean by *steep*.

Nathan: You put one end up really high like this. (Demonstrates with a section of track.)

Teacher: So, a steep ramp is when one end is a lot higher than the other end?

Nathan: Yup.

Teacher: We have quite a few blocks. I wonder how many we might need if everyone wants to try?

Nathan: I might not need them all, but I'll need a lot!

Teacher: We'll have to keep an eye out to see that everyone has what they need, won't we? How will we know how far the marble goes?

Tempest: We can stand by it.

Teacher: We could stand by it. Then everyone could see how far it went from the end of the ramp to where you are standing. Is there another way?

Nathan: I'm going to put a block where it stops. That way I can try it again. I'm going to try it lots of times. I'm going to make it go the farthest of all!

Teacher: That's another idea we could try. It will be interesting to see how far we can get it to go. What else could we try?

Tempest: I could put a piece of tape on the floor.

Teacher: That's another idea. Shall we give it a go?

Children who understand the power of close observation often move on to engage in approximations of planning and carrying out investigations based on those observations. Kindergartners in Brandy Twedt's classroom built two similar systems and observed closely to see which system produced a faster-moving marble. Their teacher photographed their work to document it and post it on the wall. Brandy asked the two children what they were doing in the photograph. One of them said, "We are having a race to see which is faster." Brandy capitalized on their interest in ramps and pathways by using their excitement to help these emergent readers and writers focus on writing down their words so they could remember what they did and others could read it (see Textbox 3.4).

TEXTBOX 3.4. BRINGING EARLY LITERACY INTO THE PICTURE

Brandy: You told me you were having a race to see which is faster. That is exciting. Let's write that down so we don't forget it. Let's first make a line for each of the words.

(Brandy drew a line for each word as the girls repeated their sentence.)

Brandy: Now we need to write each word on its line. Listen for the first word when I say it back to you again: "Charlotte and Riley have a race to see which is faster." What was the first word?

Charlotte: My name!

Brandy: Yes! You know your name. Go ahead and write it on the first line.

(Charlotte wrote her name.)

Brandy: Great! Let's say it again to see what the second word is. "Charlotte and . . ."

Charlotte: And!!

Brandy: You know we read that word earlier and put it on our word wall. Can you help me find it?

Riley: It's right there. A – n – d.

Brandy: You can write that down. You just showed it to us.

(Riley wrote the word *and.*)

Riley: Then it's my name!

Brandy: Let's see. "Charlotte and . . ."

Riley: Riley! (Wrote *Riley.*)

Brandy continued to engage in interactive writing by sharing the pen with the two kindergartners, always reading from the beginning and pointing to each word every time they needed to write the next word. The kindergartners could write down the words they knew or the sounds in the words they could hear (ras for race; wi for which; fasr for faster). By the time they were finished, both could read back the sentence they had co-constructed. Posting it on the wall, the two could revisit their event and reread it to themselves, or to other visitors to the room. Brandy had extended her kindergartners' understanding of a sense of word, sight words they could retrieve from other sources of print, beginning and ending sounds, and the vowel sounds. Brandy was accepting and celebrating children's approximations of engaging in inquiry, and also their approximations of their understanding of print (see Figure 3.15).

Racing marbles is a common focus in the beginning of Ramps and Pathways. A group of 1st-graders were interested in how similar objects performed on the same kind of inclines. They used three 2-foot tracks and three unit blocks to create identical inclines to observe how different types of objects rolled down the incline and which reached the bottom first. Three unit block arches were placed at the bottom of the ramp to contain the objects (see Figure 3.16).

Figure 3.15. Kindergartners' Interactive Writing About Their Investigation

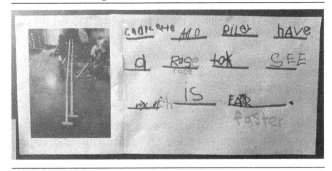

Figure 3.16. Setup for Marble Racing

Noticing how the material of the objects affected how they moved, the children began to wonder what would happen if the track was made out of different materials. They brought this question to their teacher, and she offered to cover track with different kinds of materials. The next day, the children found 2-foot lengths of track covered with either sandpaper, felt, paint, or corduroy with the ribs running the length of the track or with the ribs running the width of the track (see Figure 3.17). The 1st-graders positioned the track at the same height and began their investigation exploring how a marble's action was affected by the surface of a track.

These examples of simple investigations may not be as tightly controlled as investigations described in textbooks—with directions on what to control, what to vary, what to document, and how to document—but these examples do illustrate the authentic curiosity and agency children can have in conducting investigations. Every opportunity children have to observe, document, compare, and look for relationships within phenomena to answer their own questions will strengthen a child's use of investigative behavior.

You may have noticed that this was an investigation carried out by several children and not the whole class. In our framework for daily STEM investigations, children have the time to deepen their observations of phenomena that excite them and sharpen their skills in investigative behaviors that become part of who they are, and how they think and learn. Children's agency in conducting investigations develops best when they are allowed to have choice in what to investigate. Young children vary in their development of perspective-taking or seeing another person's point of view. To accommodate this, any environment for investigation also follows the UDL and must be flexible, allowing children the choice of working alone, in pairs, or within a group, as well as choice in the direction and intensity of their investigation.

The same goes for engineering. Career engineers work in teams whose members contribute ideas about how to improve designs or solve problems that arise in the design process of producing technology for a customer. PK–2 children are far more likely to think harder about how to solve a problem within their own lives. A child's idea of a problem that needs solving may not seem significant to adults, but the problem is important to the child. When young children are committed to solving a problem, they sharpen their abilities to (1) engage in systems thinking (how a change in one part affects another part), (2) engage in creative thought and problem solving, (3) develop self-regulation and optimism as they come to view errors and failures as an opportunity to learn, (4) communicate with others about their work, (5) collaborate with their peers, and (6) engage in ethical thinking as they consider how their actions and use of materials affect their peers as they design, build, and test (NRC, 2009). Examples of questions and problems PK–2 children have expressed are listed below:

- How can I make the marble roll faster?
- How can I make the marble roll slower?
- How does the speed of the marble affect what I want my system to do?
- How do spheres the same size, but made from a different material, move on my system?
- How can I build a system strong enough to move a large, heavy, steel ball bearing?
- How many corners can I get a marble to turn?
- How many times can I get a marble to reverse its direction?
- How many different design features can I have in one system?

Figure 3.17. Investigating the Effects of Texture

4. Analyzing and Interpreting Data

Analyzing data in K–2 builds on prior experiences and progresses to collecting, recording, and sharing observations. (NGSS, Appendix F)

What This Looks Like, Feels Like, and Sounds like in PK–2 Ramps and Pathways Experiences. Scientists and engineers use data as evidence for their ideas about how the world works. Young children can record their observations in drawings, words, or numbers to share them with others. However, before they can begin to record data, they have to have a purpose for the data. The teacher can help them realize a purpose for data by asking simply, "How will we know . . . ?" or "How can we remember . . . ?" Children may already have ideas on what to pay attention to and can direct the teacher to take down information for them. For children just learning how to represent speech through writing, the teacher can act as a scribe for the child. As children begin to grasp the rules of writing, they begin to use what they know to write on their own.

The kinds of information, or data, PK–2 children and their educators can collect include photographs, video, observational drawings, concept webs, information sorted on T-charts, counts of events recorded with tally marks, and written or dictated descriptions of observations. When children look at the data they have collected, their educator can serve as a model by noticing patterns in the data, making comparisons, or commenting on relationships that help to answer the question or problem the children posed.

When educators and children co-create ways of collecting data that are important to them, children understand the way the data are organized and are more likely to use data collection on their own. With enough modeling, the children may begin to take this on themselves. The children might make a decision to go back and restart the investigation if they find they need to collect different information or control a variable. Young children engage in approximations of recording and analyzing data when they do the following:

- ask the educator to act as their scribe to write down their ideas, questions, predictions, and reports of what happened

- record observations about materials and how they move by drawing and/or writing in science journals
- describe positional relationships of tracks and ramps in order to answer questions about how the system is able to work
- compare predictions about where an object needs to be placed on an incline in order for it to hit a target

5. Using Mathematics and Computational Thinking

Mathematical and computational thinking in K–2 builds on prior experience and progresses to recognizing that mathematics can be used to describe the natural and designed world(s). (NGSS, Appendix F)

What This Looks Like, Feels Like, and Sounds Like in PK–2 Ramps and Pathways Experiences. STEM investigations provide rich opportunities for PK–2 children to count and determine relative amounts of more or less and to use general observations or standard units of measure to determine whether objects are either taller or shorter, longer or shorter, heavier or lighter, bigger or smaller, hotter or colder.

Mathematics can be used in the collection and representation of data. Young children can use numbers to count the number of blocks supporting a piece of track to record information about the height of the ramp. Also, the construction of ramp structures affords the added bonus of developing spatial reasoning, an early childhood mathematical concept that is gaining importance in the field of mathematics but is neglected in the early childhood classroom (Sarama & Clements, 2009). In building their designs, young children engage deeply in spatial tasks such as flipping and rotating as they manipulate unit blocks to coordinate the components of their ramp structures (Casey et al., 2008). Early childhood experience and success in such spatial tasks has been linked to later success in problem solving in middle school and high school honors math courses (Kersh et al., 2008). While a high-quality school set of 720 unit blocks to use in Ramps and Pathways investigations can cost well over $2,500, their use is invaluable in concept development both in mathematics (part-part and part-whole relationships, as well as spatial reasoning) and in physics and engineering (the role of balance, weight, tension, and friction in stable construction). With unit blocks and ramps, children design and construct their own technology of ramp and pathway systems and, in the process, develop science and engineering habits of mind. Compare this with the cost of outfitting a classroom with 10 tablet computers. Analyzing the programs available on hand-held devices, we find most programs to be didactic and to require low-level thinking by users. In addition to providing low conceptual development, in a few years the computers will be outdated. In comparison, unit blocks last forever. If a choice is to be made, we would advocate low-tech for high conceptual development instead of high-tech for low conceptual development.

Computational thinking is a term not well known in the PK–2 world and can feel intimidating. It can also be narrowly defined to the point that it fits only within "learn to code" curricula. In fact, computational thinking is a thought process that can begin in the early grades when children have experiences that call on it: (1) decomposition, (2) pattern recognition, (3) abstraction, and (4) algorithms.

Decomposition is meaningful when young children are facing a problem that requires multiple steps to solve. For example, if children want to build a system of ramps and pathways, they will need to think of how they will prepare for this challenge. What should they do first? What materials will they need? How will they need to alter the materials? If they make an adjustment in one component of a system, what will need to be done with those following it?

Pattern recognition in the primary grades is often thought of as one's ability to determine a pattern (such as the basic ABAB) and continue it. A deeper understanding of pattern recognition in Ramps and Pathways experiences invites children to observe similar objects or experiences and identify commonalities or patterns in order to build a working system or expand a design by drawing on their understanding of the patterns in force and motion phenomena. By finding what objects or experiences have in common and how they differ, children can begin to understand trends and make predictions. For example, children may be invited to investigate how different types of spheres move on an incline. What do they all have in common? (They are all round like a ball.) How do they differ? (Some are solid, some

are hollow. They can be made of metal, glass, hard or soft plastic, wood, or fiber.) As children recognize patterns in how the attributes of different materials respond to starting, stopping, slowing, or increasing their movement, their awareness of the world around them expands and helps them solve future problems and predict with greater accuracy.

Abstraction is focusing on the information that is important and ignoring information that is not. Children who are building systems of ramps and pathways often select an object to move based on its attractive qualities, such as color, size, and weight. They demonstrate abstraction when they ignore an object's attractive qualities and instead focus on its functionality.

Algorithmic thinking involves sequential rules to follow in order to solve a problem. Young children can learn that the order in which steps are taken to complete something can have a significant effect. An example would be that when children adjust a component early in the system, they will need to check the following components for needed additional adjustments.

6. Constructing Explanations and Designing Solutions

Constructing explanations and designing solutions in K–2 builds on prior experiences and progresses to the use of evidence and ideas in constructing evidence-based accounts of natural phenomena and designing solutions. (NGSS, Appendix F)

What This Looks Like, Feels Like, and Sounds Like in PK–2 Ramps and Pathways Experiences. When PK–2 children are given the opportunity to pursue answers to their own questions about the natural or designed world or have an idea on how to design and build their own technology to "make something happen," they demonstrate an intrinsic desire to conduct an investigation, collect information (data) that makes sense to them, and analyze it to find an answer or a solution. When they are satisfied with their answer or solution, they can make a claim and use their data as evidence to support their claim and present it to others. When educators scaffold their children's analysis by assisting them in preparing to present their data, or by acting as scribe to construct a claim, they have rich opportunities to model writing, enhance vocabulary, and consider the needs of an audience. These are all important literacy components. Young children need opportunities to explain and critique ideas. Ramps and Pathways activities allow children opportunities to explain what they are observing and to critique other's explanations. As children gain more understanding of force and motion, they can describe causal accounts of how the marble moves on their ramp structures, and how their design accommodates the marble's movement. Again, explanations require explicit descriptions that nudge children to search for just the right word. The teacher's goal is to start with the children's current vocabulary for describing actions rather than introducing technical terms that are not relevant to the young children's levels of experience. We can add new vocabulary words gradually as children experience the relevant actions. Teachers can provide such words when the moment demands, and children will begin to incorporate new vocabulary as discussion continues over time. Educators can model how to construct a table, diagram, graph, model, or numbers to provide details about ideas or solutions. Through the gradual release of responsibility, children take on these roles, exhibiting approximations of these behaviors and improving their presentation over time.

7. Engaging in Argument From Evidence

Engaging in argument from evidence in K–2 builds on prior experiences and progresses to comparing ideas and representations about the natural and designed world(s). (NGSS, Appendix F)

What This Looks Like, Feels Like, and Sounds Like in PK–2 Ramps and Pathways Experiences. Educators are well acquainted with their role in telling and explaining. When the educator knows the content well, it is easy to assume the role of being the sole authority, telling children what information is important and confirming correct answers. In classrooms in which inquiry learning is valued, the role of educator shifts from sole authority to the interrelated roles of facilitator, questioner, listener, and learner. All these roles are important in engaging in scientific argumentation.

Engaging in scientific argumentation works best when there is a designated space for classroom conversations—a place for children to gather together,

ready to think, listen, share, and question themselves and their classmates. The educator takes on the role of **facilitator** to keep the discussion focused on the important science or engineering concept, assisting children in structuring their comments and questions to keep a meaningful and natural conversation going. In the role of **questioner**, the educator models how to respectfully disagree or to request a deeper explanation. The educator assumes the role of active **listener** by restating what children say to clarify understanding. And the educator takes on the role of **learner** by stating changes in their own thinking after a child presents their argument.

It is essential to remember that young learners arrive in our classrooms with vast differences in their experiences with engaging in argumentation. Argumentation requires considering problems from different perspectives. Some children are still struggling with taking another's perspective. If discussion is a regular occurrence in a child's family, argumentation will come more easily. For other children, only the adults engage in discussion, and young children are not invited into the conversation. In some families, there is no discussion at all, as adults make all the decisions and children are expected to follow. Some families engage in argument not to come to consensus, but to win, sometimes to win at all costs. Children will need to hear phrases modeled for them such as "I disagree . . . Have you thought of . . . ?" or "I'm confused. Can you help me understand?" It is important to introduce scientific argumentation with young children, but educators should be prepared to support children's approximations of scientific argumentation with the expectation that conventional scientific argumentation will develop over time.

Children are nurtured to ponder and discuss claims that can be supported through descriptive data or numerical data. This is done in an educational environment that accepts, respects, and considers all answers and encourages child communication throughout the argumentation process. This is possible in a classroom where children expect to think, listen, share, and respectfully question their original ideas and their classmates' ideas. The educator can act as scribe to document a claim that has been successfully argued, achieving consensus, and then post the claim on the classroom wall. Examples of a child's approximations of arguing with evidence include the following:

- The child demonstrates with materials to provide evidence collected on how the properties of a material affect its movement as it rolls down a ramp, and then after it leaves the end of the ramp.
- The child explains (argues) from evidence that the weight of a sphere knocks a system out of balance as the sphere rolls through, causing frequent rebuilds.
- The child listens to and considers explanations (arguments) that the heights of a sequence of hills need to be lower for each hill following.

8. Obtaining, Evaluating, and Communicating Information

Obtaining, evaluating, and communicating information in K–2 builds on prior experiences and uses observations and texts to communicate new information. (NGSS, Appendix F)

What This Looks Like, Feels Like, and Sounds Like in PK–2 Ramps and Pathways Experiences. We find that children are most excited about STEM when they can do STEM. When children are emotionally invested in their work, they will want to share or compare their thinking with others. PK–2 teachers can support children's development in obtaining, evaluating, and communicating information through nonfiction read-alouds, observational drawing, expert interviews, and documentation on classroom and hallway walls.

Nonfiction Read-Alouds. Many of us are accustomed to starting off a unit of study or an investigation with a good book. However, we want you to consider waiting to read informational books on ramps and pathways to your children until after they have had opportunities to engage in ramps and pathways phenomena. Starting with a STEM experience and saving the read-aloud for later has three advantages: (1) the wonder and the experience with the phenomenon are grander when children discover them on their own; (2) children's prior experiences with a phenomenon will enhance their comprehension of a book's explanation of the phenomenon; and (3) children will be able to compare their own thinking about the phenomenon with that of the author. When there is disagreement, there is the perfect context for scientific argumentation.

Observational Drawing. When teachers encourage children to engage in observational drawing, children begin to notice details and begin to document them. This allows children to compare and critique their own work, and to compare their drawings with those of their peers.

Outside Experts. Following their children's curiosity about ramps and pathways, teachers can introduce them to community members who need to consider inclines in their work. Such experts can include roofers, civil engineers who design roads with on and off ramps, and designers of ramps for accessibility. Ramps.org is an organization committed to assisting people who need wheelchair access to homes, businesses, or vehicles. Their website has a clickable map to locate local organizations that may come to talk about the thinking that goes on behind designing a ramp.

Documentation Walls. When the process of children's learning is documented through drawings, photographs, and models, as in the earlier example of Brandy Twedt and her kindergartners, a teacher can honor and celebrate children's thinking by creating a documentation wall using these artifacts. When teachers promote the process of their children's learning on the classroom walls and shelving, children have the opportunity to reflect on their work. A child can also act as a docent (a person who acts as a guide in a museum, art gallery, or zoo), serving three purposes: (1) to act as a host and welcome visitors to the classroom; (2) to be an interpreter of the documentation on the wall, helping to give the visitor a deeper understanding and appreciation of the work featured on the classroom walls and shelving; and (3) to assist in preserving the documentation in the classroom, such as cleaning up or replenishing spaces where there may be interactive work with materials. Actions of children who are engaging in obtaining, evaluating, and communicating information can include the following:

- They read nonfiction books about ramps and pathways to compare what they learned about ramps and pathways with what the authors of the books report.
- They begin to pay attention to text features (e.g., headings, tables of contents, glossaries, electronic menus, icons) and begin to explore their own use of text features in

their writing about ramps and pathways phenomena.

- They communicate information or design ideas and/or solutions with others using models, drawings, writing, tallies, or numbers to provide detail about scientific ideas, practices, and/or design ideas.

WEAVING THROUGH THE CROSSCUTTING CONCEPTS

As young children engage in science and engineering practices in Ramps and Pathways experiences, they have the opportunity to recognize similarities in concepts they formed in previous STEM investigations. The NGSS define these as *crosscutting concepts*, or themes that hold true in science phenomena across

the four domains of science (see Appendix G of the NGSS, NGSS Lead States, 2013c). In Figure 3.18 we list each of the seven crosscutting concepts, along with the NGSS definition and a brief example, and in the following text we provide a few more detailed examples of how children may engage with these concepts in Ramps and Pathways.

1. Patterns

The NGSS state that "observed patterns in nature guide organization and classification and prompt questions about relationships and causes underlying them" (NGSS Lead States, 2013c, p. 15). As children build systems of ramps and pathways, they often use patterns in their designs. Some children may not readily recognize these patterns without an adult pointing them out. Yet others pick up on

Figure 3.18. NGSS Crosscutting Concepts (CCC) Within Ramps and Pathways

CCC	NGSS definition for K–2 (NGSS, Appendix G)	Example of How a CCC May Look in Ramps and Pathways
Patterns	Children recognize that patterns in the natural and human designed world can be observed, used to describe phenomena, and used as evidence.	Children begin to predict how far an object will roll when they observe the height of the ramp.
Cause and Effect	Students learn that events have causes that generate observable patterns. They design simple tests to gather evidence to support or refute their own ideas about causes.	Children manipulate materials to cause an effect on a marble's movement. They repeat the arrangement of materials to replicate the effect in following ramp and pathways systems.
Scale, Proportion, and Quantity	Students use relative scales to allow objects and events to be compared and described (e.g., bigger and smaller; hotter and colder; faster and slower) to describe objects. They use standard units to measure length.	Children use relative scales such as bigger and smaller when referring to objects they are moving, and faster and slower to describe the speed of a marble. They use the number of unit blocks to track the height of ramps, or floor tiles to measure how far a marble rolls.
Systems and System Models	Students understand that objects and organisms can be described in terms of their parts, and that systems in the natural and designed world have parts that work together.	When children make an adjustment to one component of their ramp and pathway system, they attend to how that adjustment will impact the other components in their system.
Energy and Matter	Students observe that objects may break into smaller pieces, be put together into larger pieces, or change shapes.	Children can take down a system of ramps and pathways and reconfigure the parts to make a completely different design.
Structure and Function	Students observe that the shape and stability of structures of natural and designed objects are related to their function(s).	Components within systems of ramps and pathways can be structured to create a drop or a jump, to cause an object to reverse direction, and to function in many other ways.
Stability and Change	Students observe that some things stay the same while other things change and that things may change slowly or rapidly.	An effective ramp and pathway system is stable when it can be used many times without the need to adjust or rebuild it.

successful design patterns and replicate them in later constructions. Children also notice that patterns in form often determine patterns in movement. For example, cylinders always roll straight, while spheres roll straight but are more susceptible to other forces and can begin to curve.

2. Cause and Effect

Events have causes, sometimes simple, sometimes multifaceted (NGSS, Appendix G). Children reason about many causal relationships as they design systems of ramps and pathways. For example, they can change the speed of a marble by raising or lowering the pitch of a track. They can verify that when they want to knock down a block at the end of a ramp, a heavier marble is more effective than a lighter one. They can also figure out that a marble can roll down one ramp and up another, but the marble won't go over a hill that is higher than the start of the initial ramp.

3. Scale, Proportion, and Quantity

"It is important "to recognize what is relevant at different size, time, and energy scales, and to recognize proportional relationships between quantities as scales change" (NGSS, Appendix G). These concepts are challenging, but children begin to grapple with them when they discern differences in building with short versus long pieces of track or heavy versus light marbles. They reason about how much speed a marble needs to fly over different widths of gaps between tracks. This application of concepts builds the practical knowledge of how the world works without needing to refer to Newton's Laws specifically.

4. Systems and System Models

Defining a system and making a model of that system help students understand and test ideas in science and engineering (NGSS, Appendix G). Ramps and Pathways activities are the perfect, meaningful introduction to the concept of systems, as the activity itself consists of building systems of track placed at an incline to create a ramp or flat to create a pathway. As children connect one track with another, they have to consider the effect of the new

addition on the existing structure. Systems grow in complexity as children determine models of success to get a marble to turn corners, switch directions, or strike a target.

5. Energy and Matter

Tracking changes of energy and matter within systems helps one understand the possibilities and limitations of the system (NGSS, Appendix G). As children compare the difference between releasing heavier or lighter marbles on a ramp, they construct a working understanding of the relation of the marble's weight and its energy, an understanding precursory to reasoning in later grades about the effects of mass. They notice that heavier marbles go farther off the end of a ramp than lighter marbles. This understanding is precursory to reasoning in later grades about kinetic energy.

6. Structure and Function

"The way an object is shaped or structured determines many of its properties and functions" (NGSS, Appendix G). When children explore which objects move on a ramp and how an object moves, they are exploring the structure of the object and how its structure has an impact on the way it functions on the ramp. For example, when children put a plastic egg on its side at the top of a ramp, it usually slides to the bottom of the ramp. But if they put a heavy marble inside the egg and place it at the top of a ramp with the large end of the egg down, the egg flips end over end to the bottom of the ramp.

7. Stability and Change

In understanding a system, it is important to study its stability and how it changes (NGSS, Appendix G). As children send marbles down their systems of ramps and pathways, they may notice that each time the marble strikes a part of the structure, there is usually some movement. Some of this movement is not enough to change the action of the next marble they send down, but often it is. They begin to redesign systems to withstand the marble's impact or increase its stability, resulting in a higher-performing system.

ALIGNING RAMPS AND PATHWAYS EXPERIENCES WITH STANDARDS SPECIFIC TO AGES AND GRADES

We have just reviewed how relevant Ramps and Pathways experiences are for developing the NGSS science and engineering practices and illustrating the NGSS crosscutting concepts in PK–2. Although Ramps and Pathways experiences are part of a framework for developing STEM dispositions, and not a stand-alone curriculum, the experiences do align well with many standards specific to age groups.

In our work with Iowa preschool teachers, we can easily connect Ramps and Pathways experiences (see Figure 3.3) to Iowa's Early Learning Standards (IELS) (Iowa Department of Education, 2018), which were written in alignment with the Next Generation Science Standards. Other states have comparable standards. Here we connect Ramps and Pathways experiences to Head Start's Early Learning Outcomes Framework (ELOF), a set of preschool standards that is common across the states (Office of Head Start, 2015). We then connect Ramps and Pathways experiences to NGSS standards for kindergarten through grade 2.

WEAVING THROUGH THE EARLY LEARNING OUTCOMES FRAMEWORK

The Early Learning Outcomes Framework (ELOF) (Office of Head Start, 2015) is a set of standards designed to improve the quality of children's learning experiences and environments among five broad areas, or domains, of early learning: (1) Approaches to Learning; (2) Social and Emotional Development; (3) Language and Literacy; (4) Cognition; and (5) Perceptual, Motor, and Physical Development. Children's experiences with ramps and pathways are applicable to all five of these domains. The ELOF requires that preschool teachers use a standardized assessment system such as Teaching Strategies GOLD® (see Heroman et al., 2010) or COR (HighScope Educational Research Foundation, 2015). The GOLD® assessment is less content-specific and more oriented toward conceptual thinking and increasing young children's capacities for practical problem solving through exploration of materials. GOLD® also seeks to document young children's

abilities to carry out increasingly sophisticated actions with those materials.

Some preschool educators find it difficult to document learning in all five areas of the ELOF. Teachers who implement Ramps and Pathways experiences, however, find that they provide a meaningful and rich context to gather data to meet a variety of standards. In addition to the example of the early childhood special education teacher's documentation board illustrating standards met (see Figure 3.3), we offer these comments from another preschool teacher, Jessica Sass, who described how many standards can be met, enjoyably at that:

> Ramps is such a rich and open-ended topic that kids can take it so many different ways. I have seen students go back day after day week after week and continue to make something new and solve new problems. Not only have we been able to work on science, but the cognitive, social, and math skills that are learned within Ramps is so great to see. We work on spatial relations, taking turns, problem solving, so many of our Early Learning Standards can be met through having Ramps in our classroom, and it's just plain fun.

In the following sections, we provide a narrative of how Ramps and Pathways experiences can fit within the five domains of ELOF, and we list the ELOF subdomains aligned to objectives and dimensions of the GOLD® assessment. You will see how Ramps and Pathways experiences stimulate rich learning that aligns well with ELOF's domains and can be easily documented to satisfy GOLD® criteria.

1. Approaches to Learning (see Figure 3.19)

This domain challenges teachers to select experiences that nurture a child's cognitive self-regulation (executive functions), initiative and curiosity, and creativity. Ramps and Pathways experiences are a context in which preschool children are able to express their curiosity, interest, and initiative in playful learning to explore the environment. As they encounter difficulties in building sturdy enough structures and in getting the results they want to see when using ramps to move objects, they develop

Figure 3.19. Approaches to Learning Subdomains Aligned to GOLD®

ELOF Goal	ELOF Subdomain and Goals	GOLD® Objective and Dimensions
	Cognitive Self-Regulation (Executive Functioning)	
P ATL 6	Child maintains focus and sustains attention with minimal adult support.	11a, 11b, 11d
P ATL 7	Child persists in tasks.	11b
P ATL 9	Child demonstrates flexibility in thinking and behavior.	11e, 11d
	Initiative and Curiosity	
P ATL 10	Child demonstrates initiative and independence.	11d
P ATL 11	Child shows interest in and curiosity about the world around them.	11d, 26
	Creativity	
P ATL 12	Child expresses creativity in thinking and communication.	11c, 11d, 11e
P ATL 13	Child uses imagination in play and interactions with others.	11d

Figure 3.20. Social and Emotional Development Subdomains Aligned to GOLD®

ELOF Goal	ELOF Subdomain and Goals	GOLD® Objective and Dimensions
	Relationships With Adults	
P SE 1	Child engages in and maintains positive relationships and interactions with adults.	2a
P SE 2	Child engages in prosocial and cooperative behavior with adults.	2a
	Relationships With Other Children	
P SE 3	Child engages in and maintains positive interactions and relationships with other children.	2c, 2d
P SE 4	Child engages in cooperative play with other children.	2c
P SE 5	Child uses basic problem-solving skills to resolve conflicts with other children.	3b
	Emotional Functioning	
P SE 6	Child expresses a broad range of emotions and recognizes these emotions in self and others.	1a
P SE 8	Child manages emotions with increasing independence.	1a

persistence as they problem-solve. When they encounter challenges to their plans, they demonstrate curiosity about what went wrong and show flexibility and creativity as they work alone or with peers to try out alternative methods for achieving their goals. Many educators have remarked on how Ramps and Pathways supports this domain, such as what this teacher in a classroom of 4-year-olds told us:

> The amount of focus and attention to detail and problem solving these students can do when given some wooden ramps and marbles is incredible! To see a student's face when they are trying to get the marble to go somewhere or do something specific and when they

finally get it, the pure joy on their face is just priceless! I also love to see students who show that drive to solve the problem and stick with it until it's solved.

2. Social and Emotional Development (see Figure 3.20)

Preschool children develop a sense of self and their abilities as they build structures and experiment with force and motion to achieve the outcomes they work to create. Many educators have commented on how Ramps and Pathways experiences facilitate teamwork and coax children to manage their behaviors and emotions with the support of their teachers. A preschool teacher in a classroom inclusive of children with disabilities told us this:

> What I love most about Ramps is that it gives students an opportunity to be a leader and an expert when they might not otherwise be. I remember a student a few years ago who really took to Ramps and made such cool creations. Another group of students was having difficulty getting their ramp to work and I went up to the ramp expert and said to him, "Hey, your friends are having trouble with their ramp, can you help them?" He gave me this great big smile and said "yeah!" [and] went over to blocks and helped them solve their problem.

3. Language and Literacy (see Figure 3.21)

For preschoolers, this central domain includes distinct Language and Communication and Literacy domains. Preschoolers engage in conversation to coordinate movement of themselves and materials to serve a collective purpose of investigating ramps and pathways. Printing out photos of children engaged in building ramps and pathways invites them to engage in their development of literacy. They may dictate a description of what is happening in their photo, write their name on their photo, label their photo, or write a short story of their experience. They have opportunities to read their peers' photos and stories, as well as group photos and written records of different experiences.

4. Cognition (see Figure 3.22)

For preschoolers, this central domain includes distinct Mathematics Development and Scientific Reasoning domains. Ramps and Pathways experiences provide preschoolers opportunities to describe and compare shapes and spatial relationships, objects, and the distance and speed with which objects travel on pathways. These experiences will generate opportunities to sort and classify objects according to how they travel on ramps and pathways and to find answers to questions preschoolers have. Ramps and Pathways experiences pique preschoolers' curiosity about force and motion. As children build structures to support ramps to move objects on pathways, educators can support children's scientific investigations by offering to write down questions they have and ideas they want to try out. As these ideas are tested, educators can support the preschoolers as they describe what they notice and learn, and then record this information through photos with notes for a child to reflect on their experience or to communicate with their peers or with an outside audience.

5. Perceptual, Motor, and Physical Development (see Figure 3.23)

Children use both large muscles and fine motor control in building structures from a variety of

Figure 3.21. Language and Communication and Literacy Subdomains Aligned to GOLD®

ELOF goal	ELOF subdomain and goals	GOLD® objective and dimensions
	Attending and Understanding	
P LC 1	Child attends to communication and language from others.	8, 8a, 8b
P LC 2	Child understands and responds to increasingly complex communication and language from others.	8, 8a, 9, 9a
	Communicating and Speaking	
P LC 4	Child understands, follows, and uses appropriate social and conversational rules.	8a, 9c
P LC 5	Child expresses self in increasingly long, detailed, and sophisticated ways.	8, 8a, 9, 9a, 9c
	Print and Alphabet Knowledge	
P LIT 3	Child identifies letters of the alphabet and produces correct sounds associated with letters.	16, 16a, 16b
	Writing	
P LIT 6	Child writes for a variety of purposes using increasingly sophisticated marks.	19, 19b

Figure 3.22. Mathematics Development and Scientific Reasoning Subdomains Aligned to GOLD®

ELOF Goal	ELOF Subdomain and Goals	GOLD® Objective and Dimensions
Measurement		
P MATH 8	Child measures objects by their various attributes using standard and non-standard measurement. Uses differences in attributes to make comparisons.	20, 20b, 21, 21b, 22, 22a
Geometry and Spatial Sense		
P MATH 9	Child identifies, describes, compares, and composes shapes.	21, 21b
P MATH 10	Child explores the positions of objects in space.	21, 21a, 30
Scientific Inquiry		
P SCI 1	Child observes and describes observable phenomena (objects, materials, organisms, and events).	24, 30
Reasoning and Problem-Solving		
P SCI 4	Child asks a question, gathers information, and makes predictions.	11c
P SCI 5	Child plans and conducts investigations and experiments.	11c, 11e
P SCI 6	Child analyzes results, draws conclusions, and communicates results.	11c

Figure 3.23. Perceptual, Motor, and Physical Development Subdomains Aligned to GOLD®

ELOF Goal	ELOF Subdomain and Goals	GOLD® Objective and Dimensions
Gross Motor		
P PMP 1	Child demonstrates control, strength, and coordination of large muscles.	4
P PMP 2	Child uses perceptual information to guide motions and interactions with objects and other people.	6
Fine Motor		
P PMP 3	Child demonstrates increasing control, strength, and coordination of small muscles.	7a

shapes and sizes of blocks and a variety of sizes of track. Muscle control develops as they learn how to prevent accidentally knocking over their own or a peer's structure. In carrying blocks and track from a storage area to a work area, they learn to watch out for peers and intervening objects and to avoid hitting them by adjusting the way that they are carrying materials.

WEAVING THROUGH THE NGSS K–2 DISCIPLINARY CORE IDEAS

Prior to the NGSS, many teachers of science focused on teaching facts in life science, physical science, and earth and space science. In each of the PK–2 grades, the NGSS challenges educators to change their practice and design lessons that enable children to use science and engineering practices to increase their understanding of fundamental ideas within the four domains of science. Below, we provide examples of how Ramps and Pathways experiences fit in within NGSS core ideas assigned to kindergarten, 1st grade, and 2nd grade. It is important to note that children's experiences in Ramps and Pathways will go beyond what is expected in the standards for each grade level and improve the texture of learning within and beyond the standards.

Kindergarten, NGSS, and Ramps and Pathways

Kindergartners are expected to use science and engineering practices within experiences that would allow them to come to an understanding of how different strengths or different directions of pushes and pulls impact how an object is moved, and how they can engineer an object's movement.

Physical Science (K-PS2 and K-PS3) and Ramps and Pathways. Kindergartners are challenged to use science and engineering practices to become aware of how there are different strengths and directions of pushes and pulls. In the beginning, children may move objects on the track by pushing them or pulling them. Before long, they become aware of the relationship between an incline and an object's movement. Even a slight incline can get a marble moving. A steeper ramp can get a marble rolling even faster. When the incline is reversed, the marble rolls in the opposite direction. Kindergartners are also challenged to consider how, when objects touch or collide, they push on one another and can change motion. In Ramps and Pathways experiences, children often release a line of marbles on an incline and observe how they will roll but also collide with each other, impacting the speed of each other. They also pay a great deal of attention to how they can place blocks in the pathway of a marble. They compare what happens when a heavy sphere strikes a block with what happens when a light sphere strikes a block. Close observers will even note that when a descending marble strikes a line of marbles on a track, the marble on the far end will be the one that moves while the rest will relatively stay in place (see Figure 3.24). Children will return to this experience in upper grades when they use a Newton's cradle (see Figure 3.25) to explore how the force of a moving sphere hitting a line of stationary spheres goes through the spheres in the middle to push the last sphere upward. Kindergarten children are challenged to explore the relationship between energy and forces, such as the way a bigger

Figure 3.25. Newton's Cradle

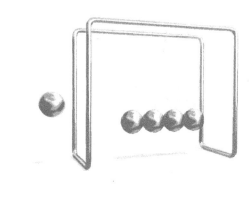

push or pull makes things speed up or slow down more quickly. Ramps and Pathways experiences are a context in which children are continuously grappling with increasing or decreasing the force of a moving marble on their system.

Engineering, Technology, and Applications of Science (ETS1) and Ramps and Pathways. Ramps and Pathways experiences are a rich context for kindergartners to engage in open-ended engineering design. Because children are so interested in making the marble move on ramps and pathways, they pose their own design problems and build increasingly sophisticated structures. The more they build, the more solutions they find to get a marble to slow down or change direction. For example, children may slow the movement of a marble by lowering the incline of a ramp, or they may place carpet or pieces of fabric at the bottom to slow the speed of the marble.

First Grade, NGSS, and Ramps and Pathways

The NGSS performance expectations for 1st grade in physical science focus on light and sound. Even though force and motion are not a focus of the NGSS 1st-grade core ideas in physical science, it is beneficial for 1st-grade students to continue their investigations into force and motion. Just because something is not listed specifically in the 1st-grade band does not mean it is forbidden. Quite the contrary. The NGSS grade expectations are the bare minimum. Furthermore, the NGSS engineering design standards are also listed as applying to 1st grade,

Figure 3.24. Colliding Marbles

and Ramps and Pathways experiences continue to be a huge interest for 1st-graders.

Engineering, Technology, and Applications of Science (ETS1) and Ramps and Pathways. First-graders are expected to ask questions, make observations, and gather information to find solutions to problems. Even when 1st-graders have had Ramps and Pathways experiences in previous years, we have found the materials to be so open-ended for possibilities that children never tire of them. We must also remember that just as young learners develop reading and writing behaviors through daily experiences in literacy, young learners also develop science and engineering behaviors through daily experiences in STEM. These behaviors align with 21st Century Skills of critical thinking, communication, creativity, problem solving, perseverance, and collaboration (Partnership for 21st Century Learning, 2007).

First-grade teachers who implement Ramps and Pathways find that the problem-solving behaviors used by children who engage in Ramps and Pathways activities transfer to other subjects. One teacher shared the frustration she had with a student who at first refused to write anything unless she knew how to spell it correctly. Because of the student's refusal to attempt spellings, the teacher could not analyze her errors to determine her understanding of spelling patterns. This limited the ability of the teacher to design instruction to elevate the child's understanding of spelling patterns. This child was drawn to the activity of Ramps and Pathways and became emboldened in the design challenges she posed to herself. As she encountered failures, she developed the behavior of analyzing what went wrong and problem-solving to fix it. This behavior began to translate into her behaviors in writing. If she didn't know how to spell a word, she became comfortable with writing down the phonemes she could hear (invented spelling) to finish her thoughts. This word was identified by a circle so she could easily find it and correct it with new information at a later time.

Another teacher noticed that at the beginning of the year when she asked children to read aloud to her to take a running record, she found some children read over unknown words very quickly in hopes she wouldn't notice they had made a mistake. However, after engaging in Ramps and Pathways experiences over time, they no longer did this, but instead would go back, take a closer look, and problem-solve the unknown word. "It was as if they had learned in building ramps systems that mistakes were an opportunity to problem-solve and learn!"

Yet another teacher found her students thinking more flexibly in mathematics. They took pride in demonstrating multiple ways to solve a mathematical problem and even engaged in argumentation regarding which method was most efficient. This classroom was once being observed by a 3rd-grade teacher. The children were being challenged with mental math problems involving adding three two-digit numbers together. As the children called out the answers, the 3rd-grade teacher walked over to their teacher, certain she was providing her children the answers. She was stunned to learn that there was no trick. These children were calling upon all three executive functions (inhibitory control, working memory, and cognitive flexibility) to mentally solve the problems. The teacher believes that her students' engagement in Ramps and Pathways enabled them to develop the habits of mind to be flexible and think creatively to solve problems. These habits will be revisited in the NGSS Engineering, Technology, and Applications of Science written for children in grades K–2.

Second Grade, NGSS, and Ramps and Pathways

In 2nd grade, experiences with ramps and pathways address and/or support understandings in the physical science domain in regard to matter and interaction. Through science and engineering practices, 2nd-graders can come to understand that different kinds of matter exist and have different properties that are suited to different purposes. Materials can be classified based on these properties. The materials can also be rearranged or assembled to make a new object with a purpose.

Physical Science (2-PS1) and Ramps and Pathways. Properties of matter become meaningful to 2nd-graders when they are provided opportunities to investigate them beyond one unit and throughout the year. Ramps and Pathways experiences are a context where 2nd-graders have an intrinsic desire to investigate properties of materials and how those properties respond to force.

When wooden unit blocks are used in Ramps and Pathways activities, children can come to understand that things are made up of different kinds of materials and that a great variety of objects can be built up from a small set of pieces. Wooden unit blocks used in Ramps and Pathways activities are cut into *unit*-based measurements of halves, doubles, and quadruples and lay the foundations for basic math and geometry. Blocks are typically found in all high-quality preschools and kindergarten classrooms and in lucky primary-grade classrooms.

As children build with unit blocks, they experience the nature of balancing weight against the forces of gravity, friction, and tension. They notice the differences of the faces of each block and explore how the side face of the half unit is congruent to the short side face of the unit block, half the length of the long side. They notice that two of the large faces of the half unit are congruent to one of the large faces of the unit block. Pattern blocks are spectacular materials that engage children in spatial thinking. Multiple studies over decades have found value in children's block play, and some have reported that—in middle and high school mathematics and in spatial thinking—children who played with blocks significantly outperform those who did not (Casey et al., 2008; Geary et al., 2000; Kersh et al., 2008; Wheatley, 1990; Wolfgang et al., 2001), influencing success in STEM subjects and STEM careers.

The objects to move on the tracks in Ramps and Pathways experiences are made up of different kinds of materials. Children observe that some are made from glass, metal, plastic, Styrofoam, and wood. In addition, children notice that the objects exhibit various shapes, sizes, and weights; are solid or hollow; and can open up or not. As children move various objects on the tracks, they become aware of how the material, shape, and composition of the objects affect how those objects move. They discern differences in how objects react when they strike another object. They detect patterns in how items with similar shapes or materials move, and they begin to select objects with specific properties for specific purposes within their systems.

SUMMARY

When administrators and their teachers recognize the power of Ramps and Pathways experiences in developing science and engineering practices and crosscutting concepts, and in supporting age level–specific standards, preschool, kindergarten, 1st-grade, and 2nd-grade children will be enabled to enjoy robust and intellectually stimulating STEM experiences. Administrators will have the opportunity to value the work of their teachers and children by noticing and naming the processes of learning documented and promoted on the walls and shelving in the classroom. The NGSS assists teachers trained in early childhood teacher preparation programs in identifying science and engineering content that is important to include in both learning with and teaching their young children. The NGSS nudges teachers trained in elementary teacher preparation programs to approach science and engineering in a developmental and student-centered way. Ramps and Pathways experiences are useful in addressing NGSS standards in ways that are exciting and meaningful for young learners throughout the year. While the NGSS identifies grade-level content for teachers' use in planning instruction throughout the year, the standards are not meant to limit children's engagement with a phenomenon when they show an interest in it.

CHAPTER 4

Arranging Space to Investigate Ramps and Pathways

The art of teaching is the art of assisting discovery to take place.

—Mark Van Doren, *A Liberal Education*, 1943

Teachers need time to think about science in a setting that is not task oriented. They need time to consider questions such as, How does science work for scientists? For children? For themselves?

—Wendy Saul and Jeanne Reardon, *Beyond the Science Kit*, 1996

If you look at history, innovation doesn't come just from giving people incentives; it comes from creating environments where their ideas can connect.

—Steven Johnson, science author and media theorist, 2010

TEXTBOX 4.1. REIMAGINING A CLASSROOM FOR STEM LEARNING

Gwen stood in the middle of her 2nd-grade classroom and scanned its contents. She had just reviewed the Next Generation Science Standards. Her traditional science for 20 minutes twice a week had allowed her to cover the disciplinary core ideas, but it didn't allow her students to develop science and engineering practices or enable them to think about relationships among the crosscutting concepts. How might she do this, and where would she find the time?

The term *foolproof* implies that something is designed so well that even a fool can make it work. One of the most derogatory phrases used in designing curriculum is the phrase *teacher proof*, that is, regardless of the teacher using the curriculum, significant learning will occur (Taylor, 2013). To suggest a curriculum is "teacher proof" is to imply that the curriculum was designed so well for student success that even a poor teacher could implement it simply by following a script. Companies that market scripted curriculum to schools claim that their standardized

approach to curriculum will ensure that all students will receive the same skills and will result in higher test scores and reduce an achievement gap. Some districts that buy into this marketing go so far as to expect all children in a grade to be reading the same text at the same time and expect all teachers in any given subject to end on the same page of the teacher's guide each day. By holding teachers accountable, they say that they believe this will result in little to no consequences when children transfer to another building in their district (Curwin, 2012). Some of the contributors to this book are witnessing with great concern the consequences as they watch districts implement this approach (see Textbox 4.1). They recall a visiting early childhood professor from China in 2003. This professor showed a video of young children in China seated in desks in a row with identical blocks on the desktops. Per their teacher's instruction, the 4- and 5-year-old children lifted the same block at the same time and positioned it in an identical manner in perfect synchronization. The professor expressed how China's approach to standardized teaching to achieve scores on standardized tests worked. The children did score well. However, this approach had drastic repercussions on creativity and innovation in their society as the children moved through school and into the workforce. The professor then showed video of current early childhood classrooms in China that looked very similar to American early childhood classrooms in the 1990s. The video showed children working in learning centers of their choice and having lively conversations with one another. China was changing its approach to education to match the 1990s approach of the United States, with the goal of nurturing the creative and innovative thinking that had benefited American society and its economy. He thought it strange that, at the same time, American schools were changing their approach to education to mirror China's approach in the 1990s, with the goal of scoring higher on standardized tests.

To counter the idea of *teacher-proof curriculum*, Taylor (2013) introduced the phrase *curriculum-proof teacher*. "The 'curriculum-proof teacher' does not ignore or sabotage the text; rather, he or she can and does use *any* given curriculum in highly effective ways" (Taylor, 2013, p. 297). Curriculum-proof PK–2 teachers use their expertise in child development, content, and pedagogy along with an understanding of every child's unique interests, strengths, and needs to engineer their classroom to provide their children with daily opportunities for STEM learning. No curriculum, scripted or not, will meet the needs of every young learner (NRC, 2004). Curriculum-proof teachers understand the importance of differentiating instruction. In this era of immense teacher shortages, curriculum-proof teachers are leaving districts that subscribe to the belief of teacher-proof curriculum and are finding positions in schools that respect their knowledge and expertise in teaching. They express great relief in once again experiencing with their children the shared joy of learning and teaching, and they look forward to their creative and innovative children's bright futures.

A question we are often asked by educators who understand the importance of a rich curriculum that includes daily STEM experiences is "What does it look like in action?" or "Where is there a school I can visit to see this at work?" These educators are seeking to learn from other curriculum-proof teachers and to envision how STEM can be a part of their children's daily learning. Curriculum-proof

teachers do exist and thrive in learning communities that give teachers the autonomy to differentiate instruction. We are fortunate to work with a nearby small public school district in Traer, Iowa (see Figure 4.1). These PK–2 teachers and their administrators understand that strong teachers never stop becoming stronger. Jill, Sammy, Vonna, Anne, Leigh, Shannon, Brenda, Makenzie, Connie, and their current and former administrators, Susan and Josh, started on this path of becoming even more effective teachers with the encouragement of another early childhood educator in their school, Lisa Chizek. Always a lover of science, Lisa introduced the idea of STEM to the early childhood teachers and invited us to be part of their learning community. Together, we reimagined, redesigned, and engineered their classrooms to be integrative STEM and literacy environments for learning.

Their school now accepts visits from public school teachers across the state who want to "see it in action." The teachers are transparent with every visitor in that everything is not picture-perfect and they are still becoming. They must also be incredibly creative and innovative to comply with increasing mandates for public schools and still provide their students with STEM every day. However, they share how learning and teaching are still joyful in their classrooms and invite visitors to the school into the integrative STEM and literacy community. While many districts are positioning middle school

Figure 4.1. Traer Kindergarten Teachers Collaborate With University Professor During Shared Work Time

and high school learning to make STEM relevant to their students and encourage graduates to pursue careers in STEM, this Iowa district is playing the long game. They understand that STEM thinking and dispositions begin to develop at the critical time of early childhood and are investing in the early years.

Becoming an integrative STEM and literacy early childhood educator will be easier for some than for others. In most preschool classrooms, Ramps and Pathways experiences fit seamlessly into center time when that time is at least 45 minutes in length. Schools that have removed centers from PK–2 classrooms to focus solely on literacy learning and mathematics will find it more difficult to re-envision independent child-led work in STEM. Administrators and educators in these schools may have been boxed in by policies that resulted in high-stakes standardized testing and a temptation to teach to the test. The longer these unfortunate policies are in place, the more research on child development and how children learn will be sacrificed. As a result, many schools return to the ineffective traditional siloed teaching of standards at each grade level.

It is important to address age- and grade-level learning standards, but it is dangerous to use grade-level standards alone to determine what is included in curriculum. Doing so narrows the curriculum (McMurrer & Kober, 2007; Nichols & Berliner, 2008), increases inequality (Berliner, 2006), and contributes to the de professionalization of teachers (Au, 2011; Luke, 2004). Expanding our view of fully integrative early STEM and literacy teaching to provide multiple experiences in multiple contexts over time provides the rigor and relevance necessary to cultivate our children's capabilities and dispositions such as critical thinking, holistic thinking, creativity and imagination, and responsibility—all of which are essential for success and well-being in the 21st century.

In this chapter, we provide examples of how classroom space can be arranged and outfitted to support children's investigations into force and motion phenomena with Ramps and Pathways experiences every day and over time. Some will include examples of standards that can be addressed within the center. We will revisit centers that may feel familiar to you and illustrate how Ramps and Pathways experiences can fit. If you've never had centers, we recommend that you and your administrator partner to begin with one. Just one. Add more as you develop comfort with children's independent learning. When you add a center for the first time, it will be rocky, but remain patiently optimistic. Your children may never have had an invitation or the expectation that they could learn how to regulate their own behavior. Stay strong. Expect failure and learn from it. You and your children will figure it out, and you will be ready for additional centers, one at a time. When we go into traditional classrooms, we often watch children tug at their teacher's shirt and say, "Teacher, I'm done. What do I do now?" We rarely see this happen in a classroom where there are high-quality and open-ended STEM centers. There is always something interesting to figure out. When you notice that children in your classroom are no longer tugging on your shirt to ask what they should do next, you will know you have arrived.

TEACHERS AS ENGINEERS

If engineering is "design under constraint," Gwen is most certainly engaged in a complex engineering design problem. Her design challenge is to build science and engineering experiences for her 2nd-graders that allow her students to conceptually understand disciplinary core ideas through their practice of science and engineering experiences. Her constraints are time, the physical size of her classroom, access to and storage of materials, state standards (NRC, 2015), and, most importantly, the unique strengths and needs of her students and her relationship with them. In this chapter, we share examples of how teachers of young students have redesigned their classrooms to accommodate integrative learning that gives their students access to STEM on a daily basis.

Throughout the history of education, theorists and philosophers in early childhood education have emphasized the importance of the physical environment and how contexts, visual and spatial arrangements, and placement of materials affect learning (Dewey, 1922/2009; Froebel, 1887/1974; Piaget & Inhelder, 1969). We have long known that when classrooms are arranged to coordinate curricular expectations, children's development, children's interests, and learning and teaching become meaningful for students and teachers alike.

Young children's need to be physically active leads to an inclusive, UDL classroom environment that allows and encourages all children to move about freely and safely. However, it is mental activity that leads to learning, not merely physical activity. Therefore, environments must be designed that provide opportunities for children to think all the time. Dr. Rheta DeVries, an expert in early childhood education, recommended that teachers evaluate the worth of every activity they offer their students with the question, "What is there in this activity for children to figure out?" Early childhood educators have long advocated an approach to curriculum that is driven by active inquiry, and that embeds important concepts and skills within an integrated curriculum that is interesting and meaningful to children.

Analyzing most kindergarten and primary classroom arrangements today, the focal point is clearly literacy. Classrooms held up as exemplary models prominently display a classroom library and writing area with centers around the periphery. The purpose of these centers is to engage children in literacy work upon arrival, keep children engaged in learning when they finish their work early, free teachers to work with small groups and individual students, and allow students to engage in literacy activities to develop into lifelong readers and writers (Morrow, 2012). The inclusion of content-area centers is often recommended as another way of getting children to participate in more literacy activities. While we believe that literacy is an important part of early education and advocate for high-quality literacy instruction, instruction in literacy should not be so dominant that it eclipses the reasons for the very existence of literacy and mathematics: to ponder and communicate our investigations about how our physical and biological worlds (science) work; to understand how our human relationships (social studies) work; to read outside authors' creative thinking (realistic and imaginary) within our world; and also to write and read our own creative thinking (realistic and imaginary) about the world. By focusing narrowly on literacy, the act of figuring out how to read and write becomes abstract and in danger of becoming a series of arduous tasks to complete rather than a desired tool to explore, revisit, or think creatively about how the world works.

For this reason, we work to design an educational environment where the focal point is inquiry in all domains: science, technology, engineering, mathematics, literacy, social studies, and the arts. Such an environment allows teachers to ponder how to address standards in a meaningful way (see Textbox 4.2).

Because learning occurs best in an integrated manner, the classroom works well when it is designed to allow children to investigate a variety of topics to their fullest. For example, an outdoor garden area works well for children to investigate plant life, but the outdoor garden area is also a space where one could find children reasoning about physics, geology, meteorology, space, life science, mathematics, literacy, and social studies. In an area for art and documentation, one could find children reasoning in the domains of physics, chemistry, reading, writing, social studies, and mathematics. This takes space. To optimize use of space, tables can replace individual desks. Children can be provided cubbies to store personal belongings. To reduce traffic and for work efficiency, community containers of materials such as pencils, markers, scissors, tape, and glue can be placed strategically around the room ready for use. When instruction requires that everyone have table space at the same time, such as during a writing workshop, students can make use of flexible table space around the classroom.

TEXTBOX 4.2. WEAVING THROUGH KINDERGARTEN STANDARDS

Anne read through the kindergarten NGSS standards for Motion and Stability: Forces and Interactions. In the Disciplinary Core Ideas column she found the following:

- Pushes and pulls can have different strengths and directions. (PS2.A)
- Pushing or pulling on an object can change the speed or direction of its motion and can start or stop it. (PS2.A)
- When objects touch or collide, they push on one another and can change motion. (PS2.B)
- A bigger push or pull makes things speed up or slow down more quickly. (PS3.C)

Anne wondered how much attention should be given to these core ideas, as her kindergartners seemed to already have a working understanding of them. When she watched them on the playground, she noticed that when they wanted to help their friend get started on a swing, they understood they needed to pull the swing back, and then push their friend on the swing each time the swing came back to them. They used pushes and pulls to get their friend in motion. When children wanted to get a soccer ball to one end of the playground, they used their feet to start, stop, and change the ball's direction (PS2.B), and they kicked the ball harder to get the ball to speed up (PS3.C) to keep their opponent from taking control of it. Anne's eyes moved to the left to read through the Science and Engineering Practices. Planning and Carrying Out Investigations is listed first. She read how kindergartners should plan and carry out investigations to answer questions or test solutions to problems and eventually progress to simple investigations based on fair tests. Analyzing and Interpreting Data is listed next. Over time and experience, her kindergartners should be collecting, recording, and analyzing information to determine if an object or tool works as intended. On the far right, Anne read that the Crosscutting Concept of Cause and Effect will be relevant in experiences involving force and motion. Anne wondered how she could build on her children's experiences with force and motion on the playground by providing more experiences in the classroom. What might be meaningful problems for children to solve that would entice them to talk about concepts within force and motion?

Anne is a kindergarten teacher who works hard to break away from a traditional task-oriented perspective of science teaching. Having read early childhood and elementary science position statements to guide early childhood teachers and administrators in providing high-quality science instruction (National Science Teachers Association, 2014), Anne knows that tasking children to follow the scientific method is counter to good science teaching. She knows how important it is to provide her kindergartners access to STEM every day, and she knows the power of integrating STEM into all the disciplines. Anne has embraced STEM teaching that aligns with child development within her kindergarten classroom. This means that as an inclusive teacher working with diverse learners, she makes instructional decisions based on what she knows about child development

and learning, what she knows about each individual child in her classroom, and what she knows about each child's social and cultural context (Copple & Bredekamp, 2009).

Like many kindergartens and primary-grade classrooms, Anne's space is set up for teacher-led instruction in large- and small-group spaces, and for independent literacy practice in others. What is novel about her classroom is that she has created additional spaces within the room for independent STEM investigations. The classroom furniture is flexible, to allow spaces to be enlarged or reduced based on what is needed for different investigations.

The remainder of this chapter provides examples of making space for learning. As you read about each space, you will find some spaces to be comfortably familiar. Others may be new. Try to begin to envision your classroom as its own makerspace and pick a new kind of space to get started. We begin with three basic spaces many teachers already have and describe how experiences in Ramps and Pathways can fit: the spaces for large group, spaces for small group, and the classroom library. We follow with two other spaces that are necessary for Ramps and Pathways experiences, and that will also enhance learning literacy, mathematics, and social studies: the art and documentation space, and the physical science space. In describing these spaces, we will include information about furniture and materials.

LARGE GROUP: A SPACE TO GATHER AS A COMMUNITY OF LEARNERS

Like many early childhood educators, Anne has engineered her classroom to accommodate a space for gathering as a large group and building community (see Figure 4.2). The space is supplied with materials that reflect the UDL principle of using multiple representations to support and enhance everyone's access to learning, including the following:

Furniture: Circular rug or carpet, easel that includes magnetic whiteboard and ability to hang chart paper (some classrooms may be equipped with smartboards that can take the place of chart paper), adult-sized chair.
Materials: Markers, chart paper, variety of sizes and kinds of paper, highlighting tape,

masking tape to hang up cocreated anchor charts or documents.

Print: Song lyrics, poetry, and books that relate to exploring how Ramps and Pathways experiences can fit into the following spaces: *large-group space*, *classroom library*, and *small-group space*. We have found that two additional spaces are important to offer children every day: *physical science space* (where Ramps and Pathways will be based) and an *art and documentation space*. In describing these spaces, we will include information about furniture and materials specific to phenomena within Ramps and Pathways experiences.

UDL considerations: Position near the teacher or a peer buddy (mediator) any child who needs assistance with following, attending (inhibitory control), and processing information (working memory and cognitive flexibility); provide cube chairs or adaptive seating for children who need posture supports; use a microphone to help project the teacher's voice, especially with children who have auditory processing challenges or a hearing impairment.

A large gathering area in the center of the room offers flexible use of space serving STEM and literacy. A large gathering area provides a place for class meetings; sharing of stories, questions, and findings; and

Figure 4.2. Anne's Large-Group Space

discussion. Placing this area in the center of the room signals the importance of collaboration and discourse. It is helpful to define this area with a round rug or carpet large enough that students and the teacher can sit on its outer edge to engage in discussions. Such an arrangement guarantees full access, inclusion, and participation by positioning every class member equitably (such as placing some children closer, depending on individual development); encouraging eye contact between speaker and listeners (a practice that is especially critical for children with varying EF development and self-regulation); and allowing all children the ability to view items placed in the center. The rug is also useful for children and their teacher to gather for whole-group instruction. An adult-sized chair for the teacher and an easel to hold big books or chart paper allow the children to view illustrations in a read-aloud, examine text in big books, or engage in modeled, interactive, or shared writing. While the gathering area occupies a large space, it can be used as a place for spillover activity from other areas, with the caution to those using it that materials cannot stay there over time but must be cleaned up to allow for the next whole-class gathering.

Ramps and Pathways and Read-Alouds

A wonderful way to build classroom community is beginning the day with songs and poetry that can be written on chart paper to include as part of the morning routine. There are also many children's picture books that can be introduced through shared reading or read-alouds. But there is a caution: It is often more effective to bring in songs, poetry, and picture books about force and motion phenomena in Ramps and Pathways experiences *after* children have had experiences with ramps and pathways. This is counter to most teachers' inclination, which is to kick off units of study with a book. However, we need to consider what is known about comprehension. Reading comprehension is best when the reader has had prior experiences with the topic. Reading is more successful when the text includes vocabulary that is already within the reader's spoken vocabulary, acquired through multiple exposures in diverse contexts (Beck & McKeown, 2007). Young readers will more readily engage with songs, poetry, and picture books when the words are part of their vocabulary. When children engage with ramps and pathways, they will search for words to describe what is happening and what they observe. This is the perfect moment to give them words such as *steep*, *slope*, and *incline*. In short, if you want strong readers of nonfiction books on force and motion, you need to give them experiences with force and motion phenomena first.

Ramps and Pathways and Interactive Writing

Early childhood teachers have found that all young learners take delight in sharing their ideas, questions, and findings in Ramps and Pathways experiences and are highly engaged in documenting them in interactive writing. As teachers write down each idea and ask children to read them back to them, they capitalize on children's desire to learn the tools of literacy in service of their learning about force and motion as they engineer ramp and pathway systems. Teachers have reported that children who struggle in small-group reading instruction learn to read more readily and willingly by engaging in and documenting STEM experiences.

CLASSROOM LIBRARY: A SPACE TO INVESTIGATE THE TOOLS OF LITERACY AND DEVELOP A LOVE FOR READING AND WRITING

Many teachers are accustomed to establishing routines for children to read to themselves, read to others, listen to reading, work on words, or work on writing. These are all experiences that can happen within the comfortable confines of the classroom library (see Figure 4.3). This space can provide resources such as the following:

Materials: High-quality books (fiction, nonfiction, and reference) at children's interest levels (including books with large print), children's magazines, newspapers, puppets, felt board, headsets and iPads or tablets with access to audiobooks, word work games, a globe, maps, paper, pencils.
Furniture: Book shelving and display shelving, child-sized table and chairs, bean bag chairs, small sofa or bench, table lamp.
UDL considerations: Audiobooks and headphones, slant boards, magnifying glasses.

Figure 4.3. Classroom Library

Children engaged in inquiry need a place to research and collaborate to develop questions, search for answers, and develop a plan for investigations. A library area provides a quiet space for such incubation, intense focus, and selective attention (inhibitory controlling). The library area should allow both privacy and collaboration as children learn to read and write together, and pore over books and magazines to investigate the world. It should include materials to facilitate development in reading, writing, oral language development, listening, and word study. The act of reading and researching print resources, and recorded findings and ideas, stimulates inquiry into how print works. Children have opportunities to explore illustration techniques and book features inspired by the UDL principle of providing children with different ways to communicate and express their own thinking through art, drama, or writing that ensures full access and participation.

Fiction and nonfiction books displayed on bookshelves with the spines showing and organized systematically, such as by reading levels, by topic, or by author, invite readers to pull them out and enjoy. Book display shelving allows a full view of book covers on a specific topic and/or magazines such as *My Big Backyard*, *Ranger Rick*, or *National Geographic*. Plants, maps, globes, and aquariums can be on top of bookshelves or walls to expand investigations, to provide children opportunities to engage in other kinds of graphic representation, or for aesthetic purposes. Comfortable seating (including adaptive seating) for both adults and children enables readers to read and research independently or collaboratively. Such seating can include bean bag chairs, a child-sized table and chairs, and a small sofa or bench for an adult and child to read together. Materials for retelling, such as a felt board or puppet theater, are helpful in creative and artful representation of stories as well as communicating ideas. Access to headsets for listening to books empowers developing readers to engage in literature beyond their reading ability but addressing their level of interest. Shelving and space for word study games and materials provide inquiry opportunities for children to independently investigate how words and various text structures work.

Tubs labeled *fiction*, *nonfiction*, and *poetry* can be placed in the library. As the teacher reads a book connected to concepts within Ramps and Pathways experiences, there can be a discussion on whether the genre is fiction, nonfiction, or poetry, and the book can be placed in the appropriate tub. This visual classification system assists all children to readily identify, locate, retrieve, and return the different types of books. Poems related to Ramps and Pathways experiences and used in the morning routines of shared reading can be collected and printed on sheets of paper. Different versions of printed materials can be easily modified using enlarged print, colored font, and highlighted words, depending on individually targeted reading skills for young readers, and can be read alone or in paired sharing, as appropriate. Other children might design a readers' theater performance. Children can be invited to collect poems they enjoy and to create their own anthology, and they can add their own illustrations in the art and documentation space. The addition of slant boards (another use of a ramp) assists children having difficulty with handwriting and may also reduce eye strain.

SMALL GROUP: A SPACE FOR FOCUSED LITERACY LEARNING

Anne works hard to meet the unique needs and interests of children in their learning. Engineering a space for small-group work (see Figure 4.4) allows her to provide specialized instruction. The space is equipped with the following:

Figure 4.4. Small-Group Instruction

Furniture: Kidney-shaped table, adult-sized chair, children's chairs, shelving unit for storage of reading materials and supplies.

Materials: Lined and unlined paper of various sizes, sentence strips, markers, individual magnetic whiteboards, magnetic letters, stapler, glue, paper clips, dry-erase pens and erasers, highlighting tape, scissors, rulers.

Materials specific to Ramps and Pathways: Children's literature on ramps and pathways phenomena, science journals.

UDL considerations: Writing grips, highlighted writing paper, audiobooks, communication boards, list of translated key vocabulary words.

Because our current culture demands that children become readers at an early age, it is necessary to provide a space conducive to small-group work in literacy. This space is also useful for small-group collaboration to plan or review STEM investigations.

Positioning the Small-Group Space

The small-group space typically uses a small kidney-shaped table with a chair for the teacher in the center and four to eight child-sized chairs for the children on the other side of the table. Positioning the small-group space next to the classroom library allows reading and writing materials to be easily shared. The placement of the small-group space should allow the teacher to see all areas of the classroom from where they are sitting to monitor safety and to observe learning in the other areas from a distance. This assures children in all areas of the room that even while their teacher is engaged in small-group literacy instruction, their teacher can notice and celebrate progress with a smile or nod, and occasionally with a spontaneous class meeting to celebrate a major breakthrough in an investigation. The low noise level necessary for the classroom library and small-group spaces can be buffered with an art and documentation space. Small-group spaces should be farthest away from the STEM spaces, which demand more physical movement and audible collaboration.

Ramps and Pathways and Small-Group Vocabulary Instruction

Work from Ramps and Pathways investigations is often a meaningful context for small-group literacy instruction. Discussing what children are in the process of investigating often brings up opportunities to introduce vocabulary suggested in Chapter 2 (see Figure 2.3). Ramps and Pathways experiences are a context for developing and using vocabulary to describe properties of objects and materials, the motion and position of objects, the condition of systems, the action of the young engineers, and the names for special features in children's ramps and pathways systems. The teacher and child can engage in interactive writing to record these words along with a cocreated definition on a large piece of paper to be posted on the wall. The children can introduce this chart to their peers in large-group instruction and then post it on the wall for future reference. For classrooms with dual language learners, the vocabulary words can be displayed in English as well as the other languages spoken by the children, along with visual cues such as symbols, sketches, or photos to enhance meaning and understanding.

Ramps and Pathways and Notebooking

The tool of notebooking can be introduced in small-group literacy sessions with mini-lessons on labeling or on making a glossary of terms the children want to use in their writing. Perhaps they need to make a list of materials they want added to an investigation space, or work on a letter inviting a community expert to come and share what they know. Observing how children take on writing can serve as a formative assessment for the teacher (formation of letters, how they are able to use conventional spelling, use of logical graphemes to represent phonemes, independent usage of punctuation, etc.).

PHYSICAL SCIENCE

Interviews with successful engineers (Turkle, 2008) revealed that many had an early exposure to construction materials such as wooden building blocks, K'nex, Erector Sets, Tinkertoys, Lincoln Logs, and LEGOs. Such materials allowed them to explore the physical properties of objects and how those properties affected the construction and purposes of their technology. These investigations fall into the area of physical science. An area of the classroom for physical science exploration allows the full integration of STEM as children engineer their own technology and deepen their working knowledge of physics. Their constructions demand they engage deeply in spatial reasoning, a mathematical skill that has huge implications for mathematical success in middle school and high school. The construction toys that many engineers used as children are not typically accessible to children of all socioeconomic levels. The classroom inclusion of construction materials that encourage open-ended investigations, along with time to build, may help to level the playing field.

Construction With Unit Blocks

Materials: Unit blocks (a "school set"); open shelving that allows children to consider the properties of each kind of block and quantity; schematic drawings of various constructions; photographs of familiar buildings, bridges, and other structures.

Note: Given the budgetary choice between quantity and variety, having a sufficient number of one type of construction toy that will enable children to build large, complex structures is better than having a small number of many different types of construction toys.

Opportunities to support NGSS: K-2-ETS1; 1-PS4-2; 2-PS4-3; 1-PS4-4; 2-PS1-1; 2-PS1-2

Unit blocks, invented by Caroline Pratt at the start of the 20th century, remain foundational to preschool and indeed to all early childhood classrooms. Noted architect Frank Lloyd Wright credited block play as an early influence on his life and career. Unit blocks are typically thought of as preschool and kindergarten materials, and their use of them as frivolous play. However, an increasing amount of research is pointing to the value of working with unit blocks by older children. Unit blocks, made of hard rock maple, will easily survive decades of hard use, outlasting multiple generations of children. The blocks are machined precisely so that each block is a fraction or multiple of every other block. Children have the opportunity to engage in part-whole reasoning as they decompose and recompose shapes to make other shapes. Because unit blocks rely on balance and friction to construct stable structures, builders are constantly grappling with force and motion and counteractions of forces to obtain balance. The ability to construct a tower that uses the builder's knowledge of balance has been linked to mathematical expertise in middle school. Organizing unit blocks on open shelving allows children to classify the blocks by properties and consider those properties before selecting them for use in construction. Orderly display also allows children to reason about how many are available for use in an imagined design (economics).

Construction With Unit Blocks and Ramps and Pathways

Materials: Ten 1-foot, ten 2-foot, and ten 3-foot lengths of wooden track; container for storage of track (such as a tall trash can or hamper with weight in the bottom to avoid tipping); objects to move and containers to catch.

A complement to unit blocks is ramps and pathways. Unit blocks are perfect materials to serve as support structures for the tracks used in Ramps and Pathways constructions, allowing systematic, incremental, and measurable adjustments to ramp systems. A variety of objects to move on tracks allows children to consider properties of these objects, and how the properties and combinations of

properties affect movement. The variety of objects can be of different shapes, sizes, textures, materials, and weights. Examples include marbles and ball bearings of different sizes; ping-pong, tennis, golf, Wiffle, and racket balls; as well as rocks, curlers, dice, pom-poms, crayons, tongue depressors, and plastic eggs. By routing three horizontal grooves on the underside of several lengths of tracks, children can design a system that involves a fulcrum. Including lengths of foam pipe insulation cut in half lengthwise with Velcro at the ends allows children to create systems with loops.

Preparing for Ramps and Pathways Experiences

The open-ended materials used in Ramps and Pathways are intriguing to humans of all ages, making it possible for teachers to facilitate UDL experiences where all children thrive. The Inquiry Teaching Model (ITM) introduced in Chapter 1 also assists us in planning experiences for all the young children in our classrooms (see Figure 1.1). The vignette in Textbox 4.3 is an example of how an educator used this model to support children's learning.

TEXTBOX 4.3. IMPLEMENTING THE INQUIRY TEACHING MODEL

Anne had **observed** her children using some of the unit blocks to make ramps for the vehicles that were added to the block center. She identified a phenomenon that was **engaging** learners in her class. Building on her children's interests, Anne thought about what kinds of materials she should place in the classroom to facilitate initial explorations and provide **opportunities** for problem solving. Reflecting on the ITM, Anne **made the decision** to create a space in the construction center for children to continue to explore force and motion. She selected a simple set of materials: unit blocks; 1-, 2-, and 3-foot lengths of track; objects to move on the track, including marbles in a variety of sizes and weights; and objects with different attributes and made from different materials.

Anne then crafted an open-ended invitation to the children to engage with the materials during the morning meeting in her classroom after giving each student three simple materials: "What can you make happen with this 1-foot piece of track, a unit block, and a marble?" Why is this important? Many of her children may have formed essential concepts in force and motion on the playground but may not have transferred these concepts into their own engineering. Anne considered one child's difficulty with balance and the space she might need to work safely and effectively. Using the UDL framework, Anne asked the children if they would need more space to investigate the track that had been added to the construction center. The children suggested that they move the large block shelves back so that there was another 3 feet of space for them to work. As a result, every child benefited by having more room to move. The open-ended nature of the materials allowed children to ask their own questions, pose their own problems, and pursue information to find answers to those questions or solve those problems. Children wanted to share and discuss how they were successful in coordinating materials to engineer a marble run.

Coordinating Children's Movement Among Spaces

In Chapter 2, we introduced a model showing how educators can engineer time to give children opportunities for STEM learning every day (see Figure 2.2). In Chapter 5, we provide examples of design challenges that young children imagined and engineered on their own with suggestions for how to support them. For now, let's explore how Anne coordinated the movement of her children among the small-group literacy instruction, the classroom library, and the Ramps and Pathways experience (see Figure 4.5).

Preschool educators are familiar with various methods of navigating the movement of children within the classroom. PK–2 educators who are accustomed to directing children where to go and what to do may be nervous about not being available to hover over every group of children. We've been asked, "How will I know if they are doing what they are supposed to be doing?" Our response: "What do you want them to be doing? And what would keep them from doing that?" Those of us

Figure 4.5. Coordinating Movement Among Spaces

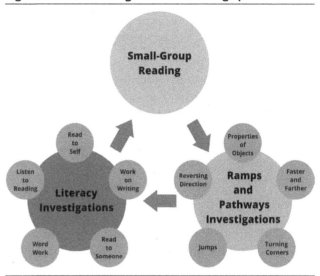

who have been teacher-directed often have a difficult time trusting children to learn without us. They can, and they will if the space is rich with potential. It is helpful to remember Dr. DeVries' question: "What is there in this experience for children to figure out?" Thinking through this will help educators mentally rehearse what children might do and troubleshoot potential problems. When educators physically play with the materials themselves, they will have a far better idea of what is possible and what they can anticipate.

Introducing Ramps and Pathways Materials

When the space is ready, bring the materials you will use to the large-group space and place them in the middle. In the example from Anne's classroom, she provided each child with a 1-foot track, a unit block, and one standard marble. She asked the children to demonstrate how they would get the marble to move on the track. She prompted them to engage in inquiry by asking, "How can you move the marble on the track without using your finger?" "How might you get the marble to move faster along the track?" "Is there a way that you could use a unit block to help you move the marble on the track?" "How can we make sure that everyone is safe when we are using these materials?"

After introducing the materials, invite the children to take a tour of the space you've prepared for them in the construction area, drawing attention to the kinds of materials you will offer, and how they are stored for student use. Include children in the decisions on how the space will operate, such as how many children can be in the center at a time, how to use the materials safely, how to care for the materials, and how to return the materials after use. Ask them if they see any potential problems. What solution do they have for handling the problem? Many teachers find it important and helpful to cocreate an agreement of how to work with the materials safely (see Figure 4.6). This is posted in the space for children to review with their peers when they find it necessary, and it can be revised as needed. Note the use of large print and different colors of markers used to write each phrase. This helps all children see and follow the words and numbered rules.

"How do I know if they are doing what they are supposed to be doing?" You've just agreed upon that.

Figure 4.6. Child and Educator Cocreated Rules

SOFT OPENING

Businesses and retail stores often have what is called a soft opening to test their operations. They quietly open their doors for passersby to trickle in. This gives the employees a more controlled environment to diagnose and correct any problems or work out any kinks. Soft openings are also beneficial for a classroom's new space. Once the new space is introduced, there can be a pilot test of how the various spaces in the room operate. The teacher can group the children into three groups of relatively the same size and write the names of the members of each group on its own paper large enough for everyone to see. Place one list of names in the Ramps and Pathways center, one in the classroom library, and one with you in the small-group space. Children will be familiar with what happens in small-group literacy instruction and literacy experiences within the classroom library, and they will all want to begin investigating in the Ramps and Pathways center. Assure everyone they will have a chance to be in the Ramps and Pathways center every day for a long time. Then begin with a group in Ramps and Pathways, a group in the classroom library, and a group with you in small group reading instruction.

Once you are finished with your small-group in reading instruction, remind them they will go to Ramps and Pathways next. Ask each child in the group what they are planning to do in the Ramps and Pathways space. Keep notes of their responses and say, "Let's go see what's happening there." Take the list of these group members and walk with them to the Ramps and Pathways space where children are still working on their structures. We have found the new builders often watch a bit before asking if they may join or continue a structure. Others will find a clear spot to begin work. Before the previous builders leave, take some photos of children at work (refrain from taking posed photos). You want to document the process of thinking. You might ask if there have been any problems that will need to be addressed at the next class meeting. Take notes if they have had problems. Take their group's list of members down and post the next group's list of members in its place. Assure them, "You might still have questions you are trying to find answers for, but remember you will be coming here every day. When you get to a place where you can stop, put your materials away and you may go to the classroom library. I'll bring your group list over there now. Go there when you are ready. These friends will be working here now, so you will need to find a place to stop your building, but remember, you will be able to come here every day."

It's important to let them make the decision on when to stop. Children may be on the cusp of figuring something out and resent having to stop. Allowing the children to make their own decision on when to end their work avoids the frustration of having to stop when they are close to a breakthrough. It also supports the development of their executive functions. Finally, walk to the classroom library space and invite the children there to your small group for instruction. These children are ready to share what they had been reading and writing, and their interest in literacy learning is primed for work in small-group literacy instruction.

Coordinating movement in this manner avoids creating frustrating abrupt stops in work when everyone has to move at the same time. Instead, there is a flow within the classroom and a healthy buzz of focused and on-task work.

CLASS MEETINGS: NURTURING A COMMUNITY OF LEARNERS

Class meetings are a time for students and teachers to gather together and reflect, discuss issues, or make decisions about how they want the class to be. Through class meetings, teachers create an environment in which their students understand that "their learning, their opinions, and their concerns are taken seriously" (Developmental Studies Center, 1996, p. 3). Class meetings are used to plan and make decisions, "check in," solve problems, or raise awareness. They can occur daily, weekly, or as needed to allow students to actively contribute to their learning of academic content and social development. To learn more about how to make class meetings a regular part of your classroom, we recommend reading a short and powerful book written by the Developmental Studies Center (1996), *Ways We Want Our Class to Be: Class Meetings That Build Commitment to Kindness and Learning.* Teachers implementing Ramps and Pathways use class meetings to accomplish the following:

1. Introduce ramps and pathways.
2. Create rules to safely and effectively work with ramps and pathways.
3. Amend rules to safely and effectively work with ramps and pathways.
4. Problem-solve any material, space, or social issues.
5. Collaboratively problem-solve students' specific design problems.
6. Highlight and celebrate what is being learned or built through questions, claims, and evidence.

STEM AS A CONTEXT FOR WRITING

Educators who provide children access to Ramps and Pathways during small-group instruction often end the morning with a writing workshop and find their young learners eager to write (see Figure 4.7). Educators often find that topic prompts are rarely needed when children have access to STEM experiences every day. An educator noted, "It's amazing what it has done to facilitate writing and spark their imagination!" Teachers have reported that children who struggle in small-group reading instruction learn to read more readily and willingly by engaging in and documenting STEM experiences. Young learners take delight in sharing their ideas, questions, and findings about the discoveries they are making in the Ramps and Pathways center and are highly engaged in documenting them in personal writing, shared writing, and interactive writing. Teachers can capitalize on their children's desire to learn the tools of literacy in service of their learning about force and motion through shared writing and interactive writing. Inquiry in STEM facilitates inquiry of the written word (see Textbox 4.4).

> **TEXTBOX 4.4. THE INQUIRY TEACHING MODEL AND LEARNING ABOUT MULTIMODAL WRITING**
>
> Multimodal writing is inextricably woven into informational texts. From trade books to maps and guidebooks, information is presented through different sign systems, such as images, color, font size, and text structure. These texts are full of diagrams, images, new vocabulary, and other features that capture children's

Figure 4.7. STEM Experiences Provide Context for Meaningful Writing

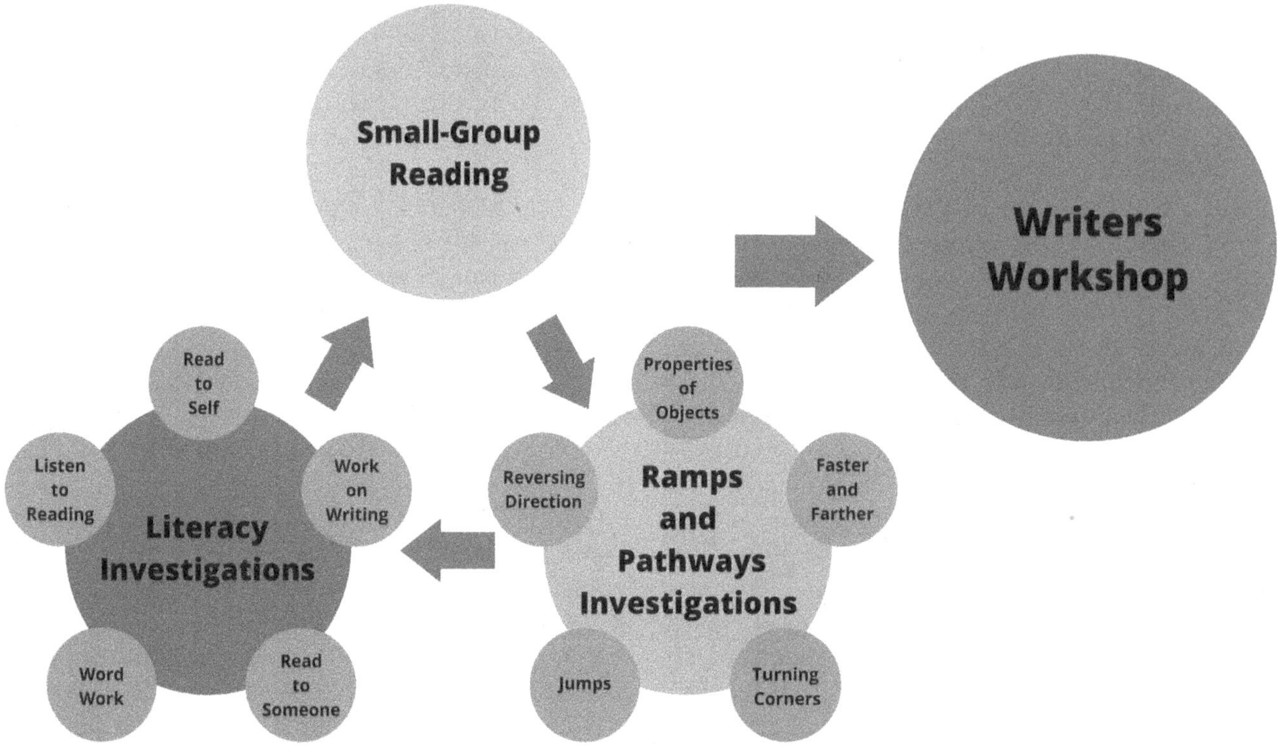

attention as readers. We can further that connection and shift the authorial role to the children themselves in authentic ways by integrating writing in STEM experiences. Already, young learners are tasked with creating informational writing beginning in kindergarten. Educators can push beyond typical projects such as grade-level creation of research books about predetermined topics (animal research is very common), which often falls flat when implemented year after year. Instead, by seeking authentic experiences and supporting documentation of authentic experiences, educators can spark informational writing, and students can produce situated and more authentic texts. STEM experiences integrated into literacy classrooms can bring the outside into the classroom and promote writing for real purposes across content areas. How words work and how messages are communicated are fundamental tenets in producing text. The production of writing mirrors the inquiry process when children are provided opportunities to explore written content from a stance of wonder, engage in novel content or areas of interest, and actively make decisions about the messages authors determine are important to document.

Shared Writing

Shared writing occurs when children talk and their teacher writes correctly. The children collaboratively dictate to the teacher what they want written, and the teacher acts as a scribe, writing on chart paper for children to see, using correct spelling and punctuation. A goal of shared writing is to invite the students into the process of writing and get them to think deeply about what to write and how to write it. To engage in shared writing:

1. Ask the children to brainstorm ideas on what they want written.
2. Let the children turn and talk to children next to them to discuss ideas to write down.
3. Verbally talk about what will be written.
4. Write down what children tell you and model the writing process thinking aloud. For example, model rereading before writing the next word or next sentences.
5. Reread and revise as needed. Ask the children for input such as: "How can

we add a detail about how differently the cube moved from the plastic egg?" "Is there something missing here? Do we need to include more information so it makes sense to the reader?"

Posting the written product on the wall invites children to return to the text and reread.

Interactive writing occurs when children and their teacher talk, and children and their teacher then write on chart paper. It serves as a bridge between reading and writing. Children write alongside an expert writer (their teacher) and read and reread as they are composing the text.

1. Decide what you want to write.
2. Write the text together, providing the children opportunities to share the pen with you.
3. Reread the text often during writing to "check your writing."
4. After writing, proofread the text together.

When teachers provide children with dry-erase boards and markers, they can write a word on their board as another child is writing the word on the chart. You can also ask them to write the word in the sky or on a friend's back.

When the piece is finished, you can model editing the writing, while celebrating children's approximations of spelling, and using opportunities to focus on beginning sounds, ending sounds, vowels, digraphs, or consonant blends. You can also model fixing punctuation. Some teachers choose to rewrite the interactive writing on another chart correctly and hang it next to the draft. Posting it on the wall invites children to return to the text and reread.

Moving Toward Integrative STEM and Literacy Learning

Ramps and Pathways experiences have been designed to introduce PK–2 educators to a framework for STEM learning every day by offering open-ended STEM experiences alongside literacy experiences within the time set aside for small-group reading instruction. There is a reciprocal relationship between STEM and literacy learning. When STEM experiences are offered every day, children's work within

the block of time devoted to science is more fruitful. Children engage in deep discussions involving questions, claims, and evidence as they develop understandings of science concepts. Children debate multiple solutions to problems they encounter as they engineer materials to produce a phenomenon or artifact to serve a child's purpose. Meeting grade-level NGSS performance standards and beyond, the educator is able to capitalize on children's interests and on developing science and engineering habits of mind that are exercised independently every day during small-group reading instruction. Children have lots of things to document and record, stimulating new ideas for topics in writing. Literacy learning becomes richer as children strive to learn the tools of literacy to document, discuss, read, and review STEM content in which they are deeply interested. There is synergy in children's development in literacy and development in STEM (see Figure 4.8).

Writers benefit from writing for an authentic audience. So much of writing in school is for the teacher, and having only one audience member can stifle message production for any writer. When children create and test Ramps and Pathways structures, they are excited to share what they discover in the moment and readily do so. However, these experiences can also be opportunities to write about meaningful experiences and share them more permanently and beyond the group in proximity at the

Figure 4.8. The Reciprocity of STEM and Literacy Development

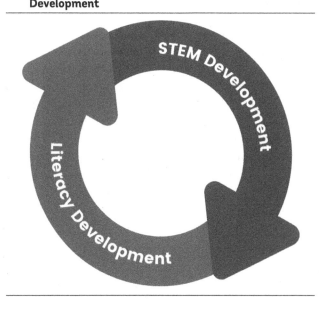

Figure 4.9. Using Speech Bubbles to Share Thinking

moment. Documenting with pictures and writing helps children produce specific messages and ensure that the messages are not too unwieldy to produce.

Taking the chance to integrate writing in STEM rotations also builds student confidence and stamina. For example, 2nd-grade teacher Makenzie provided time for her students to take photos of their early constructions and used speech bubble–shaped paper to send the message that the writing tells about the image (see Figure 4.9). Students used descriptive language, such as quantities, colors, and location, to tell peers about their construction. When exploring ramps later in the year, students in Makenzie's class had already learned how to take photos and video of their construction. They used the video as a touch point for writing and independently produced a page or two of text about their ramp challenge success and difficulties. They then recorded themselves reading their own writing for caregivers, and Makenzie was able to use school-sponsored technology (SeeSaw) to share with

families. Makenzie knew that experience with writing builds over time, just as test trials with ramps and track to round a curve do. In tandem, writing and construction build confidence. Students make multiple attempts to produce words on the page, select words to communicate the intended message, and decide what content matters for the audience. Starting with experience helps young writers share stories that matter about their intellectual lives.

The experiences in Ramps and Pathways, introduced or revisited, acknowledge young learners' attempts to understand force and motion on their own through play. These experiences tap into, guide, and focus children's interests to lead them to engage in science inquiry in a materials-rich, positive, safe, and inclusive environment for exploration and discovery. Ramps and Pathways integrative STEM and literacy experiences provide a context for children to engage in science and engineering practices and mathematics (especially spatial thinking), thus providing authentic contexts for literacy learning. Much of the print on the classroom walls promotes the intellectual life of the children who live and learn within those walls.

SUMMARY

Makerspaces for STEM are being installed in many schools, but PK–2 teachers and their children need not sign up for time. A well-equipped and mindful design of the classroom makes the PK–2 classroom itself a makerspace that provides children access to STEM learning every day. Many PK–2 teachers have already organized the classroom for literacy learning, with space for large-group instruction, small-group instruction, and literacy centers. By re-engineering the physical space to find a place for STEM investigations and making the best use of time during small-group reading instruction, STEM and literacy learning thrive in a joyful community of learners.

CHAPTER 5

Planning and Implementing Experiences in Ramps and Pathways in PK–2 Classrooms

Many schools are supporting STEM by providing a makerspace for teachers to share. The value of exploring materials in makerspaces impacts achievement in learners from ages 4 to 22 and beyond. Makerspaces promote the development of engineering design self-efficacy that can be spotted in a learner's confidence, motivation, expectation of success, and anxiety while engaging in design. When we have design self-efficacy, we seek more opportunities to apply our skills, and we persevere when things do not go well (Hilton et al., 2018). Despite the research indicating the value of time spent within a makerspace, many early childhood teachers have difficulty coordinating their instructional schedule with the availability of the makerspace. Certainly, young learners do not get access to a shared makerspace every day, compromising their opportunity to develop engineering design self-efficacy. The makerspace may also be inadequate for our youngest learners, as many of these spaces have been designed for the purposes of older children. Instead of young children traveling to another classroom for limited amounts of time, we propose that every early childhood classroom should be a makerspace. A preschool, kindergarten, 1st-grade, or 2nd-grade classroom that embraces the culture of the makerspace is a gift to every child living and learning within that classroom, as well as a source of joyful learning and teaching for the teacher. Ramps and Pathways is an example of a makerspace within an early childhood classroom. It is not a stand-alone curriculum, but an experience within a framework that supports the development of children's science and engineering practices through daily self-directed experiences in STEM.

Many of us are accustomed to writing and following lesson plans in our teaching. As a result, we teach within a paradigm that expects a sequence of actions within a specific time frame that ends with a measurable result. While tightly planned daily lessons with quantitative assessments can generate children's scores to catalog and compare, they do not accurately reflect the process of children's learning within experiences that generates creative, innovative, and critical thinking. Instead of a way to compare and sort children, the early childhood makerspace classroom is an inclusive environment that facilitates children's collaboration and cooperation in their pursuit of solving a problem that is meaningful to them. This means shifting from the paradigm of writing timed and sequenced lesson plans to writing a plan for experiences over time. We found our paradigms began to shift when we engaged in what can be called "teacher play" with Ramps and Pathways materials. As we played, fiddled around, and tinkered, first with unit blocks, and then unit blocks and track, we began to more fully understand the value of planning experiences over time rather than creating a traditional lesson plan, and we recognized the potential learning within those experiences.

BEGINNING WITH TEACHER PLAY

To fully understand the potential for learning and the development of science and engineering practices through experiences of designing and testing systems of ramps and pathways, begin with teacher play. David Hawkins (1974), a renowned scientist who was a historian of the Manhattan Project, sought to use his understanding of science to improve lives rather than eliminate them. He saw how lives could be improved when our youngest learners were allowed opportunities to engage in high-quality meaningful science. He advocated for teachers to "mess about" with materials that later would be offered to children. This is teacher play. When children first encounter new materials and ideas that are interesting, they immediately get to work exploring them. We should do the same. When educators explore the very materials they will offer to students, they are challenged to experience the materials from their own perspective and from the perspective of young children. Handle and observe the properties of objects and materials and ponder what can be done with them. Try out your ideas as you build systems of ramps and pathways and test them. Weave in what you know about your children's interests, experiences, and cultures to anticipate possibilities and different directions they might go when using the same materials. In this way, educators can plan for rich and meaningful experiences over time. If you are still required to implement commercially prepared science units in that rare 20-minute slot of time at the end of the day, you can do both. However, many teachers soon find that the experiences over time are much more powerful in developing children's use of science and engineering practices than the units and their 20-minute lessons.

Teacher Play With Unit Blocks

Unit blocks were invented by Caroline Pratt at the start of the 20th century and remain a foundational educational material in every high-quality early childhood classroom. The blocks are precisely machined so that each block is a fraction or a multiple of every other block (see Figure 5.1). Children have the opportunity to engage in part-whole relationships as they deconstruct and reconstruct shapes to make other shapes. As you engage in teacher play by handling and building with unit blocks, consider additional mathematical concepts that can be meaningful in block building (see Figure 5.2).

Building with unit blocks develops a growing understanding of how weight, balance, friction, and tension contribute to engineering a stable structure. As you build, consider how you are constantly grappling with force and motion and counteractions of forces to obtain balance. The ability to construct a tower that uses the builder's understanding

Figure 5.1. Part-Whole Relationships in Unit Blocks

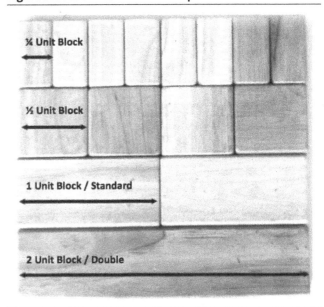

of balance, weight, and spatial thinking has been linked to high performance in math and science starting in middle school. Children who work with blocks in the early years outperform their peers who don't in math and science because of all the mathematical concepts and spatial thinking that can be developed through block play (Casey et al., 2008). Interviews with successful engineers revealed that many had an early exposure to materials such as wooden building blocks. These kinds of materials enabled them to investigate the physical properties of materials, and how those properties affected their use in design and construction (Turkle, 2008).

As you build with unit blocks, explore questions such as the following:

- How do the positions and placement of blocks impact a structure's stability?
- How can you get the same height and stability using fewer blocks?
- Are some types of blocks more useful than others?

Finally, consider your own design self-efficacy. Reflect on and describe

- your level of confidence as you build;
- your creativity expressed in building a structure;

Figure 5.2. Mathematical Concepts Meaningful in Block Building

Numerical relationships	Measurement	Shapes	Position and direction
1-to-1 correspondence	measuring	names of shapes	left/right
counting/magnitude	taller/shorter	2D/3D	vertical/horizontal
more/less	longer/shorter	pattern	on/next to
part-part-whole	length/width	sets	congruence
addition/subtraction	area/volume	angle	negative space
equivalence	estimation	categorizing/classifying	symmetry
fractions	thickness/thinness		inside/outside
seriation			over/under

- your motivation to go beyond building simple structures;
- the complexity of block building, your level of anxiety as you attempt a complex structure, and your level of perseverance; and
- how your own dispositions in block play might impact the development of your children's dispositions.

Teacher Play With Blocks and Track

Adding track to unit blocks introduces another dimension to your teacher play. Not only does a support structure need to be stable, but adding more blocks to make them higher determines whether the position of the track results in a steep slope or in a slope with a gradual incline. The slope of a ramp is an important variable to attend to when working to move marbles.

When we first began to consider how young children might respond to Ramps and Pathways materials, we engaged in teacher play with unit blocks and 1-, 2-, and 3-foot lengths of track. We gathered a variety of sizes and weights of marbles to move on the track, as well as objects with different attributes and made from different materials. As we played together, we found ourselves verbalizing and unpacking our own understandings about force and motion, and we pondered the understandings our children might develop. We surmised that children had the opportunity to do the following:

- construct a relationship between the steepness of an incline and how far an object travels when it leaves the end of the ramp

- construct a relationship between the steepness of an incline and how fast some objects travel
- use nonstandard units of measurement (such as the number of markers laid end to end) to document how far an object travels when it leaves the end of the ramp and, over time, learn to use standard units
- construct a relationship between how heavy a sphere is and how far the sphere travels
- construct a relationship between the shape of an object and how it moves down an incline (slide, tumble, wobble, wiggle, etc.), or doesn't move, or falls off

Engaging in teacher play helps educators consider how much and what kinds of materials to offer and how to visually stage them to invite children to handle them and put them to use in systems of ramps and pathways. Significant factors in how deeply children engage in Ramps and Pathways experiences include the numbers of wooden unit blocks, tracks, and objects to move. An inadequate amount of material may result in children arguing over pieces, or in children's frustration in engineering their own ramp and pathway systems. As we played, we found a full classroom set of unit blocks works best. Ten sections each of 1-, 2-, and 3-foot track seemed to be a good amount for a classroom of 15–25 children. As for the number of different kinds of materials to move on the ramps, we quickly learned that too many choices at the beginning of Ramps and Pathways experiences presented too many variables for children to sort out. A large number of variables may overwhelm children, affecting their ability to focus on constructing mental relationships.

As we played together, we thought about the kinds of questions and comments we could make that would support children's explorations. Questions and comments can help stimulate children's thinking, draw their attention to details, and assist them in constructing mental relationships. Instead of solving children's problems for them (which stifles their learning), use questions and comments to promote deeper thinking. Following are lists of possible questions you can ask, depending on what children are doing and the problem(s) they are trying to solve. These questions are based on an article written by Martens (1999) for primary grades, entitled "Productive Questions: Tools for Supporting Constructivist Learning," and enhanced by Fitzgerald and Dengler (2010) to connect younger children to variables.

Attention-Focusing Questions. These types of questions can be used to help focus children on variables they are overlooking. The attention-focusing questions may be particularly helpful in guiding and facilitating the full range of young children's active use of their developing inhibitory control and self-regulation. For young children who are easily distracted, learning to regulate their attention, behavior, and emotions is critical during STEM investigations. Attention-focusing questions can help draw their focus to what is happening in real time, enabling them to deepen their powers of observation, and, with repeated experiences over time, to increase their inhibitory control and self-regulation.

- *What have you noticed about the way this object moves down the track/along the pathway?*
- *Which sphere is your friend using in their system?*
- *What is happening when you make the ramp steep?*
- *Where do you notice the marble coming off the track?*
- *Look at what is happening when the marble comes off the track right here.*

Measuring and Counting Questions. These types of questions can be used to get children to put variables in relationship to each other. Fitzgerald and Dengler (2010) cautioned teachers to be careful not to stack these types of questions, but instead to ask for one relationship at a time. They also pointed out that these types of questions may serve as math and

problem-posing questions as well, or as math and reasoning questions.

- *How far did the marble travel or roll across the floor after it left the ramp?*
- *How far did the marble fly off the end before it landed on the floor or hit the surface?*
- *How many blocks do you need to stack to lean your ramp against to make the marble travel all the way to this target?*
- *What is different when you stack fewer blocks to lean your ramp against?*

Comparison Questions. These types of questions can be used to help younger children relate variables in quantitative ways before they have mastered numeracy or standard units of measure. They often are used in deductive reasoning questions, such as the last two in the following list, to ask the child to generate guesses, if not hypotheses, to test in action.

- *How do these objects move differently on the track or pathway?*
- *Which marble travels the farthest off the end of the ramp?*
- *What is the difference when you use a big marble versus a small marble?*
- *What is the difference when you use a heavy marble versus a light marble?*
- *Which marble goes faster, the big one or the little one? How did you figure that out?*
- *Which supports create a sturdier base? How did you figure that out?*
- *Which type of surface allows the marble to move the best? (Surface could refer to the floor or to the track itself.)*
- *Which type of surface allows the marble to travel more smoothly?*
- *Which type of surface allows the marble to go farther? How did you figure that out?*
- *How does the marble travel differently when you make the start of your ramp higher?*
- *How does the marble travel differently when you make the start of your ramp lower?*
- *How did you come to use this sphere in your system instead of the other ones?*
- *What would happen if you moved the ramp to this part of the floor?*
- *What would happen if you moved it to this side?*

Action Questions. These types of questions may help a child who is stuck. Teachers can float the answer out to a child by disguising it in the form of a question. As the child performs the action, they then may focus on relevant variables and own the success of figuring out the problem.

- *What happens if you release the marble somewhere else on the ramp?*
- *What happens if you put this one on first instead of that one?*
- *What happens if you make your ramp higher (or lower)?*
- *What happens if you add (or take away) a block to the support?* (This could refer to any particular point on the structure, not just the beginning of the pathway.)
- *What if you tried a bigger (or smaller) sphere?*
- *Is there somewhere you could you place the container so it will catch a marble as it leaves the ramp?*
- *How would it work if you position the ramp this way?*

Problem-Posing Questions. These types of questions can be used to challenge children to find a way to change a variable. They almost always include *can* or *could*, which serves to underscore the child's agency rather than following teacher directions. Notice that by using second-person *you* rather than the common teacherly *we*, trust in the child's agency also is maximized.

- *Can you find a way to make the marble move along the (flat) track without touching or blowing on the marble?*
- *Can you figure out how to make the marble stay on the ramp?*
- *How can you get the marble to travel farther off the ramp?*
- *How can you catch a marble when it flies off the ramp?*
- *Can you figure out how to make a marble turn a corner?*
- *Are there any other ways you can make a marble turn a corner?*
- *What could you do to make the marble knock down this target?*
- *What can you do to make the marble travel all the way to the end of the ramp?*

- *How can you make the marble go faster?*
- *How can you make the marble go slower?*
- *Can you build a ramp within this (confined) space?*
- *Can you make a marble go uphill?*
- *Can you build a ramp so that the marble has to jump from one part of the track or pathway to another?*
- *Is there anything else you could use to make that work?*

Reasoning Questions. These types of questions can be constructed to ask children to **predict** (deductive reasoning) or **generalize** (inductive reasoning) about variables. When asking children to reason by making predictions, teachers can have the child stop and answer, perhaps by having the teacher write down the prediction or by the child making a drawing of what would happen. (If the child just goes ahead and tries a response without actually predicting, the question reverts to being an action question rather than one supporting deductive reasoning.)

- *What do you think will happen if you use the ball bearing instead of the marble?*
- *What would happen if you made the start of the ramp higher?*
- *What will happen if you remove the block at the corner?*

When guiding children to reason by asking them to generalize their findings, teachers may pose questions like these:

- *What have you learned about making the marble move fast?*
- *What can you tell me about systems that use a slow-moving marble?*
- *What do you know now about how to get a marble to turn a corner?*
- *What can you tell me about how the different kinds of spheres work on ramp and pathway systems?*

In our work with preservice teachers, we provide the following advice on their preparation of questions:

- Avoid stacking. Ask one question about one variable at a time (particularly applicable to early math questions). Make "What is the same and different about these balls?" into separate questions: "What is different about these balls?" and then "What is the same about these balls?"

- Avoid taking agency away from the child. As you craft your questions, turn first person into second person. For example, instead of asking "What will happen if I/we . . . ?," ask "What will happen if you . . . ?" Early childhood educators often use "we" to signal that they also are learners, but too often children hear "we" and assume the adult will be doing the work.

- Yes/no questions are not productive of thinking. Children can say yes or no and just stop the conversation, or else pick one or the other without really figuring out the answer.

- Teacher-test questions (with one right answer, the one in the teacher's mind) are not productive of children's process and discovery.

- Be flexible in your thinking about what "should" be happening, and ask your questions.

- You can make responses to children's questions and statements in the form of questions, such as "What do you think?" or "I wonder how that happened?" or smile, nod, or give thumbs-up. (Sometimes no comment at all is appropriate.)

- Consider yourself a failure if your tongue does not bleed at least once from biting it to prevent yourself from just giving an answer to a child, or telling them what to do, or even just asking a teacher-test question.

Lessons From Our Children

After introducing Ramps and Pathways to our children, we found our predictions of how engaged they would be with the materials to be correct, and our prepared questions and comments to be fruitful. However, we found we significantly underestimated what children would do with the materials. The children independently took on many more design challenges that were incredibly creative and complex. Intrigued, we again engaged in teacher play to replicate their design challenges and quickly learned just how difficult these child-initiated

challenges were. Of the 13 examples of design challenges we offer in this chapter, we had predicted only four of them. Nine challenges were generated by young children themselves. Young children are highly creative with open-ended materials in Ramps and Pathways experiences, and you may find your children challenging themselves with additional unique inquiries. Every time we work with children, always one or more of them show us yet another creative twist to a design.

ASSESSMENT IN RAMPS AND PATHWAYS

Engaging in teacher play with Ramps and Pathways materials will make it apparent that a typical approach to assessment will not capture the creativity, innovation, critical thinking, and engineering and science practices children would be employing. This calls for reexamining the purposes for and uses of assessments. Attention to assessments not only provides a window into the learning and teaching occurring within the classroom, but it also is essential for educators under pressure to prove they are addressing grade-level standards.

Many educators are required to administer specific assessments that quantifiably measure a child's performance in a specific task. They are expected to track children's performance using these quantifiable measures to compare the score of one child to the score of another. What results is a very narrow school experience for children. Not everything that is important for children to learn and be able to do can be measured with numbers. Frank Serafini (2010), a former elementary educator and now professor of literacy education at Arizona State University, empathized with educators who were frustrated by how much time was lost to administering required assessments that had little impact on their teaching and children's learning. He introduced classroom-based assessments for educators to "inform our practice, enrich instruction, and generate the artifacts and data we need to remind various stakeholders that students' intelligence and capabilities can't be captured in a single test" (p. xiii). Such assessments allow educators to come to know each child as a unique individual in their quest to understand what is in the world, how it works, and how they can engage in its workings. When educators know their children well, they are intentional in their pedagogical moves as instructors and can more accurately anticipate children's next moves as learners. While Serafini is an expert in assessing literacy learning, his ideas about assessment are of great use in other domains of learning as well, such as STEM. Serafini recommended the use of four criteria to determine whether a classroom-based assessment is useful. Classroom-based assessments must

1. help children learn more effectively, not serve as a tool to compare one child to another;
2. help educators teach more effectively;
3. help educators articulate their understandings of their children to external audiences; and
4. be efficient, so they interrupt learning and teaching as little as possible.

Using these criteria, we can craft assessments that make children's thinking about force, motion, and design visible without interrupting that thinking. We can use our understanding of how they think to make instructional decisions that deepen children's interest and understanding. We can use assessments to make our children's thinking visible to the children themselves, and then to outside audiences. Once their process of learning has been made visible, audiences can view children as budding scientists and engineers. Following Serafini's lead in classroom assessments, we can look to three sources of information that help us understand our children's development in STEM thinking and learning:

1. *Artifacts:* The products children create as they examine and explore objects and phenomena. These might include drawings, photos, video, clay representations, structures, or creations of their own technology.
2. *Observations:* The notes we generate and collect when we passively observe children at work in STEM experiences.
3. *Interactions:* "The active discussions and communications we have with students on a daily basis." (Serafini, 2010, p. 23)

PREPARING FOR A PARADIGM SHIFT

In this chapter, we provide our insights into how educators can support the development of their children's science by making changes in how they currently engineer the environment of their classrooms. We challenge educators to shift away from preparing a lesson plan that ends with children stating that an object needs a push or a pull to move. Instead, we invite you into preparing experiences over time where children perceive patterns within the world of motion and learn how to engineer motion. Within the last 25 years of working with young children engaging in Ramps and Pathways experiences, we have noticed general patterns in children's design interests, but there is no one specific sequence to follow. However, we do list them in a somewhat ascending order of experience, with children developing basic understandings as foundations for later design challenges. The first few challenges are good starts for everyone, but the later ones are for the more experienced. We offer examples of design challenges that were initiated by children from ages 3 to 8. As we describe each design challenge we include the following:

- the title of an engineering experience written from the perspective of an adult learner
- an example of a teacher's open-ended invitation to their young learners to take on a challenge (if they aren't already challenging themselves)
- an explanation of why this experience matters in a child's development of science and engineering practices and critical thinking
- suggestions for materials that may be useful in building and testing a design
- guidance for engaging in teacher play within the engineering experience
- suggestions for documentation and assessments to make thinking visible

To fully capitalize on children's interest and engagement with the phenomena within Ramps and Pathways, each engineering experience provides guidance in considering the four aspects of a high-quality early childhood environment (see Figure 1.3) that will help a teacher transform their classroom into a makerspace classroom. Those four aspects of the classroom environment are the following:

1. physical environment
2. intellectual environment
3. social–emotional environment
4. promotional environment

In Figure 5.3, you will see a synthesis of the Ramps and Pathways experiences. To the right of each

experience, we feature an assessment that is useful in documenting children's learning and making their thinking visible. In the discussion of each experience, we explore how the suggested assessment is useful for educators and their children within the context of Ramps and Pathways. However, each assessment can be used in any of the design challenges.

It is essential to understand that your and your children's experiences with Ramps and Pathways may look similar to what we have witnessed and experienced, or they may look very different. Your children's work in designing within Ramps and Pathways will

Figure 5.3. Children's Engineering Experiences and Featured Assessments

Engineering Experience	Featured Assessment
1. Engineering Sturdy Structures *How can I arrange blocks to make a sturdy structure that will stay standing?*	Observational Records
2. A Unit Block, a Track, and a Marble *What can I make happen using one block, one track, and one marble? How could I get the marble to move without touching it?*	School-to-Home-to-School Communication: Family letter to encourage exploration of ramps and/or pathways in children's neighborhoods or places they visit
3. Engineering a Ramp Using a 2-Foot Track to Move a Marble *How far does the marble roll after it leaves the end of the 2-foot ramp? How can I get it to roll farther?*	Science Journals
4. Engineering an Incline to Move Objects With Different Attributes *Will all of these objects move down the ramp the same way?*	Softball Interview and Sorting
5. Engineering Ramps, Roads, and Pathways *How can I use tracks to add a road to the end of my ramp and keep the marble rolling straight?*	Teacher Reflection Journal
6. Engineering Ramps of Different Lengths to Move Different Types of Spheres *How do different kinds of spheres affect the designs of my systems?*	Engineering Habits of Mind
7. Engineering a System of Hills and Valleys *How can I get a marble to roll up a hill?*	Engineering Behaviors
8. Engineering a System With Corners *How can I get a marble to turn a corner?*	Observational Records With Productive Questions
9. Engineering a Jump: A System to Transfer a Marble From One Track to Another Over a Gap *How can I get a marble to jump over a space in the pathway?*	Time-Lapse Video and/or Photo Series
10. Engineering a Drop: A System to Catch a Marble *How can I design a pathway that ends with the marble dropping into a bucket?*	Science Journals
11. Engineering a System to Reverse the Direction of a Marble *How can I design a pathway that causes a marble to move backward?*	Science Concepts
12. Engineering a System to Work in Odd Spaces *How can I construct a pathway that fits in this small space?*	Teacher Reflection Journal × Engineering Habits of Mind
13. Setting Off a Chain of Events *How can I aim a marble to knock down objects?*	Time-Lapse Video and/or Photo Series for Documenting Progress

be enhanced and personalized by their own unique interests, experiences, and curiosities, as well as your classroom environment. The children's work will be influenced by your own and your families' cultures, languages, and histories. We found the first four examples of experiences to be typical of beginning builders among both children and adults. Again, there is no correct sequence of challenges to take on. As you observe your children at work, use the Inquiry Teaching Model (see Figure 1.1) to understand how to support children's inquiry and advance children's learning in Ramps and Pathways experiences.

EXPERIENCE 1. ENGINEERING STURDY STRUCTURES

How can I arrange blocks to make a sturdy structure that will stay standing?

Why This Experience Matters

Building with unit blocks challenges children to think about weight, balance, friction, and tension as they construct stable structures. The more experiences students have with block building, the stronger their spatial thinking will be (see Figure 5.4). When children are able to build stable structures to support track in Ramps and Pathways experiences, they will be able to give more attention to engineering the movement of marbles or other objects on the track.

Materials:

- classroom set of wooden unit blocks
- shelving to hold and display unit blocks

Design constraints or things for the teacher to hold constant:

- the children's use of only wooden unit blocks
- building within the space designated for block building

Figure 5.4. Engineering Sturdy Structures

Things that children can vary or change:

- the types of unit blocks used
- the positions of blocks in use
- the size of the structure
- the use of symmetrical features of structures or asymmetrical features
- ideas for testing stability

Mental relationships children have the possibility of constructing:

- between the properties of a block and how those properties affect its use in a structure
- between a block placed vertically or horizontally and a structure's stability
- which blocks can be substituted for another

Example of a teacher's invitation to focus:

I've seen a lot of different kinds of interesting structures you have been building. Some stay standing and some fall down easily. How can you arrange blocks to make a sturdy structure that will stay standing?

Before You Introduce, Engage in Teacher Play

Explore blocks from your adult perspective as you build. Consider the following:

- how a block's placement and position impact your structure's stability
- how you would define *stable*
- how you could test your structure's stability
- how you can get the same height and stability using fewer blocks
- which kinds of blocks are more useful than others
- the number of blocks you have available for children, and whether you wish you had more of a specific type
- the level of sound as you build and when structures topple, and how noise may impact other learners

Consider your own self-efficacy with engineering thinking with respect to your:

- level of confidence as you build
- creativity expressed in building a structure
- level of anxiety as you attempt more complex structures
- motivation to try something even harder after you build a satisfying structure
- surprise at how complex block building can be and how to go beyond simple structures
- perception of opportunities to apply your growing skills and to persevere when things do not go well
- dispositions in block play and how they may influence the development of your children's dispositions

Now think from your children's perspective:

- What might they try to attempt?
- What might be some of their frustrations?
- What kinds of problems would be important for them to work through?
- How could you support them without telling them how to solve their problem?
- What specific comments could you make or questions could you ask to deepen their thinking?

Attending to the Four Aspects of the Environment

Physical Environment: Arranging the Classroom to Promote Inquiry

Prepare a traffic-free area with adequate space in your classroom for children to engage in block play. If there is a part of your classroom that needs quiet, place the block space on the opposite side of the room, because children will be using a lot of language as they build. Add a low-pile carpet for children to build upon. A low-pile carpet will not interfere with the stability of a structure and will soften the sound of structures that collapse. Choose a carpet with a neutral, natural color and without a pattern. Brightly colored carpets fight for attention and details in children's structures. Bright carpets will challenge children's ability to focus and solve intricate problems, and they will make it more difficult for you to document with photos and video. If you have a bright carpet, consider placing a large

canvas drop cloth used by house painters over the bright rug.

Some children may have physical–motor considerations due to differences in the range of motion and control of their muscles, joints, and bones occasioned by contributing medical conditions such as cerebral palsy, spina bifida, or muscular dystrophy. If this is the case in your classroom, it may be necessary to use specific blocks that are easier for children to grasp and manipulate, such as large cardboard or foam blocks. If sitting on the floor is difficult due to posture concerns or children who need adaptive equipment such as gait trainers or wheelchairs, a large table at the correct height for ramp building may provide them with the support needed to build. One teacher introduced ramps in an empty water table. She used one wall of the container as the means to elevate the ramp and the wall on the other side as the way to stop the sphere. No chasing it across the room.

Prepare adequate shelving to house the blocks. Sort and arrange the blocks on the shelves in categories, positioning them in a way that invites children to contemplate the different properties of the blocks, and consider the number of each kind of block (see Figure 5.5). Photograph and laminate a picture of the stocked block shelf. Place it near the shelf to use as reference for when the blocks need to be put away. A well-designed dedicated space for block building will be in high use all year long. The younger the children, the more apt they are to build directly in front of the shelving. This may hinder other children from access to the blocks, so having a large enough space is important for preschoolers.

Figure 5.5. Arranging Blocks to Invite Building

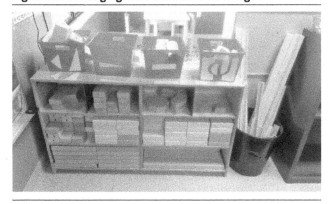

Intellectual Environment: Opportunities to Ask Questions, Predict, and Reason

Children naturally engage in engineering as they design and build with unit blocks (Petroski, 2003). In block play, children have the opportunity to engage with rich, open-ended materials that support the development of inborn intellectual dispositions (Katz, 2015). Block building inspires them to engage in the intellectual life of reasoning, predicting, posing questions and problems, developing ideas, and having a drive to understand (Katz, 2015). Blocks support play that affords critical thinking skills and opportunities to which all children need full access, including those with cognitive delays. Consider questions and comments to support children's intellectual work of reasoning, predicting, analyzing, and questioning as they build sturdy structures. Dodge et al. (2016) encouraged teachers to support and honor children's work in block play by commenting on what they are doing by offering descriptions of what teachers notice, or by asking open-ended questions to begin a conversation about the children's work. These comments and questions can be based on a child's choice of blocks, their arrangement, the number used, the similarity (to each other) of blocks used, and noteworthy designs. Below, we include some suggestions from Dodge et al. (2016), as well as additional questions that focus on sturdy structures.

Question or comment on their choice of blocks:

- *I notice you are using all the same kinds of blocks.*
- *What kinds of blocks make the sturdiest towers?*
- *Which blocks are not very useful in making sturdy structures? Why do you suppose that is?*
- *I see you are using mostly rectangular blocks. Some are long, and some are short.*

Question or comment on the arrangement of blocks:

- *I notice your blocks make a space in the middle.*
- *When you push on this side to make the edge on this side even, what happens to the edge on the other side?*
- *Some of the blocks in your structure are laying down, and some are standing up. How might that make the structure sturdy, or shaky?*

- *What would happen if you turned the blocks on their sides?*

Question or comment on the number of blocks:

- *If I count the blocks on their sides, I can say your structure is two blocks high. I wonder if it could get even higher.*
- *I see you've begun a pattern of two on their sides, one flat on top. Two on their sides, one flat on top. How many times can you repeat that pattern and still have a sturdy structure?*
- *What other patterns have you tried? How well did they work?*

Question or comment on the similarity of blocks in use:

- *I notice all your blocks are rectangles, but they're not all the same size.*
- *I see you selected all the same kinds of blocks to build this. How would it work with different kinds?*

Question or comment on noteworthy designs:

- *You made the top block balance. I bet that wasn't easy.*
- *Your blocks are way out at the edges without peeking out. You made the edges flush or even. How important is this in making a structure sturdy?*
- *It looks like two windows when I look through it from the ends. When I look at it from this side, I don't see any windows.*

Suggest additional challenges for confident builders:

- *How could you test the structure to see if it is sturdy?*
- *How could you build this high using fewer blocks?*

Social–Emotional Environment: Nurturing Healthy Learning Dispositions

Navigate conflict in the block area by co-constructing an idea of how the block area should operate. Learning to resolve conflict is an essential part of a classroom designed for inclusive inquiry (see Textbox 5.1). Adult–child relationships are at the heart of this kind of classroom community. When children participate in rulemaking in the classroom they begin to formulate ideas about the reasons for rules, what rules might be needed to make their classroom work, and why rules are necessary to make a classroom a great place to learn and grow (see Figure 5.6). Some teachers may choose to begin with a few simple classroom rules, stated positively: Be safe; listen; be a friend; use polite words. Teachers who understand the value of cocreated classroom rules may wait until there is a need for rules before asking the children to participate in rulemaking. For example, when children were leaving the block area with blocks on the floor, their teacher brought this problem to their attention at the next morning meeting. They generated ideas for taking care of the blocks and how to put them away. The teacher wrote their ideas on chart paper to be placed in the block center, and children could refer to them when the center was in use. Some teachers find it helpful to use photos or children's drawings as visual cues to help children to understand and independently apply the rules during their block play and ramp investigations.

TEXTBOX 5.1. THE VALUE OF COCREATING RULES WITH CHILDREN

Learning to resolve conflict is an essential part of an inclusive classroom designed for inquiry. Classroom conflict is inevitable among young children engaged in an active curriculum that embraces early STEM experiences. We have learned that there are positive aspects to conflict and its resolution, such as the following:

- Conflicts provide rich opportunities for children to be confronted with the perspective of others.
- Children's desire for good relationships with their friends motivates them to persist in solving problems.
- Engaging and supporting children in resolving their own conflicts fosters mutual respect in the classroom.

Our goal is for children to have a personal conviction about basic values so that even when adults are not present they will follow the rules and expectations.

Children can learn to self-regulate when they see that we believe in their abilities to do so. We can support their development of self-regulation by taking steps such as these:

- providing a place in the classroom for resolving conflicts and coaching children at the beginning to learn how to resolve conflict
- sharing decision-making in the development of classroom rules
- voting to make decisions

Promotional Environment: Promoting and Celebrating Children's Thinking and Ideas

To promote children's thinking, photograph a child working on a block structure, and take a photo of the structure without the child after it was completed. Print out the photos and interview the child about their process.

- *Tell me about your structure.*
- *What was the most difficult part of building this structure?*
- *How did you work through that difficult part?*
- *What would you want others to know about your structure?*

Post the photo with the child's words on the wall for others to read and enjoy.

It is important to communicate to families and administrators the children's ownership of how the classroom is operated. This can be done by calling attention to the rules developed for the Ramps and Pathways center (see Figure 5.6). Promote children's ownership to outside audiences by placing a label describing the value of ownership (see Textbox 5.2) above the co-constructed rules for the Ramps and Pathways center.

TEXTBOX 5.2. WHO WRITES THE RULES?

These rules (see Figure 5.6) for working in the Ramps and Pathways center were written by the learners in this classroom. Research shows that when children have a voice in how decisions are made and how the classroom is operated (within parameters), they hold themselves and their peers more accountable. In our discussion on how to operate the Ramps and Pathways center, the children considered what the action in the center should be (building). We were concerned about losing the marbles, so the children made a rule about having a way to catch the marbles at the end of a system. As with most rules they are used to following, they included listening to directions, and the need to take care of materials. If more than one person wanted an object in the center, they would share. Finally, to keep the classroom in shape and make sure all the materials are not lost, they added a rule about putting everything away where they found it. Participating in decisions in how to learn together in our classroom supports children's development of responsibility and an awareness of how others respond to our actions.

Featured Assessment: Observational Records

Use a software program that allows you to print each one of your children's names on a sheet of mailing labels. Make sure to observe each child at least once within the week and write your observations on the child's mailing label. The empty labels will remind you of who yet needs to be observed. Date and document a child's actions, a language sample, questions they are posing, problems they are posing, and relationships they are forming. At the end of the week, pull off the labels and put them on a page for each child. Over time, you will have a sequenced record of each child's thinking and their use of science and engineering practices, with specific examples.

Make your observations more specific by recording what you notice and how children respond

Figure 5.6. Classroom Rules

to questions designed to explore their thinking. Dodge et al. (2016) encouraged teachers to support and honor children's work in block play by commenting on what they are doing with descriptions of what they notice, or by asking open-ended questions to begin a conversation about their work. The comments and questions can be based on a child's choice of blocks, their arrangement, the number used, the similarity (to each other) of blocks used, and noteworthy designs, as mentioned earlier in the section on Intellectual Environment.

EXPERIENCE 2. A UNIT BLOCK, A TRACK, AND A MARBLE

What can I make happen using one block, one track, and one marble? How could I get the marble to move without touching it?

Why This Experience Matters

Children's growing understanding of how the world works includes observing how objects move and detecting patterns. This experience may be brief, but is important for sparking conversations about what makes objects move, and it frames the macro question of "How can I move this marble in an interesting way?" Children may suggest blowing on the marble or shaking the track. These answers are not wrong and should be honored. No matter how hard it may be for you to keep from telling your children to lift up one end, try equally hard to resist the urge. This reminder is especially important within diverse settings, working with children who fall along the full range of learning and development. Young children with developmental delays may require more repetition, additional practice, and multiple observations before they are ready to construct new relationships related to slope and motion. With time (which can vary widely), space, and patience, all children with differing abilities can eventually begin to elevate one end of the track on their own. And if they do it on their own, they truly will own that knowledge.

Materials (see Figure 5.7):

- unit blocks
- 1-foot tracks
- standard-sized marbles

Figure 5.7. Unit Blocks, 1-Foot Track, and Standard-Sized Marbles

Design constraints or things for the teacher to hold constant:

- one unit block, one 1-foot track, and one marble per child

Things that children can vary or change:

- the position of the unit block
- the elevation of one end of the track
- where to let go of the marble on the track

Mental relationships children have the possibility of constructing:

- between the position of the block and its height
- between the height of the block and the steepness of the slope
- between the steepness of the slope and how fast or far the marble will roll

Example of a teacher's invitation to focus:

I noticed you have been thinking hard about how to position blocks to build a sturdy structure. I've watched you explore what happens when you stack blocks in a vertical position, and what happens when you stack blocks in a horizontal position. I want to add some other materials to the blocks. I have these tracks that are all the same length. They are all 1 foot long. I also have these marbles. I'm wondering what you can make happen using one block, one track, and one marble. How could you get the marble to move without touching it?

Before You Introduce, Engage in Teacher Play

After your children have had ample time to build sturdy structures and interest starts to wane, your children may be ready for Ramps and Pathways. Explore from an adult's perspective what you can make happen with a unit block, a 1-foot piece of track, and a standard-sized marble:

- How many ways can you make the marble move without touching it?
- How can you make the track into a ramp with a steep slope? A gradual slope?

Investigating Ramps and Pathways With Young Children

- What three ways can you change the position of the unit block to get three different kinds of slope?
- What surface allows the marble to move the farthest?
- What can you use to keep the marble from rolling too far?

Now think from your children's perspective:

- Have you noticed any use of ramps in the school or community setting that may be familiar to the children? If so, how might that prior experience affect how children engage with these materials?
- What solutions might your children have for moving a marble on the track without touching it?
- Are there any dangers in your children's use of these materials? If yes, how might you mitigate that danger?
- Do you have a child who still mouths objects? How can you adapt materials to allow all children to safely engage in this experience?

Attending to the Four Aspects of the Environment

Physical Environment: Arranging the Classroom to Promote Inquiry

In this introductory experience, we have found it effective to have a class meeting to introduce the materials and pose the open-ended question in the large-group meeting space. Using a round rug helps children form a circle for discussion and group exploration. Choosing a rug with neutral and natural tones helps children focus on the phenomenon without visual distractions. An easel with chart paper and markers close by is useful in documenting children's ideas and questions.

Intellectual Environment: Opportunities to Ask Questions, Predict, and Reason

In the NGSS, kindergarten children are expected to understand that an object needs a push or pull to move it. In your introduction of this experience,

you might capitalize on children's use of language by rephrasing their ideas using the words *push* and *pull*. For example:

- *You can use your finger to push the marble to make it move.*
- *You can use your finger to pull the marble toward you.*
- *You can push the marble with the air you use to blow on it.*
- *You can use a toy or other object to push or pull the marble.*

Sooner or later, children will have the idea they can lift one end of the track to make the marble move (see Figure 5.8). What is making the marble move? The answer is the pull of gravity. Children can learn to say, "The pull of gravity makes the marble roll down," but young children will not have a conceptual understanding of gravity. In fact, many adults do not have a deep conceptual understanding of gravity. In our own teacher play, we struggled to explain gravity and finally Googled it. While children may not understand the concept of gravity, they can still notice patterns in how objects move. They are incredibly interested in engineering the movement of objects, making subsequent experiences meaningful in developing science and engineering practices.

Our friend Peggy Ashbrook is an expert in learning and teaching science with young children. She has authored several books on early science and was the Early Years Columnist with National Science

Figure 5.8. Constructing an Incline

Teaching Association's journal *Science and Children*. Peggy likes to introduce Ramps and Pathways by placing one unit block, a 1-foot piece of track, and one marble in front of each child in a circle with the request to look at it, but not to touch it—yet (see Figure 5.9).

Peggy then poses the question, "How could you make your marble move using just a track and a block? Try out your ideas." In a matter of seconds, children begin to place the track on the block to make a ramp. Children begin to vary the position of the unit block, finding that they can elevate and lower the slope by placing the block in three different positions (see Figure 5.10). Many children begin collaborating, combining their materials to make a ramp and pathways.

Reminder: Do not rush children in placing track at an incline. There is much for them to learn in

Figure 5.9. Introducing Ramps and Pathways

Figure 5.10. Unit Block in Three Positions

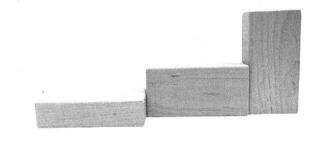

designing and constructing pathways. Resist showing them how to make an incline. Allow them to discover this way of moving objects on their own, and their conceptual understanding will be deeper.

Social–Emotional Environment: Nurturing Healthy Learning Dispositions

We have found it helpful to sit on the floor next to children in a circle instead of in a chair above them. Sitting above them suggests to the children that we are the keepers of all knowledge and have all the correct answers. In this situation, children will provide only responses that they believe the teacher will agree with. Sitting alongside children encourages them to talk with one another rather than only to the teacher. Positioning ourselves at children's level likewise supports communication and engaged discussions, allowing children to make better eye contact with greater attention and focus while increasing their ability to hear and subsequently listen in order to understand, which may be critical to children with visual and hearing impairments. We can lessen our role as the expert to create a community of inquiry with suggestions such as these:

- *Who has questions for Davaceah about his idea?*
- *Jaylaun shared an idea with me of how to get the marble to go farther. Jaylaun, could you explain your idea to all of us?*
- *Turn to the person next to you to talk about this idea.*

Promotional Environment: Promoting and Celebrating Children's Thinking and Ideas

Feature the children's thinking by cocreating a list of how to get the marble to move, or by using a Language Experience Approach (LEA). Reading and writing are reciprocal processes. Implementing an LEA with young children capitalizes on the relationship between the two to help children become stronger readers. The children share an experience with ramps and pathways, such as how to get a marble to move, then they describe the experience out loud, dictate to the teacher what to write, and finally read what they said. In the process, children develop a sense of ownership of reading and writing. For very young children, this process helps them recognize that what they say can be recorded in print.

These are some actions that teacher's can take in an LEA:

- capitalize on students' interest and experiences in getting a marble to move
- prompt the students to reflect on different ways to move a marble
- ask questions to elicit details about the experience through more explicit language
- help students to mentally and verbally rehearse the ideas they will be writing about

Once they are comfortable with saying the vocabulary words out loud, children move to the written part of the strategy as teachers and students work together to cowrite text explaining what they observed in making the marble move. The written work is then promoted by posting it at the children's eye level on one of the classroom walls. The piece becomes a tool for reading practice and a way for children to reinforce the vocabulary they used earlier.

To prepare for an LEA, the teacher photographs children engaged in making marbles move. The photos are not posed, but focus on the acts of building, acts of confronting a problem, and acts of problem solving. The children use the images as prompts to describe what they were figuring out in the experience. The teacher then writes those moments on chart paper, modeling the writing process and using sound–symbol relationships while forming the words. After each sentence is completed, the teacher and children read the whole story from the beginning.

LEAs turn experiences into oral language, and then turn the oral language into the written form. Reading back the story then returns the written language back into oral language. In the process, children are able to

- draw on their own personal experiences;
- learn to recognize words in print that are orally very familiar to them;
- enhance their expressive vocabulary;
- boost writing skills;
- read their own work; and
- reinforce their reading skills and build confidence in their writing abilities.

Featured Assessment: School-to-Home-to-School Communication

To learn what experiences children have with ramps and pathways around their homes, write or cocreate a letter to send home inviting families to share. You can then use this information to build on the everyday experiences of children with their families outside of school. See Figures 6.3 and 6.4 for examples of drawings sent back to the teacher in response to this invitation.

Dear Families,
We have become interested in how we move things from one place to another, such as pathways outdoors and ramps we use to get up or down without stairs. We would like to find out what kinds of ramps and pathways your child has near or even in your home. Please have your child draw one or more pathways or ramps in your neighborhood or home to share with our class as we begin to explore ramps and pathways.
Sincerely,
Teacher

EXPERIENCE 3. ENGINEERING A RAMP USING A 2-FOOT TRACK TO MOVE A MARBLE

How far does the marble roll after it leaves the end of the 2-foot ramp?

Why This Experience Matters

A child's ability and confidence to launch investigations begin with many small trial-and-error experiences such as this one. Some children will want to lean their track against a shelf. Others will use unit blocks for supports and be more iterative in their testing (see Figure 5.11). It is okay that they are focusing on different concepts. That is the beauty of working with open-ended materials. All can enjoy them as a challenge that is just right for them. Educators who have experienced teacher play with the materials will likely recognize the different concepts being explored. When you see your children starting to do this on their own, the information in this experience will be helpful in shifting from direct instruction to facilitating children's learning.

Materials: These materials should already be available to the children, but you might offer only one size of track. In this example we use 2-foot tracks.

- unit blocks
- shelving to store unit blocks

Figure 5.11. Two-Foot Tracks, Unit Blocks, and a Marble

- 2-foot tracks
- standard-sized marbles

Design constraints or things for the teacher to hold constant:

- standard-sized marbles
- 2-foot tracks

Things that children can vary or change:

- the shelf or surface the child uses to support the start of the ramp
- the elevation of one end of the track
- where to let go of the marble on the track

Important: Children may be changing these variables without knowing it. You can use attention-focusing questions to help them observe their actions more closely. For example, "I noticed the first time, you let go of the marble here [point to the place on the ramp] but after that, you let go of the marble here [point to place on the ramp]. I wonder if that makes a difference in how far the marble rolls. How could you find out?"

Mental relationships children have the possibility of constructing:

- between the height of the block stack or shelf and the steepness of the slope
- between the steepness of the slope and how fast or far the marble will roll

Example of a teacher's invitation to focus:

I noticed Danton and Whitney are investigating how far the marble rolls after it leaves the end of their ramp. Danton and Whitney, can you let us know what you've been thinking about? (Danton and Whitney share their ideas. Teacher engages in shared writing to record their comments and posts them near the Ramps and Pathways area.) *Danton and Whitney are finding that the marble goes really far when they use the 2-foot track to make ramps. I'd like to explore this a bit more with you, so I've put out all of the 2-foot-long tracks. Let's investigate a bit more and then talk about it this week.*

Before You Introduce, Engage in Teacher Play

First, explore from an adult's perspective using one 2-foot piece of track, unit blocks, and a marble. Investigate the following:

- How does an incremental increase in the height of a slope impact the speed of a marble?
- How could you measure that speed?
- You have two ramps made with the same length of track leaned against the same number of stacked unit blocks (see Figure 5.12). You want to learn if the marble will roll at the same speed on both. Would this be a fair test? If not, how could you make it a fair test?
- How does an incremental increase in the height of a slope impact how far a marble rolls after it leaves the bottom of the ramp?
- How could you measure that distance?
- How could you get the marble to roll even farther?
- How high must the start of the ramp be to get the marble to roll the farthest? Ten unit blocks high? 11? 12? 13? 14?
- At which point of height does the marble just fall off or bounce?

Now think from your children's perspective:

- They will be interested in moving the marble both faster and farther.
- They may observe that a marble rolls faster on a steep slope, but backing up that observation with data may be too difficult.
- How might they compare and talk about speed?
- How might a slow-motion feature on a recording device help children observe speed?
- How might they compare and talk about distance?
- Would it be better to mark the stopping points of marbles with a Post-it and then compare distances? How might I suggest this to them? Or should I not?
- Which would be easiest for them to observe? Differences in speed or distance?
- Would this be a good time to introduce nonstandard units of measurement using items familiar to children? For example, markers, pencils, unifix blocks, unit blocks.
- Would this be a good time to introduce formal standard units of measurement to 2nd-graders? Should we use informal standard units of measure such as how many markers long the marble rolled? Or should we focus on comparing distances by marking a marble's stopping point with a sticker on the carpet or floor and compare the points?
- Are they ready for the idea of fair tests (see Figure 5.12)? Some children will notice the difference in the steepness of the slope depending on how they lean the 2-foot track on a stack of unit blocks. Some will not, as they are only focused on getting the marble to go faster and/or farther. Only you know your children well enough to decide if they are ready to think about fair tests.

Attending to the Four Aspects of the Environment

Physical Environment: Arranging the Classroom to Promote Inquiry

Decide whether this experience would work best in a large group or in a small group. Consider the placement of tables and chairs and how they may affect children's testing to learn how to get a marble to travel a great distance. Can the classroom furniture be rearranged to make a large space for the class to explore together? Or could it be arranged to enable children to explore with the materials in an area that keeps marbles from rolling into other parts of the classroom? Prepare a way to store marbles when they are not in use. Some teachers use an egg carton and put a marble in each section. Children can check to see if all 12 marbles are accounted for,

Figure 5.12. Considering Fair Tests

or if some are missing. This can be a meaningful context for mathematical reasoning. Three sections of the egg carton are empty. How many marbles are left? There are two rows of six in an egg carton, or six rows of two. Make clipboards available to children with paper and pencils for them to use to document what they are learning.

Intellectual Environment: Opportunities to Ask Questions, Predict, and Reason

If you started out as a traditional teacher like we did, you may be tempted to turn this experience into a lesson with children following your direction. We challenge you to resist this temptation and let go of the idea that all of the children should learn the same concept on the same day. UDL reminds us that it is imperative to make the necessary adaptations and modifications needed to ensure that instruction is guided and informed by children's individual rates of learning and development. The idea of all children proceeding through a lesson at the same pace turns rich, intellectual goals into academic tasks that can influence teachers into comparing one child with another, often in ways that are more harmful (from a deficit view) than helpful (using a strengths-based approach). Instead, take 5 minutes to observe a group of your children at work (see Figure 5.13).

Children's actions can often reveal the questions they are trying to answer. Watch for details like these:

- Who has figured out that the steeper the ramp is, the faster the marble goes?
- Who has figured out that at some point in steepness, the marble no longer rolls down the ramp but just falls to the floor?
- Who has figured out that the length of a ramp leaned up on a stack of blocks increases or decreases the steepness of a ramp? (see Figure 5.14)
- Who is focused on how far the marble travels?
- Which children are focused on racing two marbles using two pieces of track? Is it a fair race?
- What kinds of materials are getting in the way of children's development of concepts?

Figure 5.13. Exploring Fair Tests

Figure 5.14. Comparing the Steepness of Different-Sized Ramps

- Which kinds of materials could be added to enhance the development of concepts?

Social–Emotional Environment: Nurturing Healthy Learning Dispositions

Exploring ramps is a highly engaging experience and a cause of great excitement. In their excitement, children may accidentally knock down another's ramp. Someone may step on a marble or get into the path of another's moving marble. We teachers know enough to expect conflict, but the work of Piaget challenges us to reframe conflict as a positive rather than negative aspect of learning and teaching. Piaget (1932/1965) described two kinds of conflict: inter-individual conflict and intra-individual conflict. Inter-individual conflict is what we are most familiar with. It occurs between two or more individuals and involves a clash between the individuals' goals, behaviors, beliefs, knowledge, or expectations. Intra-individual conflict occurs within the individual child and involves a contradiction between what the child knows or believes and what they experience or observe. Conflict actually plays a central role in the development of a child's knowledge when it prompts the child to change how they think and feel. A child's efforts to resolve conflict lead to the development of logic and the construction of new understanding (Piaget, 1932/1965).

Early childhood teachers who plan for the development of the social–emotional environment in their classrooms enhance the interpersonal relationships of their students as well as provide for intellectual development. Teachers can establish such an environment by providing a place where children can go to work out a problem together when on-the-spot problem solving is not possible. Encourage children to use their words to solve a conflict and give them words to use when they struggle to find their voice (see Textbox 5.3).

TEXTBOX 5.3. HELPING CHILDREN USE THEIR WORDS IN CONFLICT RESOLUTION

Teacher: Brice, are you upset that your ramp got knocked down? Tell Faith, "I didn't like that you knocked down my ramp."

Brice: Faith, I don't like it when you knock down my ramp!

Teacher: Faith, did you mean to knock down Brice's ramp? Do you wish you hadn't? Tell him, "I didn't mean to knock down your ramp."

Faith: Brice, I didn't want to knock your ramp down. I wish I didn't do it.

Teacher: Brice, Faith said she didn't mean to knock your ramp down and she wishes she hadn't. Is there something Faith can do to make you feel better?

Brice: Yes.

Teacher: What do you want her to do?

Brice: Help me build my ramp back up.

Teacher: Faith, would you help him build his ramp back up to help him feel better?

Faith: Yes. Let's go build it.

This amount of effort takes a lot of time, but it is time well spent when children learn to navigate their own conflicts. Teachers tell us that setting up the classroom to embrace conflict to solve it at the beginning of the year creates a positive learning environment for the remainder of the year. An authentically inclusive UDL setting is one in which all children are equally valued community members. The more children are able to resolve conflicts, the greater the likelihood that they will develop and maintain meaningful friendships that will in turn grant them full access to, and participation in, group play, projects, and investigations.

Promotional Environment: Promoting and Celebrating Children's Thinking and Ideas

As you observe children, photograph them in the process of working rather than asking them to pose. Try to get a camera angle that allows them to observe the steepness of their slope, which may require you to lie on the floor to take photos or video. After printing the photo, share it with the children. Seeing themselves in the process of building may help them focus on how hard they were thinking, or it may nudge them to observe the steepness of the ramp more closely.

Invite children to document their thinking. You may want to act as scribe for children who are still constructing an understanding that their spoken words can be represented by marks on a page. Others may be ready for the challenge to put their words into print. Posting these mini-stories on the wall enables children to read and revisit their thinking. Copies could also be placed into a class book that the children can read to themselves or each other. A collection of mini-stories with a common concept can be grouped together. For example, under the heading of "We are learning we can control how fast and how slow a marble goes by changing the height of the ramp," you can place photos of children at work with captions underneath:

- Brayden found he could make the marble go fast by making the start of his ramp four blocks high.
- JaQuaisha found she could slow down the marble if she only used one block at the start of her ramp.
- Shaleah found that when she made the ramp too steep, the marble just fell to the floor and bounced.
- Martavius noticed that the faster a marble went, the farther it rolled after it left the ramp. He kept track of how far it rolled with Post-its.
- Kenneth found that using the slow-motion video-recording on the tablet helped him figure out which marble got to the bottom of the ramp first.

By providing a label describing the concept children are developing along with the standards being addressed, educators can inform outside audiences such as families and administrators of the rigor of playful learning.

Featured Assessment: Science Journals

Some educators introduce the idea of science journals using purchased bound composition notebooks. When one educator grew frustrated by her children's entries on random pages in the notebook, she began a system of using a binder clip to fasten all the new pages on the right, leaving all the used pages on the left. After reading a child's entry, she would remove the binder clip to release

a fresh page for the child's next entry and refasten the rest of the new pages on the right. She found this helped some children begin to understand that print concepts of reading from front to back applied to their own writing as well as published books. She encouraged her children to use the date stamper from observational drawing to date a new entry. This allowed her to view her children's growth in their observations and data collection. It also provided a way for her to track children's development in their concepts of print, their spelling patterns, their use of digraphs and blends, their vowel usage, their capitalization and punctuation, and their use of text features outside formal instruction. It was an indicator of how children were applying literacy skills to their everyday writing. The journal was used as an artifact at conferences with families to illustrate a child's growth. She bought each child two notebooks, one for the start of school through the end of December, and one for the month of January through the end of the school year. She kept the fall notebooks until the end of the school year. When she handed them out to the children in the last week of school, the children took delight in how much they had grown in their writing and documentation. "Look how I used to spell this word!" "Look how hard it is to read what I wrote back then!"

Other educators prepare blank books (see Figure 5.15) and make them available for children to use as science journals. To construct the blank books, they cut 8½ × 11 sheets of copy paper and cardstock in half. They count five pieces of the copy paper halves and place them on top of one piece of cardstock that serves as the cover. They fold the pages and cover in half to find the middle. Using a long-arm stapler, they put two staples in the center to bind the pages to the cover. The result is a blank book with 20 pages. Teachers of more prolific writers simply construct blank books with more pages. Children like how the small book feels in their hands, and many find these custom-made books more personal than stock notebooks and therefore are more encouraged to use them. They take delight in reading their book to themselves and others. The educators find opportunities to talk about text features such as the title page or the use of boldface print as they assist children in adding their own words to the pages. When some children began to

Figure 5.15. Little Blank Book

take note of how some authors include a dedication page, they began to include a dedication page in their own books. Some children take note of how they are creating their own little library or book series!

No matter which kind of book you choose to use, invite children to log their experience and thinking in a science journal. What children choose to talk about, write about, photograph, or draw is a window into their process of inquiry. Educators can support children's use of science journals in a variety of ways.

Supporting Children's Use of Science Journals

Educators support children's construction and use of science journals when they do the following:

- Take a series of photos of children working, print them out, and cut them apart so children can sequence and paste the photos in the science journal (printing photos on large mailing labels eliminates the steps of cutting and gluing).
- Ask the child to explain what they were doing in the photos and what they were thinking.

- Glue a photo on the left side of the page and ask the child to describe what is going on in the photo (glue the photo on the right side for left-handed children).
- Act as scribe by writing down the child's words and reading them back for the child's approval.
- Encourage emergent writers to do their own writing.
- Invite children to sketch what they observe.
- Glue an observational drawing on one side of the page and write about the child's thinking on the other.

Accommodations to match a child's development of fine motor skills can include increasing the size of the book, offering a range of writing utensils, or adding lines for text.

Analyze a Child's Science Journal for STEM Learning

- Are they asking questions, or still messing about with the materials?
- Are they figuring out how to work collaboratively with peers, or preferring to work alone?
- Are they using the journal to record what they did, or to record what they are thinking?
- Are they noticing any cause-and-effect relationships?
- Are they noticing any patterns?
- Are they recognizing a system, or how parts work together?
- Are they still curious about the phenomena and exploring the questions they have, or are they ready to move on?

Reflect on Your Pedagogy

- What adjustments do you need to make in your teaching to deepen the child's understanding?
- What additional materials do they need?
- What materials should you remove?
- What changes need to be made in the physical environment?

Analyze a Child's Science Journal for Literacy Learning

- Are they using the journal for the purpose of documenting their STEM thinking, or are they using it for the purpose of telling a story about their experience? (Either is fine.)
- Are they able to explain what they are doing from photos?
- Are they able to read back the words they dictated to you?
- Are they able to sequence photos to explain what they did?
- Are they able to use beginning sounds to write about what they are figuring out? Beginning and ending sounds? Beginning, middle, and ending sounds?
- Are they writing from left to right?
- Are they allowing spaces between their words?
- Are they writing more than one sentence to go with a picture?
- Are they using punctuation?
- Are they able to read back what they wrote?

Analyze the Promotional Environment

- What are the children spending time viewing? Is it at an eye level where they can observe it?
- How does a child respond to seeing their ideas on the wall or shelving?
- How do children respond to their peers' work on the wall or shelving?
- How can you categorize what is featured on the walls or shelving?
- Is there a place that features and honors children's published writing in science journals?
- Are children finding satisfaction in "publishing" their thinking in science journals?
- Are children interested in reading a peer's science journal?

EXPERIENCE 4. ENGINEERING AN INCLINE TO MOVE OBJECTS WITH DIFFERENT ATTRIBUTES

Will all of these objects move down the ramp the same way?

Why This Experience Matters

When children work to move objects that are not spheres, they have an opportunity to consider how the shape of an object affects how it moves down an incline. A basic first exploration for young children is shapes. Providing children with a set of three-dimensional (3D) shapes such as a cube, cylinder, rectangular prism, sphere, cone, and pyramid allows children to think about how the shape of an object affects its movement. They can notice that the face of a three-dimensional object can affect how it does or doesn't move. For example, the sphere will always roll. The cylinder will slide when positioned on the face that is flat, and roll when positioned on its side. The cone will slide when positioned on the face that is flat, and begin to roll when released on its side, but will roll to the right or left and then either stop or slide the rest of the way down. The pyramid, cube, and rectangular prism have only faces that are flat and will always slide. This is a time when a wider incline than a track is helpful (see Figure 5.16). When children tire of exploring the geometric objects, add items familiar to them that can be classified as one of the three-dimensional shapes (see Figure 5.17).

Figure 5.16. Comparing the Movement of Three-Dimensional Shapes on a Ramp

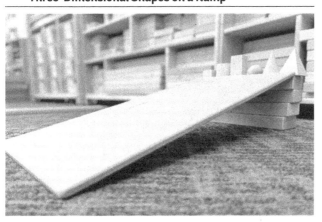

Figure 5.17. Classifying by Shape

Sphere	Cube	Rectangular prism	Cone	Cylinder	Pyramid
marble	dice	domino	golf tee	spool	5-sided dice
ping-pong ball	building block	juice box	drinking cup	tin can	
golf ball	Unifix cube	unit block	condiment cup	paper towel roll	
			funnel	crayon	
			top		

Figure 5.18. Preschool Discussion on Shape and Movement (With Video)

As children demonstrate their understanding of which of the contrasting characteristics make the most difference in how an object will move (from predictions or generalizations they make, either aloud or in action), gradually add more complexity to the choices of objects for them to observe. A video of preschool children explaining their ideas to each other and their teacher can be accessed by scanning the QR code in Figure 5.18.

Materials:

- unit blocks
- 2-foot tracks or wide boards to make into ramps
- set of 3D geometric shapes (cube, rectangular prism, sphere, cone, pyramid, cylinder)

- sets of everyday objects with shapes similar to the 3D geometric shapes, such as the items suggested in Figure 5.17

Design constraints or things for the teacher to hold constant:

- 2-foot tracks and/or a wide board of one size for everyone
- a specific set of objects to compare in action on the ramp for everyone

Things that children can vary or change:

- the height of the ramp
- the object selected from a set to be placed on the ramp
- how the object is positioned at the top of the ramp (e.g., cylinders on end or on their side)

Mental relationships children have the possibility of constructing:

- between the properties of the object and how those properties affect movement
- between the height of the ramp and the ability to move each object

Example of a teacher's invitation to focus:

I noticed Tanajah and Carl were rolling different objects they gathered from the classroom. Tanajah brought a crayon and an eraser to send down the ramp, and Carl brought a jingle bell and a popsicle stick. Tanajah and Carl, can you tell us what you were thinking about? (Children explain how they were noticing how things moved differently.) *I've gathered some other objects for you to try to move. I wonder if they will all move down a ramp the same? If you want to try other objects on a ramp, bring them to the Ramps and Pathways space and put them on this tray on top of the shelf. Let's talk about what you are figuring out later this week.*

Before You Introduce, Engage in Teacher Play

Collect a variety of objects to try to move on a 2-foot ramp or a flat board. Look for a variety of shapes (spheres, cubes, cones, cylinders, pyramids, rectangular prisms) of different materials (glass, hard and soft plastic, foam, wood, metal), types of construction (hollow or solid, rigid or flexible), and weights (heavy, hefty, light, lightweight). Think from the perspective of an adult as you explore how these objects move, or don't move, on a ramp. Consider the following:

- What kinds of words can be used to describe how each object moves? Let's write them down: roll, slide, wobble, wiggle, jiggle, bounce, tumble, somersault, flip-flop, cartwheel, turn, rotate, slide, glide, skate, skid, slither, shake, tremble, quiver, fast, slow, steady, stable, teeter, jerk.
- Which objects will always move down a ramp?
- Which objects will only move when the ramp is steep?
- Which objects move in the same way?
- How do the objects differ in their movement once they leave the bottom of the ramp?
- How do the properties of objects impact how they move?
- Which objects continue to move after they leave the bottom of the ramp, and which objects come to a stop?
- If you have objects that are the same size and shape, but made from different materials, do they move in the same way? How are they different?

Think about this experience from the perspective of your children:

- What kinds of materials might be most appealing to children to try?
- Your children may bring toy cars to send down ramps. Try some of these on the ramps. How might you position them on a ramp? Explore using two ramps to move toy cars with a front and back wheel positioned on each ramp.
- How might your children respond if you put all the objects out at once?
- How might your children respond if you limited the number of variables by putting together sets of objects for them to use? (same-sized spheres, but of different weights; spheres of the same material, but of different sizes; different objects with similar shapes . . .)

- How could you offer the materials in a way that invites children to be intentional in the object they select to move?
- What additional comments and questions can you add to this list to inspire their reasoning? (See Textbox 5.4).

TEXTBOX 5.4. QUESTIONS AND COMMENTS

Questions and comments that are appropriate for PK–2 children:

- *How can you get this object to go down the ramp?*
- *What do you need to do to get all the objects to move down the same ramp?*
- *Is there a way to get this object to go down the ramp?*
- *How can you describe how this object is moving?*
- *I notice this object seems to wobble and tumble down the ramp and stops, while this other one slides and then turns at the bottom.*
- *Which one goes the farthest?*
- *I wonder why these objects all slide and these other objects all roll?*
- *This one won't go all the way down. What do you think is happening?*

Additional questions and comments that are appropriate for older children:

- *I wonder why this is so hard to move.*
- *Which objects are interesting to watch?*
- *Which objects are the most interesting to use? What makes them interesting? Does everyone agree with you?*
- *Which objects are not interesting to use? Why? Does everyone agree with you?*

Attending to the Four Aspects of the Environment

Physical Environment: Arranging the Classroom to Promote Inquiry

For younger children, you may consider working with three to five children during small-group time to allow for more hands-on learning. Working with a smaller group may better help to engage all children. Older children may be able to handle larger groups. Prepare a space for children to explore away from

high-traffic areas. Provide containers to house each kind of object you will offer children or place the objects on a tray on top of the block shelf. You may want to label each container to add to your print-rich environment. Place a pan-balance scale nearby for children to use should they want to compare weights of two objects. Be aware of the continuum of motor skills, social–emotional, and cognitive development in your classroom as you choose materials for children to investigate. Limiting the number of objects and variables children have to choose from may assist those who have difficulty with inhibitory control or cognitive flexibility to be able to attend to, and focus on, the specific variable(s) that matters. Scaffolding children's experience by adding objects with additional variables as they are ready for a new challenge supports all children as they construct relationships related to how the different variables affect motion.

Intellectual Environment: Opportunities to Ask Questions, Predict, and Reason

In this experience, children have the opportunity to think about the different properties of materials such as glass, metal, plastic, wood, ceramics, fibers, and composites that are made from two or more materials combined together. As you observe how students respond, and their knowledge level, you may gradually add more materials. With younger children, the introduction of different types of materials may be more gradual over time. Observation and responding to what you see children saying and doing with materials will help guide you to the next steps in the investigative materials. In this experience, children's thinking goes much further than being able to name different materials and categorize them. They are inspired to think about how those properties can be put to use in a system of ramps and pathways. We have observed children respond to objects with different attributes moving in different ways and report on what they are noticing. They may make the following kinds of observations:

- A system designed and built for a wooden sphere may not accommodate the steel ball bearing even if they are the same size. The heavier ball bearing will knock against supports and barriers with more force, resulting in the need to rebuild the structure.

- A cylinder-shaped object can be positioned at the top of a ramp to either slide down or roll down. Children may also notice that a cylinder will roll in a straight direction while a sphere can veer to one side or the other.
- A plastic Easter egg can also be positioned at the top of a ramp to slide or roll down, but when it leaves the end of the ramp, it will roll in a circular path instead of a straight path. Children may notice that a glue bottle lid, a pinecone, a small plastic top, or a small wooden figure also move in a circular path. Comparing them, they may begin to perceive that all are cone-shaped, or have one end larger than the other.
- A plastic Easter egg is hollow. So is a ping-pong ball or a pit ball or Whiffle ball. Children can take apart the plastic Easter egg, place different objects inside, and explore how the contents in the Easter egg affect the egg's movement.
- A small bouncy ball is solid like a shooter marble and may be the same size, but it responds very differently.

The open-ended nature of this experience provides many opportunities for children to reason, predict, analyze, and question, which leads to creative and innovative designs. Young children have independently designed systems to accommodate the properties of an object.

Social–Emotional Environment: Nurturing Healthy Learning Dispositions

In our work with young children, we often find children first selecting the heavy shooter marble to move on their system. When we ask them the reason for choosing it, they might respond that it was their favorite color, or that they picked it because of how it moves on an incline. You may hear them say, "The metal one has the most power!" or "It will go the fastest!" This fits within their worldview. Faster wins races. They are soon confronted by the fact that the biggest and heaviest spheres are not the easiest to use in building an intricate, complex system. Before long, they leave the large shooter marbles on the shelf and select the standard-sized glass marble or wooden sphere. In a subtle way,

they learn that fastest is not always best. Slow is also sometimes best.

Promotional Environment: Promoting and Celebrating Children's Thinking and Ideas

When children begin to compare how objects move, there is an opening for a meaningful experience with shared writing (see Figure 5.19). Educators can begin to model using a T-chart with the actual objects, pictures of the objects, or a labeled bar graph. In Figure 5.20, note the effective use of photos to enhance and support children's understanding. Posting these visual representations of data collection in the space for Ramps and Pathways is evidence of intellectual work within the classroom.

A powerful example of documenting children's thinking occurred when a preschool teacher made a T-chart of "Roll Vs. Not Roll" on butcher paper on the floor. When children began to sort the actual objects, they noticed that some objects moved without rolling. The teacher stopped the children for a brief meeting and asked for a word to describe a third option. She did not give them the word, but let them find it. One child offered "slide," so they got another piece of butcher paper, taped it alongside, and wrote "Slide" at the top and then re-sorted some of the "Not Roll" objects into the new column.

Figure 5.19. Documenting Children's Observations

Figure 5.20. "Roll or Slide" T-Chart

Featured Assessment: Softball Interview and Sorting

As you observe, you may want to probe to learn more about how a child is thinking. A softball interview is one way of finding out. Select a moment to enter the child's space, taking care your questions will not interrupt the child's work. The tone in your voice matters: Make sure the tone is inviting the child to a conversation, not an interrogation. Using the system of mailing labels explained earlier (in the Engineering Sturdy Structures experience), you can document the child's responses.

Examples of Questions

- *Tell me about these objects that you are sending down the ramp. Are there any other objects that roll the same way?*
- *What do you notice about the objects that go down all the way? What do you notice about objects that just sit there and do not go down? What do you notice about objects that move in a different way?*
- *Would you sort these into three piles so we can talk about this with the rest of the class?*

Examples of Noticing

- *I notice you are not sending these objects down the ramp at all. Can you tell me about that?*
- *I saw that you put some containers along the side of the ramp. Help me understand how you are using the containers.*

Analyze Your Observational Records

- What cause-and-effect patterns are the children noticing?
- What patterns are they finding in the shape of the material and how it moves or fails to move?
- Do they show an understanding that an object's shape and/or the material from which it is made affect its movement?
- Are they paying attention to the materials' different properties to pick the objects that will go faster? Farther?
- How are they describing how the materials move? Did they come up with "roll," "not roll" without your suggestion? Did they add "slide" or a similar word as a kind of not rolling but moving anyhow?
- What questions do they seem to be asking?
- What problems do they seem to be posing?
- Who is drawing and/or writing in their journal? Are they using it to record their thinking, or are they using it so they can tell you they are using it?
- Who is ready to be introduced to a more rigorous style of investigation?
- Whom do you need to interview to get a better understanding of how they are thinking?

Analyze the Promotional Environment

- What are the children spending time viewing? Is it at an eye level where they can observe it?
- How do children respond to seeing their ideas on the wall or shelving?
- How do children respond to their peers' work on the wall or shelving?
- How can you categorize what is featured on the walls or shelving?

EXPERIENCE 5. ENGINEERING RAMPS, ROADS, AND PATHWAYS

How can I use tracks to add a road to the end of my ramp and keep the marble rolling straight?

Why This Experience Matters

We have observed that when children begin to notice that a sphere does not always roll in a straight direction once it leaves the ramp, they begin to use the track to add roads or pathways to the bottom of the ramp. This is often the beginning of engineering systems with different components. In Figure 5.21, you can see a three-component system: the first component of a ramp, and second and third components of pathways. Changing one component will almost always require a readjustment of other components. Without the readjustment, the system will not work. Children who are just beginning to become aware of this will often leave a gap at the connection of two pathways, or overlap them in a way that interrupts the action of the marble rather than allowing it to continue (see Figure 5.22).

Always keep in mind that children with varying abilities may require more time and multiple attempts before they figure out what they need to do to resolve the problem. It is imperative to allow them the opportunity to find the solution. After many attempts, the teacher can point and ask the productive attention-focusing question, "What do you notice when the marble rolls to the end of the incline?" to help guide and facilitate the child's thinking without providing the answer. Over time, checking the connections becomes a regular habit.

Materials:

- unit blocks
- tracks
- standard-sized marbles
- 2-inch squares of vinyl shelf liner

Design constraints or things for the teacher to hold constant:

- using standard-sized marbles

Figure 5.22. Overlapping Track

Figure 5.21. Ramps, Roads, and Pathways

Things that children can vary or change:

- the different lengths of tracks used in the system
- the height of the ramp
- the length of the ramp

Mental relationships children have the possibility of constructing:

- between the joining of the track and the continued movement of the marble
- between the length of the road or pathway and the distance the marble rolls
- between the steepness of the ramp and the smoothness of how the marble moves onto the next component

Example of a teacher's invitation to focus:

I've noticed some of you are beginning to place track at the end of your ramp. Can you help me understand why you are doing this? (Some children may say it keeps the marble going straight. Others may say it makes the marble roll farther.) *I see Clyde used three tracks to make his system. He used a long piece of track to make a ramp, and he used two middle-sized tracks to make a road. I think I want to draw that so I can remember how Clyde built his system.* (Teacher models making a drawing of his system.) *Clyde, would you explain how your system works so I can write it down under my drawing?* (Teacher uses shared writing to document Clyde's thinking.) *I'm going to post this here on the wall so we can read it. I wonder what other kinds of systems we can build and then draw.*

Before You Introduce, Engage in Teacher Play

Explore the differences of a marble's speed and distance by varying the height of the ramp. Take note of where two tracks connect and when you need to overlap track to keep the marble rolling smoothly. At times, you may become frustrated when tracks start to slide rather than stay in place. Some 6-year-old children taught us what to do when they needed to solve that problem. One of them ran to the first aid kit to retrieve a nitrile glove. They cut the glove into pieces and placed a small piece under the tracks at the junction where

the two tracks were slipping. The properties of the nitrile glove material provided just the right amount of friction to hold both tracks in place. From then on, we followed the children's lead and began to provide 2×2-inch squares of vinyl shelf liner that has properties similar to that of the nitrile glove for children to use. Later, we found children were folding the pieces of vinyl and placing them under a track to give it just the right amount of lift to allow a sphere to pass from one component to another.

Also pay attention to where you release the marble on the ramp. How does this affect the action of the marble? When young children are releasing the marble in different places on the ramp, think about how you might draw their attention to this variable. An example we have seen from teachers:

> *I notice that when you try your marble out on your system, sometimes you release the marble here* (point to the track) *and sometimes you release the marble here* (point to the track). *I'm wondering if that makes a difference in how far the marble rolls. How might we investigate that?*

Some children and their teachers have placed colored dot stickers at different places on the ramp, and then compared how far a marble rolled with a starting point at each sticker.

Attending to the Four Aspects of the Environment

Physical Environment: Arranging the Classroom to Promote Inquiry

When children start adding roads and pathways, they take up a lot of the classroom space (see Figure 5.23). Many want to see if they can get a marble to move across the length of the classroom. Think about how furniture might be moved to give them some of this needed space without interrupting learning in other parts of the classroom.

Intellectual Environment: Opportunities to Ask Questions, Predict, and Reason

These types of systems are easy for children to document using lines on paper. Children are able to represent their system with a side-view drawing. For young children, representing a long ramp and pathway

Figure 5.23. Considering Space

system on a piece of paper challenges them to think about how to scale it down to fit on that paper.

- *How do you want to position your paper to start to draw it? Do you want the paper to be tall? Or laying down?*

When children run out of room on their drawing, support their problem solving. Have tape and additional paper close by for them to retrieve.

- *It looks like you need more room to draw your whole system. You've run out of paper. What could we do to finish drawing the rest of your system? What do you need?*

Once the drawing has been made, teachers can support children in communicating information about their system using labels. In the drawing, they can label the components.

- *Show me where you used long pieces of track.*
- *Where did you use a middle-sized track or short track?*

- *How many pieces of track did you use in all?*
- *If you want people to know how tall the beginning of your ramp is, how could you show them in your model?*

In addition to children's documentation of ramp structures and systems captured in paper and pencil drawings, young children who have challenges with motor skills or visual impairments might use popsicle sticks or paper strips glued to construction paper to create a diagram of their ramp system. As structures become more complex, children can use the popsicle sticks to create three-dimensional models of their structures. Children with more severe disabilities might be paired with another student and encouraged to share ideas by using a low-tech or high-tech communication system.

Social–Emotional Environment: Nurturing Healthy Learning Dispositions

Some engineering curricula require children to draw a plan of a system before they build the system. Linear ramps such as the ones being used are relatively easy for children to draw. However, requiring a drawing before building too early may be frustrating for young learners, especially those with limited physical mobility. In the beginning of engineering thinking, builders need the experience to build a working understanding of how the physics affects the design of a structure before they can use a drawing to show their plans.

We have found that when children grow increasingly confident in their designs and know their systems work in the way they do because of their designs, this is a moment when drawing becomes meaningful. Children may be interested in sharing their drawings and challenging their peers to use the drawing to replicate their system. In a sense, these behaviors can be viewed as a precursor to using blueprints.

Promotional Environment: Promoting and Celebrating Children's Thinking and Ideas

As children begin to document their own work with drawings, honor their work by providing space on the classroom or hallway walls to display their work. Including the children's explanations of their drawing through shared writing provides environmental print

Figure 5.24. Builder's Drawing and the Ramp System

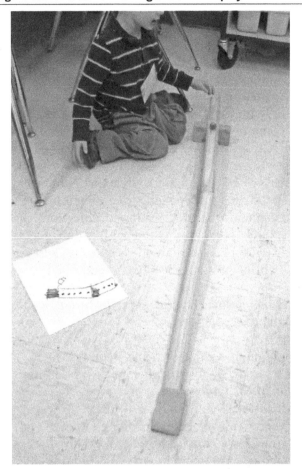

that children will return to reread again and again. Peggy Ashbrook often takes photos of the drawing alongside the actual structure and the builder. Rather than posed photos, she captures the children deep in thought as they demonstrate their system (see Figure 5.24).

Project Zero (pz.harvard.edu) was started at the Harvard Graduate School of Education in 1967 to better understand learning in and through the arts. It has grown into "an intellectual wellspring, nourishing inquiry into the complexity of human potentials and exploring sustainable ways to support them across multiple and diverse cultural contexts" (McHugh et al., 2022). The site is a wellspring for teachers who want to use documentation (data) as a tool to deepen and extend learning. One powerful data source Project Zero promotes is photographs of student-generated artifacts from the work in the classroom. Posting photos of individual children's work (block and ramp structures, drawings, notes on a whiteboard, information collected on chart paper) as well as work of small groups and the whole class reinforces children's sense of belonging in the classroom.

Featured Assessment: Teacher Reflection Journal

If you do not already keep a reflection journal, consider starting one. Such a journal is meant to inspire reflection on successful events as well as failures. Reflect on the growth and development of your children as engineers by using a teacher reflection journal.

Reflect on the Class as a Whole

- Who is and who isn't engaging in the challenges?
- How is the class handling the materials? Do I need to remove some of the materials to help them to focus, or do I need to add more to provide more options?

Reflect on a Specific Child's Response to This Challenge

- How long does it take this child to find a problem with the joint between two pieces of track?
- What productive questions did I have to ask to support the child's reasoning?
- Did the child observe a peer or ask a peer for help?
- Once the child was successful, did the child help a peer with the same problem?
- How did the child document the resulting pathway?

Reflect on the Promotional Environment

- What are the children spending time viewing? Is it at a level where they can read and observe it?
- How do the children respond to seeing their drawings on the wall?
- How do the children respond to their peers' drawings?
- How could I add to the display of observational drawings to help an outside audience understand the reason for the drawings?

EXPERIENCE 6. ENGINEERING RAMPS OF DIFFERENT LENGTHS TO MOVE DIFFERENT TYPES OF SPHERES

How do different kinds of spheres affect the designs of my systems?

Why This Experience Matters

Engineers must understand properties of materials and objects to make effective decisions in their designs. Ramps and Pathways materials are a meaningful way for children to grapple with properties. Children may understand how spheres are easiest to move on ramps and on pathways. Adding spheres of different materials but of same size challenges them to think about how weight affects movement, as well as the kind of material (see Figure 5.25).

Viewing this challenge from the perspective of UDL, it may be necessary to scaffold how many spheres of the same size children can successfully attend to (inhibitory control) as they compare and contrast the different materials, simultaneously using their cognitive flexibility. Any child who is still mouthing objects must be carefully supervised at all times and should only have access to large spheres that cannot be swallowed. Depending on their development, some children may need to observe just two or three spheres at a time. Children may first select the metal ball bearing, as it is heaviest. Or they may select the bouncy ball because they like the rubbery feel of it. However, the very properties that are attractive to children are not always the best in constructing systems to move spheres effectively. Depending on children's fine motor and eye–hand coordination skills, accommodations may need to be made with regard to choosing sizes of spheres (using larger marbles) and surface textures (e.g., selecting rubber balls) that could be easier for children to grasp, allowing for ample success before challenging them with smaller spheres that have a smooth surface area. Spheres with bright and contrasting primary and secondary colors, or that are black and white combined, may be easier for children with visual impairments to track and follow as they roll along ramp pathways, in comparison to wooden spheres.

The movement of the heavy glass shooter marble and the heaviest metal ball bearing makes it more difficult to keep the system stable. The system needs readjustments or rebuilding almost every time the ball bearing is used. The bouncy balls are lighter, but when they strike another object, their movement is more unpredictable and more difficult to control. They bounce unexpectedly rather than roll along the pathways. The large wooden sphere is lightest. It is not visibly attractive, but it is more useful on different systems and is less disruptive to the pathway design. As children observe each type of sphere, they also exercise their working memory as they compare and contrast, recalling what happens as each sphere rolls along the same pathways.

Materials:

- unit blocks
- tracks
- shooter marble and other spheres the same size (metal ball bearing, wooden sphere, rubber bouncy balls)
- standard-sized marble and other spheres the same size (metal ball bearing, wooden sphere)
- pan balance

Design constraints or things for the teacher to hold constant:

- spheres made of no more than four different materials and of the same size
- spheres made of the same material and in different sizes

Figure 5.25. Ramps, Blocks, and Spheres

Things that children can vary or change:

- the type or size of sphere
- the length of track
- the height of the ramp
- the number of tracks used
- the supports used in elevating track

Mental relationships children have the possibility of constructing:

- between the weight of a sphere and how far it rolls
- between the weight of a sphere and how difficult it is to stop
- between the type of material and the weight of the sphere
- between the type of material and how it responds to ramps and pathways

Example of a teacher's invitation to focus:

I noticed many of you are choosing spheres to move, or things that are round like a basketball (not round like a pancake). I've got some spheres made out of glass, metal, plastic, and wood. I'm wondering what we can find out about building systems for spheres of different sizes, and for spheres made from different kinds of materials.

Before You Introduce, Engage in Teacher Play

Before you begin, jot down some predictions you may have about how each sphere will move on a ramp and pathway system. Then begin to build. Keep in mind the following considerations:

- Build a system to move a sphere and try the different types of spheres on your system. How do the spheres compare?
- If your children are already building systems with corners, build a system with one corner and compare how the system responds to the different types of spheres.
- What are some of the challenges in moving the large spheres? The smaller ones?
- What kinds of changes do you need to make to your system so that all of the large spheres can be used?

- Go back to your predictions. How accurate were they? What surprises did you have?

When we work with other teachers, we find that most teachers select a wooden large or small sphere or a standard-sized marble as the easiest to use in designing a system to move the object. Even with such humble material, many of the systems that are designed are elaborate. In the system shown in Figure 5.26, the first marble's movement sends two other marbles in opposite directions; a video of the system in action can be accessed by scanning the QR code.

A bouncy ball sphere is often left to the side, as the bounces are difficult to control. This didn't stop a group of teachers in Des Moines, Iowa, who built a system for moving a bouncy ball that came to a surprise ending (see Figure 5.27; scan the QR code to access a video of the system at work).

As you engage in teacher play, if you are like us, you may be tempted to use the word *momentum* to describe how the spheres move differently. As our physics expert, Dr. Lawrence Escalada, explained in the Inquiry section of Chapter 1, we learned that momentum is a concept much more complicated than what we had believed. Momentum is defined

Figure 5.26. Splitting Marbles' Directions (With Video)

Figure 5.27. System for a Bouncy Ball (With Video)

as the mass of an object multiplied by its velocity, but let's keep it simple and use *speed* instead. So momentum equals the mass of an object multiplied by its speed. Then we found we had a misconception about mass. We believed mass and weight to be the same thing, but this is not accurate. A marble's mass, which can be defined as the amount of matter it has, is the same regardless of where it is in the entire universe. If we traveled to the Moon and weighed ourselves on it, our weight would change, but we would have the same amount of mass. The mass of an object can also be considered the amount of resistance (inertia) an object has in changing its motion. For example, the more mass that a marble has, the harder it is to get it to move or to get it to stop. In general terms, we can consider momentum as how much matter or stuff is moving and how fast it is moving. Thus, a heavy marble that is moving at the same speed as a lighter marble has more momentum than the lighter marble. This may explain why children might say, "The heavy marbles are harder to stop," assuming the marbles are moving at the same speed. Escalada suggests that the term momentum and other related terms (mass and velocity) can be useful in adult discussions about force and motion provided the adults understand the definitions of the terms, but they should not be used with the children because these terms are formal and not appropriate for children at this age. The language in a child's statement, "The

heavy marbles are harder to stop," is descriptive and in line with children's investigations in force and motion and should be honored.

Think about this experience from the perspective of your children:

- How much space did you need as you explored? How does the classroom need to be arranged for the children to explore?
- How many of each sphere would be enough to put out for them?
- What would be a good way to house the spheres when not in use?
- Do they have the word *sphere* in their vocabulary, or could you introduce it to them as being "all things round like a basketball and not round like a pancake"?
- How might they describe the action of the marble?
- What safety concerns do you have, and how might you address them?

Attending to the Four Aspects of the Environment

Physical Environment: Arranging the Classroom to Promote Inquiry

Some teachers are reluctant to use the heavier spheres like the ball bearing and the shooter marble. Teachers might challenge the children to find ways to control the spheres after they leave the ramp. Children have responded by lining the paths with block walls or using blocks to contain a marble at the end of the track. Children tend to do this anyway when they get tired of chasing marbles across the room.

Egg cartons are useful for storing the spheres after exploration. Empty cells will inform children how many spheres they will need to find before they leave the center. Labeling the egg cartons "glass shooter marbles, metal ball bearings, plastic bouncy balls, and wooden spheres" add to a print-rich environment that enhances literacy learning.

Making a pan balance available near the center may invite children to compare the heaviness of the spheres. Older children may be drawn to making sense of standard units of measurement in regard to weight.

Intellectual Environment: Opportunities to Ask Questions, Predict, and Reason

Offering this experience to children provides them with opportunities to explore different properties of materials, and consider how those properties will influence the design of a system to move them. It is a context where you might see primary-grade students begin to discuss what engineers call *trade-offs*. They may want to use the metal ball bearing, which is more difficult to control. The trade-off in using the ball bearing is the need for a simpler design, or the need for additional blocks to build a system sturdy enough to handle it. As children build their systems, their predictions on what the system needs to be successful will become more accurate over time as they refine their working understanding of physics.

Social–Emotional Environment: Nurturing Healthy Learning Dispositions

Because of safety concerns when using large, heavy spheres, facilitate a discussion with the children about the importance of keeping everyone and the materials safe. How to carry and move longer track is another important discussion, especially for helping children with visual–motor and spatial awareness needs to develop an understanding of how to transport materials without hitting or bumping other children or their ramp structures. Co-construct rules or routines that will keep the spheres accounted for. Post the rules in the center for children to revisit when the need arises.

Promotional Environment: Promoting and Celebrating Children's Thinking and Ideas

Take a photo of a system and print it out on a large piece of paper. Invite the children to diagram the different components (ramp, corner, pathway, etc.) and then add a description of what is important to think about when assembling each component. Offer a variety of materials, as previously discussed, for children to use to create their diagram. Collect a video of the system in action and create a QR code to allow outside audiences to scan the code and view the video. Downloading a QR code app on tablets and making it available to children will allow them to revisit the action on systems they have designed in the past.

Create a sphere museum for visitors, complete with labels. Prereaders and prewriters may be able to connect to beginning letters of each descriptor (glass, wooden, metal, plastic). Emergent writers may be able to connect with beginning sounds of each descriptor and a short list of its properties (glass: heavy and smooth; wooden: light and smooth; metal: shiny, very heavy, and smooth; plastic: light, smooth, and a little bit squishy). The labels will support early writers who want to label their own papers by using the labels as a source for correct spelling. Beginning readers and writers may be able to read co-constructed descriptions of what a builder needs to think about when using an object, and responsive readers and writers may independently begin to create labels and descriptors on their own. A co-constructed classroom dictionary may support spelling words they are using as they learn. Alternatively, the words can be placed within a word wall in the classroom.

Featured Assessment: Engineering Habits of Mind

The most important manner of supporting young children's engineering thinking, surpassing the engineering design process, is to focus on the development of engineering habits of mind. These habits of mind include systems thinking, creativity, optimism, collaboration, communication, and attention to ethical considerations. In Appendix A: Engineering Habits of Mind in Ramps and Pathways, the middle column provides descriptions of each habit of mind (Katehi et al., 2009, pp. 5–6). The third column describes how these habits of mind are observed in children's actions as they engage in Ramps and Pathways experiences. Educators who observe children in these actions can be assured they are providing effective high-quality STEM experiences for their children. Educators can use the checklist in Appendix B to monitor children's development of engineering habits of mind over time.

EXPERIENCE 7. ENGINEERING A SYSTEM OF HILLS AND VALLEYS

How can I get a marble to roll up a hill?

Why This Experience Matters

When children are confident in engineering ramps and pathways to get marbles to go down fast and roll far, they may be ready for the following challenge: "This marble goes down the ramp nicely. Do you suppose you can make a marble roll up a ramp?" This challenge requires children to construct a mental relationship between the slopes of the first and second hills, and the amount of speed the sphere needs to ascend a hill (see Figure 5.28).

Materials:

- unit blocks
- three different lengths of tracks
- standard-sized marbles

Design constraints or things for the teacher to hold constant:

- the necessity of having a hill after the initial ramp that gets the ball moving

Things that children can vary or change:

- the type of sphere
- the length of track
- the height of the ramp

Mental relationships children have the possibility of constructing:

- the height of the starter ramp and the speed of the marble as it crests the top of the hill
- the energy lost in the impact of the marble at the bottom of the starter ramp (if the starter ramp is too steep)

Example of a teacher's invitation to focus:

I noticed you are pretty good at getting a marble to go down a ramp fast enough to get it to roll far. I wonder if there is a way to get a marble to roll up a ramp.

Before You Introduce, Engage in Teacher Play

This design challenge is fascinating to builders of all ages. Once the first hill is achieved, there is almost always a desire to add more (see Figure 5.29). Use all three sizes of track and unit blocks to build a series of one-, two-, and three-hill systems. As you build, consider the following:

- What length of track makes the best starter ramp?
- What problems might you have in connecting the starter ramp with the track positioned to send the marble back up?
- What pattern do you notice about a series of hills in a successful system?
- Which kind of sphere is easiest to use in a system with hills and valleys?

Figure 5.28. Hills and Valleys

Figure 5.29. Teacher Play With Hills and Valleys

- How do you know when you make the hill too high? Too low?

Think about this experience from the perspective of your children:

- What spheres would be best to set out for children to use?
- What kind of space will they need to build?
- What kinds of questions and comments might be helpful? A few we have generated include the following:
  » *How could you build a ramp with many hills?*
  » *What supports work best for you in building a hill?*
  » *Is there a way to build that support without using so many blocks?*
  » *I wonder if we can figure out how to make that support more sturdy.*
  » *How do you know when you make the hill too high?*

» *How do you know when you make the hill too low?*

Attending to the Four Aspects of the Environment

Physical Environment: Arranging the Classroom to Promote Inquiry

These types of systems do not take up as much space as the systems built to make a marble roll far, but they will require a configuration of the classroom to provide builders a large amount of space (see Figure 5.30). You may want to reduce the selection of spheres with this challenge, offering only the standard-sized marbles or similar-sized wood spheres at first. Include a tablet for children to video-record in slow motion to help them review the action of the marble as it transfers from one component to the next.

Intellectual Environment: Opportunities to Ask Questions, Predict, and Reason

Engineering systems to send a marble down one component and then up the next one requires that children consider the speed necessary coming down that will leave the marble with enough speed to make it up and over the crest of the second component and onto a third. Engineering this design challenge requires the children to make iterative tests and adjustments to all three components of the system. When successful, children often go further into the challenge by designing and engineering more complex systems of hills and valleys, such as using seven components to get a marble to ascend two hills and end with an incline that slowly tapers down (see Figure 5.31).

Figure 5.30. Space Needed for Hills and Valleys

Figure 5.32 shows two 6-year-olds challenging themselves to make a series of hills and valleys. A close look at the connections among the components reveals their technique for moving the marble from one to the next. These two engineers became so confident that they asked their teacher to make a quick line drawing of a system, and they would build it. After a series of successful designs and builds, their teacher wanted to see how they would respond to a design that was physically impossible: the starter ramp being at a lower incline than the second component (see Figure 5.33). Their teacher watched as the girls took the line drawing to the building site. They talked together for a bit and then returned to the teacher and said, "I'm sorry, but your design won't work. You will need to give us another." The teacher responded that she wanted this design and asked why they wouldn't build it. The girls patiently explained to their teacher that the starter ramp was too low, and the marble wouldn't have enough speed to make it up the second component.

Curious to know whether other 6-year-olds understood this concept, the teacher asked the girls to assist her in replicating the design on chart paper and bringing the question to their peers. Quickly, the others explained what was wrong with the design. Aireus provided wording for a recommendation for others wanting to build a system with hills and valleys (see Figure 5.33). Clearly, many were now ready to begin to draw plans before building, and to use the plans to build a system. They were able to use inductive reasoning to generalize across their experiences in order to determine the necessary components for the plan. To make sure the full range of learners understand the relationship between slope, incline, and crest with each consecutive hill, the teacher can use the UDL principle of multiple representations, using the design sketch to complete a three-dimensional structure. This requires children to complete the engineering design process by following the plan, constructing the design, identifying the design problem, adjusting the ramp, and testing the design in order to see whether the issue has been resolved.

Social–Emotional Environment: Nurturing Healthy Learning Dispositions

In this challenge, we ask children to design a system that can send a marble up a hill. At first, children's responses may be, "It's not possible. Marbles go down a ramp, not up." We found when we said that it was possible, they would reluctantly go work on the challenge without a great deal of confidence. However, when we said, "I once saw another 6-year-old get a marble to go up a hill. How do you suppose she did that?" they went to work with a bit of excitement that they, too, could meet this challenge. If another 6-year-old could do it, why couldn't they?

Promotional Environment: Promoting and Celebrating Children's Thinking and Ideas

When debriefing on the hills and valleys challenge, we used simple line drawings of systems to discuss what was necessary in designing a successful

Figure 5.31. Designing More Complex Hills and Valleys

Figure 5.32. Connecting a Series of Hills and Valleys

Figure 5.33. An Impossible Design

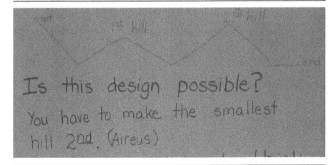

system. This was a natural way of using models to explain thinking, which is one of the NGSS science and engineering practices. Featuring the drawings and explanations on the wall was an amazing testament to outside audiences of the deep thinking required in building ramps and pathways.

Featured Assessment: Engineering Behaviors

As you coach a child to share their structure, document examples of behaviors the child exhibited that are consistent with the NGSS science and engineering practices. Supporting children's approximations of the practices over time leads to their conventional use of the practices. It is not recommended that you assess a child on all eight practices in one sitting. One checklist can serve one child throughout the school year and can be reviewed in the fall, winter, and spring. In Appendix C, we list three of the engineering practices described by the NGSS alongside examples of how they relate to student behaviors in Ramps and Pathways experiences. Appendix D is an example of a checklist that allows teachers to take notes.

EXPERIENCE 8. ENGINEERING A SYSTEM WITH CORNERS

How can I get a marble to turn a corner?

Why This Experience Matters

Designing a system with corners (see Figure 5.34) requires children to integrate their understanding of slope and speed with a working understanding of how to counter the force of a moving marble with blocks so that it bounces onto another track. Children are gaining a working knowledge of Newton's First Law of Motion: A body remains at rest, or in motion at a constant speed in a straight line, unless acted upon by a force to cause it to change direction. The NGSS recommends Newton's laws of motion be addressed in middle school. It is important to know that it is not developmentally appropriate to ask young learners to explain Newton's First Law of Motion in the context of their system. But it is appropriate to ask them to explain what they did to change the marble's direction using their own words.

Caution: Not all young learners may be ready for this challenge in the time you have with them. Young builders may believe the marble will turn a corner simply because they laid the next track to make a corner (see Figure 5.35). They may take on this challenge in following years.

Materials:

- unit blocks
- three different lengths of track
- a variety of spheres

Figure 5.34. Turning a Corner

Figure 5.35. Young Learner Making Corners

Design constraints or things for the teacher to hold constant:

- the use of only a standard-sized marble

As children master their designs of corners, they can be offered spheres that are the same size but made of different materials, or made of the same material but are different sizes.

Things that children can vary or change:

- the length of track
- the height of the ramp
- the arrangement of blocks to knock the marble onto the next component
- the system's design of a square corner, a sharp corner, or a wide corner
- the number of corners in the system

Mental relationships children have the possibility of constructing:

- between the speed of the marble and the number and position of blocks needed for the marble to bounce onto the next component in the system
- between the heaviness of a marble and the number and position of blocks needed for the marble to bounce onto the next component in the system

- the difference in difficulty of making a sharp corner (acute angle), a square corner (90° angle), or a wide corner (obtuse angle)

Example of a teacher's invitation to focus: Children may begin challenging themselves to engineer marbles to turn corners on their own and may not need an invitation. If children are beginning to lose interest in linear ramp and pathway systems, you might reignite their interest by inviting them to focus on the challenge of engineering a system with corners.

I've noticed you are pretty successful in making systems that are straight. I wonder if there is a way to get a marble to turn a corner.

Before You Introduce, Engage in Teacher Play

Explore making systems with corners using spheres of different sizes and materials. Once you are able to make one corner work, explore adding others. In Figure 5.36, you see two teachers who have built a system with five corners. Engaging in teacher play to build systems with corners will help you understand the difficulty in getting a marble to turn a corner and will result in your admiration for young children who are able to figure this out! Considerations for this task include the following:

- How does the speed of a marble affect the ease of getting it to turn a corner?

Figure 5.36. Making Corners in Teacher Play

- How does the second component need to be positioned to accept the oncoming marble?
- What ways can you keep the marble on the track without it bouncing off?
- What is the difference in difficulty in building a system with a wide corner, a square corner, or a sharp corner?
- How does the weight of a sphere impact how you design the structures at each corner?

Think about this experience from the perspective of your children:

- Consider your children's understanding of the properties of objects and how those properties might interfere with an object's ability to turn a corner. If they are still focused on using cars, would it be beneficial to offer cars and spheres at first? Or do they only need spheres to try?
- Think about how your students may visualize a corner. Would they think of a wide, sharp, or square corner? Their life experiences in their environments will impact how they will visualize corners.
- How can you support children as they problem-solve a design with corners without telling them what to do or fixing it for them?

Attending to the Four Aspects of the Environment

Physical Environment: Arranging the Classroom to Promote Inquiry

Long, linear ramps take up a lot of classroom space. We have found that young children often begin to challenge themselves to change the direction of the marble on their own. This new design element may pique the interest of other children. As more children become interested in including corners in their structures, less space will be needed. However, other children may still be interested in the long, linear ramps. It is essential that you allow their explorations to continue alongside those of the children interested in changing a marble's direction.

Intellectual Environment: Opportunities to Ask Questions, Predict, and Reason

As children begin to design structures to change a marble's direction, they will be confronted by the physics of inertia, that is, objects that are denser will be more difficult to put into motion, change in direction, and stop. Children may begin to develop a working understanding of density by thinking about how much "stuff" is packed into a sphere. The denser a material is, the more mass (or stuff) it has. We encourage you *not* to use the words *mass*, *density*, or *inertia* with children. It is best for them to use their own language to describe their reasoning. For example, a child may state, "I don't like using the shooter marbles. They are solid and heavier than the regular marbles. It's hard to get them to turn a corner because they want to keep going straight. They have more power and just knock the blocks down. Then it goes on the floor instead of on the next track. I have to keep rebuilding my system when I use them." In this statement, the child is beginning to make sense of solids and how some solids are heavier, making their movement more difficult to control. In later grades, they will be able to be more specific in their descriptions of the phenomenon using words like *inertia*, *mass*, and *density*. Typically for young learners, we would rather have them use as much of their own language as possible to enable us to more fully comprehend their conceptual understanding. Requiring young children to use the words *inertia*, *mass*, and *density* in their explanations may make them sound more intelligent, but it does not make them more intelligent. Understanding the concepts and relationships is what makes them intelligent. Introducing these words too early, before they have gained conceptual understanding, runs the risk of them giving the right answer without the conceptual understanding.

Noted physicist Richard Feynman was disturbed by a 1st-grade science textbook's attempts to teach 6-year-olds about energy. On one page was a picture of a wind-up toy dog with the question "What makes it move?" According to the teacher's guide, the answer was "energy." The textbook went on with more pictures with the same question and the same answer: "Energy makes it move." Feynman saw no problem with the question "What makes it move?" If a young child is provided an opportunity to deconstruct a wind-up toy, they have the possibility to observe what happens when they turn the wind-up key, and what happens when they let go of it. "Take apart the toy; see how it works. See the cleverness of the gears; see the ratchets. Learn something about the toy, the way the toy is put together, the ingenuity of the people devising the ratchets, and other things. That's good" (Feynman, 1969, p. 317). Feynman had a problem with the answer "Energy makes it move." He argued that teaching definitions of words like *energy*, *gravity*, *inertia*, or *friction* does not result in learning. He proposed a test for teachers to discern whether they have taught an idea, or only the definition. He suggested teachers ask

> Without using the new word which you have just learned, try to rephrase what you have just learned in your own language. For example of friction, without using the word "friction," tell me what you know about why the soles of your shoes wear out. To simply say it is because of friction, is sad, because it's not science. (Feynman, 1969, p. 317)

If the child explains that the soles of shoes rub against the notches and bumps of the sidewalk and leave bits of them behind, the child is grasping the concept of friction. When we ask young children the reason why they place a lot of blocks at the end of a ramp to force a heavy shooter marble to change its direction, we need to value a child's response of "Because it's harder to stop the big marble. If I don't put more than one block there, it will push the block over because the marble hits it so hard. The smaller marbles can't hit it hard enough to push the block over."

A lovely mouthful of descriptive language is used when children are able to engage in STEM!

Social–Emotional Environment: Nurturing Healthy Learning Dispositions

Because of your own teacher play (or your lack of teacher play), you may be tempted to tell children how to solve a problem or adjust the structure out of your own curiosity about how to make it work. Exercise your own inhibitory control and let children figure this out. Fixing it for them robs them of the learning that comes from making mistakes, and the satisfaction of being able to solve problems on their own. If you have your own questions about what might work better, return to teacher play to satisfy your own questions.

If you are concerned about children's frustrations, you can nurture their self-regulation by narrating their emotions to engage them in self-talk. "I see you are upset that the marble keeps tipping over the blocks, but I notice you are not getting angry and giving up. You take a deep breath and try again."

You can nurture collaboration by suggesting they ask for help from another child who is having success. "You are working hard on this. I noticed Tanajah has gotten it to work a few times. I wonder if she can help you out if you ask her."

Promotional Environment: Promoting and Celebrating Children's Thinking and Ideas

Evanshen and Faulk (2019) challenged teachers to evaluate what was featured on the walls and shelving in the classroom by asking themselves, "In what ways does this object represent or enhance the children's engagement in the process of learning?" If the objects, charts, bulletin boards, and posters promoted on the walls and shelving of the classroom are commercially or teacher produced, reconsider how the space on the walls and shelving is being used. Observing children at work as they build systems of ramps and pathways, teachers can document children's movements through photographs and video recordings. Analyzing these artifacts often reveals children's understandings and ideas. Giving these artifacts space on the classroom walls and shelving promotes their value and serves as evidence of children's processes of learning as they access prior knowledge, plan and investigate, and elaborate their thinking (Krechevsky et al., 2013). The artifacts become tools in the classroom environment to support continuous learning (Evanshen & Faulk, 2019).

Document children's thinking as they challenge themselves to change the direction of the marble on a ramp structure, using photography and video from a smartphone or a tablet. Instead of asking children to pose with their ramp structure, photograph them as they are in the process of constructing and testing their systems. Photograph the structure from the top

as well as the sides. Interview the builders to learn what their strategies are in building a structure to get marbles to turn corners. If there is a problem area, ask them to show it to you and explain what is happening. Photograph the problem area.

After school, print the photos and examine them. Considering the audience of the builders, select and arrange the photos to tell a visual story of the children's work. The next day, invite the children to examine the photos. Ask them what they remember about the building in the photos. Did your photographs tell the whole story? What do they remember about building their structure that isn't in your photos? Take down their words as they revisit their work. Ask them to help you label each photo they want to use to tell their story. Ask them what was hard, surprising, or exciting, and what they most wanted to share with the rest of the class and the school community. Keep children focused on revisiting the learning going on, not just something they did (Krechevsky et al., 2013). Revisit this documentation with the rest of the class to launch a discussion of ideas on how to get marbles to change direction or turn a corner. Post the series of photos and explanations at children's eye level for them to revisit (see Figure 5.37). Continue to add to the documentation as children take on other design challenges.

Figure 5.37. Displaying Children's Work at Eye Level

Featured Assessment: Observational Records With Productive Questions

Use observational records to document children's responses to questions as they take on the classic challenge of getting a marble to turn a corner. We include examples of productive questions that take children's thinking forward. These questions allow educators to meet children where they are in their thinking and provide the kind of support they need at any given moment (Fitzgerald & Dengler, 2010; Martens, 1999). Reviewing our overview of these questions from the beginning of Chapter 5, here we give examples specific to the challenge of getting a marble to turn a corner.

Examples of Questions

Attention-focusing questions help children turn their attention to significant details and focus on variables they might be overlooking.

- *What do you notice about where the marble goes off the track?*
- *What is your friend doing with her blocks along the side of the track?*
- *Where is your friend putting the next piece of track?*
- *What is happening when the marble hits the block?*

Measuring and counting questions help children be more precise about their observations. For younger children who do not yet know standard units of measure or know how to count accurately, approximations like simple comparisons are acceptable as early math.

- *How many turns did you make in your track?*
- *How far did the marble go before it stopped rolling?*
- *How fast did the marble go after you added another block to the support?*

Comparison questions nudge children to analyze and classify.

- *What is different when you make a wall at the corner?*
- *What is the same when you make a tunnel and when you make a wall at the corner?*
- *How is this corner different from that corner?*

Action questions urge children to actively explore properties of materials and are particularly good at helping a child who is stumped to focus on more relevant variables without the teacher just solving the problem for the child.

- *What happens if you change something where the marble is going off the track?*

Problem-posing questions help inspire children to plan investigations to find solutions. The challenge questions usually are problem-posing questions.

- *Can you find a way to make the marble turn a corner?*
- *Can you find something that will stop the marble from flying off the track at the corner?*
- *Can you figure out how to slow down the marble?*

Reasoning questions help children process their experiences and construct understandings.

Predicting (deductive reasoning): After you ask for a prediction, try to get the child to respond before trying something. The response for less verbal or less adept speakers of English could be to choose between two or more pictures of potential outcomes. Tell them to wait while you write their answer down so you can check to see if their prediction (or guess) happened after they try it.

- *What do you think will happen if you use this heavier marble?*
- *How fast will the marble go if you use the longer track piece before the turn?*
- *What would happen if you made the track flatter?*

Generalizing (inductive reasoning) about variables: These types of questions often make good prompts for the "L" in a KWL chart ("what have you learned") using a Language Experience Approach (LEA). "Show me" is a good prompt for children with challenges in their ability to verbalize.

- *Show me how you made a structure that helped a marble to make a turn.*

- *What have you learned about how to make a marble turn?*
- *What can you tell me about what happened when you used the heavier marble?*
- *What do you now know about the best way to make a turn for your little car?*

Causal reasoning is hard for younger children to express sensibly until they have constructed stable cause-and-effect relationships. Children who have demonstrated cause-and-effect understanding can be asked "why" questions such as "how come, what is the reason for, what makes, what causes, what made you decide, what is your purpose for, how does this make that happen." Even so, asking children to predict or to generalize often is more productive than asking "why" questions.

Analyze Your Observational Records

- What cause-and-effect patterns are they noticing, even if only in their actions rather than in answers to "why" questions?
- What understanding of the properties of materials are they relying on in their selection of materials to use?
- How are they describing the properties of the materials?
- What questions do they seem to be asking?
- What problems do they seem to be posing?
- Who is ready to be introduced to a more difficult design?
- Whom do you need to interview to get a better understanding of how they are thinking?

EXPERIENCE 9. ENGINEERING A JUMP: A SYSTEM TO TRANSFER A MARBLE FROM ONE TRACK TO ANOTHER OVER A GAP

How can I get a marble to jump over a space in the pathway?

Why This Experience Matters

When the teacher notices a gap between two linear ramp sections (see Figure 5.38), they may ask the child if there is a way the marble can jump across the gap. Children who take on the challenge of building a system that includes the feature of a jump, or a gap between two components of track, grapple with the relationship between speed and inertia, and with coordinating that relationship with the force of gravity. It is best not to coach them to use the words *inertia* and *gravity*, but instead encourage them to use their own language to describe the challenge. In this challenge, you may overhear children saying things like the following:

- The marble has to go fast so it flies over the gap and doesn't fall between.
- The marble is going down the first ramp fast, then slows down as it goes up this one, but still goes fast enough to go up and over the gap and onto the next track.
- I want to see how wide I can make the gap.
- I need to make sure the tracks are all lined up. If I stand at the end of the system and look to the beginning, I can tell where I need to adjust the track to get it all in a straight line.

Materials:

- unit blocks
- tracks
- a variety of spheres

Design constraints or things for the teacher to hold constant:

- At the beginning, the teacher may guide students to use one kind of sphere until they are successful. After success, the teacher may offer or suggest using other sizes or weights of spheres to see if the design is still successful. This will allow children to explore the properties of the spheres within the context of a different design problem.

Things that children can vary or change:

- the width of the gap between the two pieces of track
- the steepness of the incline

Mental relationships children have the possibility of constructing:

- between the need for an uphill track and the ability of the marble to make a jump
- between the speed of the marble and the arc of the marble as it leaves the end of a suspended ramp
- between the steepness of the incline and the arc of the marble as it leaves the end of a suspended ramp

Figure 5.38. Engineering a Jump

- between the ricochet effect of the marble dropping onto a flat track versus the ricochet effect of the marble dropping onto a downward incline

Example of a teacher's invitation to focus:

I notice you have a gap here, but the marble makes it across. I wonder why it isn't dropping down into the gap and stopping? How wide a gap do you think you can get the marble to jump across?

Or

Your marble is moving really fast across these connecting tracks, and almost looks like it's barely touching the track! I wonder what would happen if you made a space between two tracks instead of connecting them. I'm curious to know if it would go over the space and on to the next track.

Before You Introduce, Engage in Teacher Play

Explore the complexity of designing a system with the feature of a jump (see Figure 5.39). As you talk yourself through problem solving, consider how you might craft questions or comments to support your children in this challenge. Record the questions on a clipboard and place them in the center for you to refer to when needed. Questions such as these might be included:

- Which length of track works best to start the movement of a marble?
- How can you adjust the steepness of the downward and upward ramps to give the marble enough speed off the upward ramp to make it across a gap?
- How do you decide where the third track is placed?
- What happens when you position that third track as a downward ramp? Upward? Level?
- Which kind of marble works best for you?
- How might your children respond to this challenge?
- If it is too difficult for the child to land the marble onto a third track, might they be

Figure 5.39. Building a Jump in Teacher Play

interested in placing a bucket for it to land in after it leaves the second track?

Attending to the Four Aspects of the Environment

Physical Environment: Arranging the Classroom to Promote Inquiry

Consider adding a Berber or loop area rug to the Ramps and Pathways center. Berber carpet is generally flat and allows blocks to stack evenly. It also dampens the noise and slows down the movement of escaping marbles.

Intellectual Environment: Opportunities to Ask Questions, Predict, and Reason

Young children may have watched video of stunt drivers jumping cars and motorcycles over gaps or of ski jumping in the Olympics. All use a ramp to send the driver or skier up and over. The speed (or lack of it) often determines the success of the landing. Young children may be interested in exploring this phenomenon using ramps and pathway materials. The interest may begin unintentionally when a child has inadvertently left a gap between two pieces of track, but the speed of the marble helps the marble overcome the gap. A teacher may draw a child's attention to this through questions and comments such as these:

- *What is happening to the marble at the gap?*
- *If you wanted to keep the gap, is there a way the marble could cross it and land on the next track?*

Other times, children may come to school inspired after watching video of bike stunts or a car, truck, motorcycle, or skier using speed and an upward ramp to get airborne. Some use a downward ramp in landing, and others do not. Children may want to bring this design feature to their systems of ramps and pathways. Getting a marble airborne may be the first challenge to meet. As children build, you can support their problem solving by preparing questions and comments to deepen their ability to think critically and to track the progress of their designs. These are some examples:

- *I wonder how you could get the marble to go faster before it goes up the ramp to make it jump a greater distance?*
- *I saw your marble land here and then roll. I'm going to mark where it landed with this dot sticker. I wonder if you can get it to go even farther?*

It is even more difficult to land the marble on another track and have it continue on in a system. You might ask the following:

- *I see the marble crosses the gap, but then bounces off the next track. Is there something you can do*

with the first or second track to keep the marble from bouncing off?
- *Can you get the system working if you make the gap even wider?*

Children may want to document the distance between the gap using nonstandard units of measurement. In one teacher's classroom, the children challenged each other to build a ramp to jump over the most cars. This challenge was measured by the number of cars jumped (see Figure 5.40).

Social–Emotional Environment: Nurturing Healthy Learning Dispositions

Building a system with jumps often works best when children collaborate by observing the system from different perspectives during testing. A child positioned at the end of the system can spot where the tracks and ramps do not align. They can direct another child to make adjustments by moving the track a bit to one side or another. Another child can view the system from the side and take note of where the marble lands or bounces off the receiving track. They can provide directions to widen or close the gap. Giving and receiving directions requires perspective-taking. Considering both the side and the head-on views at the same time exercises a child's working memory.

Promotional Environment: Promoting and Celebrating Children's Thinking and Ideas

When children come to school with the idea of mimicking a motorcycle or car jump, it may be helpful

Figure 5.40. Jumping Over Cars

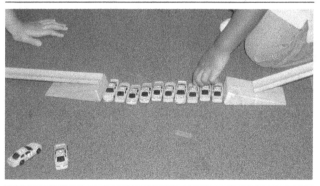

to print out pictures of stunt drivers making a jump and post them on the wall. Class discussion on what the stunt drivers may need to do to be successful can be captured in writing and posted next to the pictures. Teachers should be sure to photograph and record unsuccessful systems occasionally, so that reviewing those can help children to understand their progress in constructing successful systems as they work along. This formative assessment helps support children who may be struggling in other challenges—teachers can remind them of their attempts that eventually became successful. Examples of children's systems with successful jump features can be photographed and posted alongside photos of unsuccessful attempts. Children can either dictate or write a blurb explaining challenges, failures, and successes they had in building.

Featured Assessment: Time-Lapse Video

Perhaps children initiate trying to follow a model seen on video, or instead you might provide a video at some point during their work on this challenge. Either way, or with no video model at all, making time-lapse documentation of children's attempts can add an extra dimension to observational data you collect, in addition to helping children identify what is and what is not working. Set your cell phone or tablet to capture a time-lapse video of activity during the experience. View the video while talking about the details of the construction and the choices made in the construction. To prompt discussion of attempts that have not yet succeeded, use attention-focusing questions such as these:

- *What do you notice about how high the marble goes when five blocks support the track?*
- *Where is the end of the second piece of track?*
- *What do you notice about where the last piece of track is placed?*

Alternatively, ask children to compare the video of a failed attempt to one of a successful jump, using a slow-motion feature, if available, with questions such as these:

- *What is different about how high the end of the second track is between the one that completed the jump and the one that did not?*
- *How fast was the marble going in the successful one? How could you get the marble to go faster for the one that fell into the gap?*

EXPERIENCE 10. ENGINEERING A DROP: A SYSTEM TO CATCH A MARBLE

How can I design a pathway that ends with the marble dropping into a bucket?

Why This Experience Matters

Children as young as 3 years old think creatively to design and build systems where a marble drops into a catcher such as a bucket (see Figure 5.41). Other items to use as catchers can include a margarine tub, basket, mayonnaise jar, empty can opened with a safety-edge can opener, or other available containers. Children frequently are surprised that the sphere does not just drop straight down from the end of the ramp into the catcher. Puzzling over that contradiction to their working hypothesis, students grapple with the following mental relationships:

- the steepness of the ramp and the speed of the sphere
- the speed of the sphere and its trajectory after it leaves the end of the track
- the placement of the sphere on the ramp and its trajectory at the end of the track
- the properties of the sphere and how it lands in the catcher (ping-pong balls and rubber balls bounce significantly higher and possibly out of the container)
- the size of the catcher and the difficulty landing the sphere inside it
- the properties of the catcher and the sound it makes as the sphere drops into it

Figure 5.41. Dropping Into a Bucket

- the catcher's hardness or softness and how the sphere responds when it drops into it

Materials:

- unit blocks
- tracks of different lengths
- a variety of spheres
- catchers (buckets, plastic jars, empty cans opened with a safety-edge can opener, margarine tubs, boxes, baskets)

Things that children can vary or change:

- the type of sphere
- the length of track
- the pitch of the ramp
- kind, location, and size of catcher

Example of a teacher's invitation to focus: The teacher can introduce the idea of using catchers in the Ramps and Pathways center in a class meeting at the beginning of the week or introduce it by building upon the work of children who are already exploring this design feature.

I've noticed you can connect tracks to make a long pathway for the marble to roll. I wonder if you can do something with the tracks to get a marble into a catcher.

Lacy and John are working with a very interesting challenge. They are trying to get a marble into a catcher, and they are noticing that they have to think about where the catcher needs to be. Let's listen to what they are figuring out. Perhaps you might want to try this too.

Before You Introduce, Engage in Teacher Play

Explore building systems with a drop using different types of spheres and catchers. Can you predict where the catcher will need to be to catch a marble rolling fast on a ramp? A marble rolling slowly? What kinds of catchers would be best to offer to your children? Think about this experience from the perspective of your children to prepare questions and comments to support your children's creativity and problem solving.

Attending to the Four Aspects of the Environment

Physical Environment: Arranging the Classroom to Promote Inquiry

Choose two or three different kinds of catchers to start with and position them on a shelf that helps children consider their size (small, medium, and large) or material (metal, wood, plastic). Provide a container to store spheres for children to use. Building on a Berber rug will help slow escaping spheres.

Intellectual Environment: Opportunities to Ask Questions, Predict, and Reason

A simple description of the *trajectory* of an object is the path it follows once in flight or in motion. In Ramps and Pathways experiences, trajectory becomes meaningful when children position catchers for a sphere to land in after it leaves the end of a track. In class discussions on experiences with trajectory, teachers can model drawing a diagram of what the children are building and use dotted lines to symbolize the predicted path of a sphere after it rolls off the end of a track. Examples of questions and comments to inspire reasoning and explanations, or to focus attention, include the following:

- *What happens when you release the marble up here? Will it fall into the bucket?*
- *What happens if you release the marble halfway down the ramp? Will it fall into the bucket?*
- *How big of a catcher do you need?*
- *The ball keeps bouncing out of the catcher. I wonder how you could get the ball to stay inside the catcher instead of bouncing out.*
- *Where do you think I should put the bucket to catch the marble? Why not right underneath the end of the track?*
- *I'm wondering why you put the catcher way out here. Can you help me understand?*
- *Can you draw a picture of the path of the sphere after it leaves the end of the track?*

Once children begin to coordinate the speed of the sphere with the trajectory, you may see students designing systems where the marble will drop some distance onto a track below rather than into a catcher. As children gain control of engineering the trajectory of a sphere into a catcher, older children may enjoy an even harder challenge: to drop the sphere onto a track below and have it continue to roll (see Figure 5.42). You might offer them a challenge like this:

I've noticed some of you have been getting pretty successful at getting marbles to drop into a catcher at the end of a track. Do you think it would work to

Figure 5.42. A System With Three Drops

have the marble drop onto another track below and continue to roll? Do you have any ideas?

Questions and comments to inspire reasoning or focus attention might include these:

- *I noticed the marble is bouncing off when it lands. I wonder how you could contain it to keep it on the lower track.*
- *This drops the distance of one block! Is there a way to get the marble to drop two blocks down?*
- *What would happen if you slowed the marble as it rolls down the first ramp? How could you slow down the marble?*

Social–Emotional Environment: Nurturing Healthy Learning Dispositions

We have seen children as young as 3 years old grappling with trajectory and, through trial and error, predict where to place a catcher. Narrating the child's actions, affirming their feelings of frustration, and then following up with a suggestion that compels them to keep working can help young children gain control of frustration. You might use comments such as these:

- *It didn't make it into the catcher. How frustrating! Will you move it closer to the end of the track, or farther away? Now let's try it again and watch.*
- *It missed again! I couldn't quite see where the ball hit the floor. Could you watch closely if I release the ball?*
- *I see you aren't giving up! I wonder if using a different size of container will work?*
- *You got it in the catcher! You tried eight times before you got it to work. You can do hard things!*

Promotional Environment: Promoting and Celebrating Children's Thinking and Ideas

- Assist or encourage children to draw diagrams of a working drop using dotted lines to indicate the pathway of the sphere as it moves from the end of the track to the catcher. Write down their explanations of how the system works or encourage them to write their own explanation. Display it on the wall along with their drawing.
- Cocreate and display a table to document the sounds the catchers make when a sphere lands in them.
- Cocreate and display a table to record how the different spheres land in the catcher (bounces out, stays inside).

Featured Assessment: Science Journals

Here is an opportunity to use science journals to get children to record some of their predictions or guesses about where to place catchers and then record the results. You can take a photo of a child's successful system, print it out to paste in the journal, and then caption the child's description of the process, or help the emergent writer to do their own writing. Use these journal entries to help you document progress in engineering habits of mind, engineering practices (especially "Notices, observes, and analyzes areas of failure," "Views failures as an opportunity to problem-solve and perseveres," and "Explains design and communicates through oral or written documentation"), and awareness of the science concept of force, such as in working with slope to move the marble farther, faster, or slower.

EXPERIENCE 11. ENGINEERING A SYSTEM TO REVERSE THE DIRECTION OF A MARBLE

How can I design a pathway that causes a marble to move backward?

Why This Experience Matters

This feature is difficult for upper elementary children, but we have observed some 1st- and 2nd-graders master this design feature. Children who successfully use this feature in their ramp and pathway system draw heavily on their working memory. They coordinate their understanding of the speed of a marble and its trajectory, the greater ease in engineering a slow-moving marble's drop onto a lower ramp positioned at an incline opposite of the first, and the forward movement of the marble up that opposite incline until the marble reverses its direction (see Figure 5.43).

Materials:

- unit blocks
- tracks
- a variety of spheres
- catchers

Things that children can vary or change:

- the type of sphere
- the length of track

- the degree of incline of the ramp
- the number of reversals in a system

Mental relationships children have the possibility of constructing:

- the speed of the sphere and the ability to control its action as it drops onto a ramp below
- the steepness of the second ramp and how quickly the marble reverses its direction
- the position of the second ramp to allow room for the marble to slow down and change its direction before it rolls off the top of the second ramp
- the difficulty in slowing and changing the direction of a heavy sphere
- the difficulty in transferring a sphere that bounces easily onto a second incline

Example of a teacher's invitation to focus:

I've noticed when your system lands a marble on a track below, the marble begins to slow down. I wonder if there is a way to position the track so that the marble doesn't just slow down, but rolls backward.

Before You Introduce, Engage in Teacher Play

Experiencing your own difficulty in building your own system to change the direction of a marble will

Figure 5.43. Moving Backward

Figure 5.44. Reversing Direction in Teacher Play

develop in you a respect for children who take on this challenge (see Figure 5.44). Reflect on the difficult aspects of this challenge and what helped you make sense of all the variables in play. As you build, note the incremental adjustments you make to align the two ramps. Think about the blocks you use to create the support structures and how you position the blocks to allow the marble to move under the first ramp. Take note of how much space you need to build comfortably.

Attending to the Four Aspects of the Environment

Physical Environment: Arranging the Classroom to Promote Inquiry

This challenge requires precise incremental adjustments. Be sure to provide a space away from classroom traffic, and allow enough space for two or three builds to be going on at one time. Encourage children to get their supplies (blocks, track, spheres, and catchers) and carry them to their building space. Provide children with tablets to record the action on their system so they can review and problem-solve.

Intellectual Environment: Opportunities to Ask Questions, Predict, and Reason

Consider language that serves to coach children to engage in critical thinking and help them persevere in mastering this feature. Examples might include the following:

- *Is it easier to control a slow-moving marble or a fast-moving marble? How slowly can you get a marble to move without stopping?*
- *Remember when you were making hills and valleys? I remember you worked hard to get the marble to have enough speed to go over the hill and not roll back down. But now you do want it to roll back down.*
- *You got it to land on the track below, but it kept going straight and it rolled off the end. Is there a way to position the track below so the marble will stop before rolling off the end? If you can get it to stop, is there something you could do to get the marble to move backward?*
- *I notice you got the marble to roll backward, but then it got stuck under the first ramp. Is there a way to make more space for the marble to roll underneath?*

Social–Emotional Environment: Nurturing Healthy Learning Dispositions

First- and 2nd-graders may be comfortable taking on this challenge, but not all 1st- and 2nd-graders. Children who are not interested in this challenge will have ideas they want to pursue and should be allowed space and materials to do so. Children who do take it on can be encouraged to share their work through writing. Figure 5.45 shows a photo of a child and his ramp, which he named "The Chicken Nest." He documented his experience by describing the sequence of his build:

> First I put a long block and a square block on top of each other. When the ball went in the place where you can't see it, it hit a block and went backwards into the cup. The end!

Promotional Environment: Promoting and Celebrating Children's Thinking and Ideas

Encourage children to share video of their process with the rest of the class and facilitate a discussion of what is working and what is not. Audio-record this discussion to document the collaborative problem solving that unfolds. Create a QR code for a child's video, along with a photograph of their structure. Place the photo and the QR code in the hallway to communicate the critical thinking going on inside

Figure 5.45. The Chicken Nest

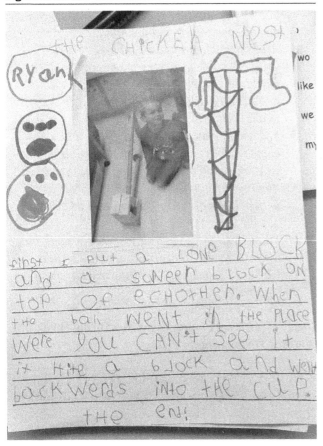

the classroom. Listening to and reflecting on the audio recording of the discussion will help you write a paragraph to provide an outside audience an understanding of critical thinking within the context of Ramps and Pathways. Include examples of how the experience meets standards.

Featured Assessment: Science Concepts

Children's playful learning in Ramps and Pathways experiences results in a working understanding of science concepts. The table shown in Appendix E can assist teachers in recognizing children's development of these concepts by observing their actions in playful learning. Educators can monitor children's growing understanding of these concepts by documenting children's behaviors over time using the form in Appendix F.

EXPERIENCE 12. ENGINEERING A SYSTEM TO WORK IN ODD SPACES

How can I build a long pathway that fits inside this small space?

Why This Experience Matters

This experience challenges children to design increasingly complex systems within an oddly shaped space (see Figure 5.46). This design challenge was born out of a problem within a 1st-grade classroom. The children had been building many long, linear systems that were taking up a lot of space in the classroom, which intruded on other learning areas. At a regular class meeting, some students pointed out that they didn't like having to work around the systems when they were engaged in other learning. The idea of staying in your own yard bubbled up in the discussion. The children and their teacher decided they would create "yards" for building using masking tape to create "lot lines" on the carpet used for building.

In the beginning, all the yards were identical and shaped as squares. The children were content to build simple structures within their yards for a while using the shorter pieces of track, but they soon lost interest. To inspire interest, the teacher placed three 2-foot sections of track inside each of the identical squares, along with 10 unit blocks. She

Figure 5.46. Building in Odd Spaces

challenged the builders to design a system using all three tracks but to stay inside of the square. They could use as many of the 10 blocks as they wanted.

At first, the children simply stacked the track and the marble would roll down only the top ramp. In a class meeting, the teacher explained the challenge in more detail. The builders were challenged to design a system to move a marble on all three tracks without stopping, and the structure had to stay in their own yard. Since all the children had the same-sized yard, same number of unit blocks, and same number and lengths of track, they began to share ideas about how to build a system that met their teacher's requirements. Over time, they began to combine features such as turning corners and reversing the direction of marbles to build successful structures.

When interest started to wane, the teacher placed a combination of different lengths of track inside each yard, along with 10 unit blocks. As children entered the classroom in the morning, they noticed each of the sets of track was different, and they were eager to take on the design challenge. They found there were many different ways to configure the tracks to design a working system in the same amount of space. What was so interesting is that once the children got a system to work, they wanted to add to its complexity. The teacher observed this, and when the children went home for the day, she pulled up the masking tape and put new tape down in different odd configurations, where each yard had a different shape and size, but she left the yards empty, leaving the children to choose their own numbers and lengths of track. What followed was amazing. Children began to build increasingly complex systems that included combinations of features such as a jump and a corner, or three corners and a drop. They designed a system with obtuse and acute corners, learning that acute corners were much more difficult to get to work. Once again, when the children designed a successful system, they didn't quit. They continued to add to the complexity. Figure 5.47 shows three 1st-graders building side by side, but each at their chosen level of complexity. Two boys decided to work together to build in a yard and were focused on the aesthetics of their design over complexity. The boy in the front of the photo elected to work alone and designed a system that changed

Figure 5.47. Complex Builds in Odd Spaces

the direction of a marble three times. Tucked into the background of the photo, the teacher and four children are engaged in small-group reading.

The following year, with a new classroom of students, the teacher waited for children to complain about the long linear ramp systems, but they didn't. She decided to bring up the problem herself in a class meeting. She found that the children responded to the challenge in a similar way, and she reintroduced the challenge every year after that. Within this challenge she was able to take note of student behaviors such as the following:

- Who takes the lead in designing?
- Who is comfortable taking direction from another child?
- Who takes risks in their designs and tries new approaches to building?
- Who stays with simple and safe designs?
- Who prefers to work alone?
- Who prefers to collaborate with others?
- Who is comfortable with asking another child for help?
- Who likes to help other children problem-solve?

The teacher discovered that children's behaviors illustrated their development of engineering habits of mind (systems thinking, creativity, optimism, collaboration, communication, attention to ethical considerations).

Materials:

- unit blocks
- different lengths of track
- a variety of spheres
- masking tape
- catchers

Design constraints or things for the teacher to hold constant:

- the size and configuration of the yard, or space for building
- at times, the length and number of track pieces to be used in a system

Things that children can vary or change:

- the type of sphere used
- at times, the length and number of track pieces used

Mental relationships children have the possibility of constructing:

- among the size of the yard, the size of the track to be used, and the features and corner angles used to build a successful system
- between the speed of the marble and the success of moving through the features of a system

Before You Introduce, Engage in Teacher Play

Grab a colleague after school lets out and explore building within the space of a yard. In the process, you will learn how large a yard should be and what size and number of track pieces should be provided at the beginning to allow success. You can gradually shrink the size of the yard to make the challenge more difficult.

Challenge yourself to build a system with acute corners, obtuse corners, and corners with 90° angles. Take note of the following:

- Which angles are easier to get to work?
- Which type of sphere works best in rolling through different types of corners?

- Which type of sphere is harder to use in a system?
- How many unit blocks should be placed in the yards? Should you include more than 10? Fewer than 10?

Think about this experience from the perspective of your children. Where might they become frustrated? Is it possible for children to work together to comfortably build at different levels of complexity with success? How could you encourage children who become frustrated? Would your children want to be part of writing the specifications of a design challenge?

Attending to the Four Aspects of the Environment

Physical Environment: Arranging the Classroom to Promote Inquiry

A large rug with a short nap works well for building. As you lay down masking tape to create the yards, consider the spacing between the yards to allow a builder to work outside of the yard without interfering with the work of their neighbor. Some teachers who have linoleum floors buy carpet squares from a home building supply store and use four carpet squares to create a square shaped yard, or an L-shaped yard, or an S-shaped yard. Children can also create their own shape of yard using the squares.

Intellectual Environment: Opportunities to Ask Questions, Predict, and Reason

This challenge, which was born out of necessity, is one that allows children to take control of their own decisions on design and to solve problems in building their design. The open-ended nature of the challenge is rich with design possibilities and problem solving at a difficulty level the child self-selects. We find when children are at this level of building, the interest stays for weeks and weeks, as each time they get a system to work, there is always another layer of complexity to add to make the system more interesting.

Social–Emotional Environment: Nurturing Healthy Learning Dispositions

There are times when children need to pause in a design challenge and turn their focus on a different question they have, or a design they want to see come to fruition. Figure 5.48 shows a teacher sitting alongside a 1st-grader who is building in his own yard but wants to explore the aesthetics of a structure. Attracted to a set of blocks that inspire the building of castles, he brought these blocks to his yard to build a castle with ramps. In his approach, he built the castle first, and then worked to add ramps within the castle. He has constructed two ramps and one long pathway with none of them connecting. The teacher watches him build and asks questions to learn his intent in building. Rather than telling him he needed to stick to the design constraint of having all the track connected in one system, she knew this child needed to satisfy his desire to build a castle containing ramps and pathways. Taking the time to observe and question to learn from the child sends a message to him that his thinking and ideas are important and valued. After a time, he rejoined his classmates in the shared challenge. He became one of the most creative and successful builders that year.

Promotional Environment: Promoting and Celebrating Children's Thinking and Ideas

Select one or two children to feature in a day, and photograph and/or video-record them in the act of building. Photograph or video-record them at work from different perspectives and at different points of time in their construction. At the end of the day, review the photos or video and select anywhere from one to five photos for each of the children. The next day, present the photos to the child and ask them

Figure 5.48. Placing Ramps Inside a Castle

to use them to tell a story about what they were thinking as they worked, or about problems they had in building their design. You might ask them to sequence the photos as they tell their story. Once they are comfortable with their story, you and the child can cocreate, or let the child write, the text of the story. For the audience of the child and their classmates, post these stories on a wall at children's eye level for all the children to read. To address the audience of other teachers, administrators, or families, link the photos to the standards, translating how these experiences addressed those standards.

Featured Assessment: Teacher Reflection Journal × Engineering Habits of Mind

Use this challenge to document the engineering habits of mind (Appendix A) for individual children and to reflect on what you are doing to support them, noting the following:

- What changes might you make to help children who are struggling with systems thinking? Do they need one-on-one attention from you with questions that you have found to be particularly productive? Would they benefit from working in a team?
- For particularly creative children, are you finding ways that they can document their designs to share in the promotional environment?
- Which children might need more support with optimism rather than perfectionism or rather than giving up after one failure?
- What are the pros and cons of having children tackle this challenge in a team?
- How can you incorporate more literacy into this experience, whether with oral communication for which you serve as a scribe, or with emergent writers making and captioning their own documentation?
- What, if any, ethical considerations have arisen in coordinating the use of space or materials among peers, or safety concerns?

EXPERIENCE 13. SETTING OFF A CHAIN OF EVENTS

How can I aim a marble to knock down objects?

Why This Experience Matters

As children build working systems that include features to change the direction of a marble, they encounter problems. In their working understanding of physics, they begin to notice relationships such as the greater difficulty in changing the direction of a fast-moving marble over a slow-moving marble, or the difficulty in changing the direction of a heavy marble over a lighter marble. They observe how the blocks they use as barriers to prevent the marble from going straight will be knocked over after a heavy or fast-moving marble strikes the barrier. In iterative tests, they often line up more blocks behind the first to create a stronger barrier. Children's interest in cause and effect often turns into design challenges to set off a chain of events.

Fascination with cause and effect may begin when children line up a series of marbles on a ramp and release them together. They notice that they don't all roll at the same speed at the same time and instead knock against each other, causing some to slow down and others to speed up. Figure 5.49 shows how children have lined up a collection of objects with different properties. Over time, or with guidance from their teacher, they reduce the variables by working with groups of identical objects to observe their interaction, and then more closely explore a lineup of similar spheres to observe their collective movement.

Interest may also start with a simple investigation to see how marbles can be sent down a ramp to knock down objects. Shown in Figure 5.50 is a construction where four boys have set up a line of small cylinders and are exploring moving the ramp to different spots to send a marble down to knock down the cylinders. They are seeking to answer the question, "Where can we place the ramp to send down the marble to knock down the most cylinders?" Other children may begin by keeping the ramp stationary and exploring how the arrangement of objects to knock down affects how many fall in one act of sending down a marble (see Figure 5.51).

Figure 5.49. Observing Colliding Objects

Figure 5.50. Knocking Down Blocks

Before long, children begin to set up materials to set off a chain reaction, a sort of Rube Goldberg machine (see Textbox 5.5). Figure 5.52 shows that a child has built a steep ramp, and then lined up and spaced four unit blocks and a metal container holding a sphere. When he released the marble at the

Figure 5.51. Placing Objects to Knock Down

Figure 5.52. Initiating a Chain of Events

top of the ramp, the marble struck the first block, creating a domino effect ending with the last block tipping over the metal container and letting the sphere out.

TEXTBOX 5.5. RUBE GOLDBERG

Rube Goldberg was a Pulitzer Prize-winning cartoonist and inventor who drew cartoons depicting extremely complex and ridiculous solutions to solving a simple problem. In 1949, two engineering fraternities at Purdue University developed an extremely competitive Rube Goldberg Machine Contest. The competition was revived in 1983 with the first challenge of designing a Rube Goldberg Machine that poured an 8-ounce cup of water. The contest became so popular that in 1988 the competition went national. This engineering contest is now Purdue University's largest media event (Purdue University, 2018). Video of past Rube Goldberg contests can be viewed on Purdue's website (https://www.purdue.edu/newsroom/rubegoldberg/history.html). Despite Rube Goldberg's death in 1970, his influence is still visible in today's society. In fact, he is the only person whose name is an adjective in Webster's Dictionary. The Rube Goldberg Institute for Innovation and Creativity invites innovative thinkers of all ages to enter its Rube Goldberg Machine Contest (https://www.rubegoldberg.org/rube-goldberg-contests/).

One group of 1st-graders wanted to put a moving piece in their system of tracks. They balanced a track on the peak of a triangular block with the intent of having the marble roll slowly across the fulcrum, causing the weight of the marble to tip the track down to deposit the marble onto the second ramp (see Figure 5.53), which reversed its direction and dropped to the third ramp, which reversed its

Figure 5.53. Incorporating a Fulcrum

Figure 5.54. Ramp and Pathway Specialty Pieces

direction and dropped to the fourth ramp, which, once again, reversed the marble's direction.

Children will add other materials to these Rube Goldberg–type systems. Jordan Redig received a gift card from one of her students and used it to purchase more materials to add to the Ramps and Pathways center. She purchased some 1-inch pipe insulation, PVC pipe and elbows, and household trim. She and her father spent an afternoon in her dad's shop and constructed specialty pieces for children to use (see Figure 5.54). Figure 5.55 shows children investigating what happens when they roll a sphere down a PVC tube, then drop it down another tube with an elbow at the end. When they held the system just right, the ball would pop up out of the end of the elbow.

Children may create a system with some action at the end. One boy created a system using one ramp to start the motion of the marble, and at the end, he placed two wedges under the last track. He worked to incrementally add or delete the wedges, and move them in and out, to give the final upward ramp just enough lift to project the marble through the block with a hole (see Figure 5.56).

Before You Introduce, Engage in Teacher Play

In classrooms where teachers have taken time to build a cooperative and collaborative learning community, chances are the children will not wait for their teacher to introduce the idea of adding additional materials to their systems. They will just do it. We have found young children lead with innovation and we find ourselves adopting their ideas. Children desiring to include a feature with a fulcrum inspired us to add sections of track with three grooves cut horizontally in the bottom (see Figure 5.57) to help keep the track on the fulcrum.

We now offer the children's design feature on our STEMware Marketplace e-commerce site for teachers wishing to add it to their classroom set of track (https://uni.estore.flywire.com/products?store Catalog=1352). We advise teachers to engage in teacher play to first replicate what they have observed children doing to understand the complexity of getting the feature to work. Then continue to engage in teacher play to generate your own innovative ideas for features. As you play, you will likely come up with some interesting materials to add to the Ramps and Pathways center.

Figure 5.55. Using PVC Pipe

Attending to the Four Aspects of the Environment

Physical Environment: Arranging the Classroom to Promote Inquiry

As children introduce new materials into their systems, create shelving to house them, making it easy for children to access when needed and put away when finished. We have seen teachers and children add tambourines and drum heads, bells, large clear plastic tubing, boomwhackers, funnels, and cardboard tubes to the center. You and your children will have more ideas.

Intellectual Environment: Opportunities to Ask Questions, Predict, and Reason

Adding materials to the center and incorporating them into ramps and pathways systems requires cognitive flexibility, or the ability to view materials in unlikely and surprising ways. As children work

Figure 5.56. Using Wedges to Elevate the Final Ramp

Figure 5.57. Tracks With Grooves

in their systems, you can support them with questions and comments such as these:

- *Which piece is the beginning of your system?*
- *Can you explain where you think the marble will go before you try out the ramp?*

- *Where will you start your marble?*
- *Where will the marble go after that?*
- *If you take a tour of what other builders are doing, could you get some new ideas?*
- *I notice the marble keeps rolling off this section of the ramp. Would you watch it here and help me figure out why?*
- *I wonder what you could do to keep the marble from stopping on this ramp section?*
- *Why do you suppose this corner works when this one doesn't?*

Social–Emotional Environment: Nurturing Healthy Learning Dispositions

When innovative teachers think creatively in offering children open-ended materials, STEM is experienced by all children. The child shown in Figure 5.58 has limited mobility and yet she is participating in the action by releasing a ball into the tube. Her classmate helps adjust the other end to direct the ball into the enclosure they have made. Jordan Redig fosters a compassionate and collaborative learning community that works well:

Figure 5.58. A Collaborative Community of Learners

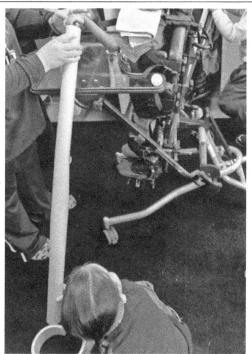

My kids always help me make decisions in changing toys and activities. They bring me stuff to put away, and then at a circle time, we think about options of what to put back out. However, if I want something specific, I kind of help guide them towards my "fun" idea. Then during a part of that day, they help bring the materials out and place them around the room.

Jordan's mom teaches kindergartners nearby. Her mom has offered Ramps and Pathways to her kindergarten children, but was amazed by the discoveries her daughter's preschoolers were making. Through conversation, Jordan learned that her mom only gets their science Ramps kit for a week and a half. "I was like, Mom! My kids get the ramps for free-choice time every day for weeks and months! Your kids can't learn all there is to learn in less than two weeks!" Jordan had a discussion with her preschoolers the next day, and they decided to share their ramps with their kindergarten friends for the month of January.

Promotional Environment: Promoting and Celebrating Children's Thinking and Ideas

As you and your children investigate force and motion, take time to meet as a group and discuss what you are noticing, and what you are still wanting to figure out. Brandy Twedt and her kindergartners adapted a KWL chart to list "What we have learned" and "What we are wondering" (see Figure 5.59). Brandy wrote the children's contributions in alternate colors and listed the name of the contributor behind to help her emergent readers recognize their contributions more easily. Placing these documents on the wall provides children with a sense of history in what they have figured out, and what they want to focus on in the future. In this classroom, the teacher and her children are comfortable with learning as a process. It is a way of being. We end this chapter with a story of Brandy's work to integrate literacy with the STEM work within Ramps and Pathways.

Featured Assessments: Time-Lapse Video or Photograph Series

This potentially complex challenge, which might continue over a stretch of time, can be a rich

Figure 5.59. Documenting Findings and Wonders

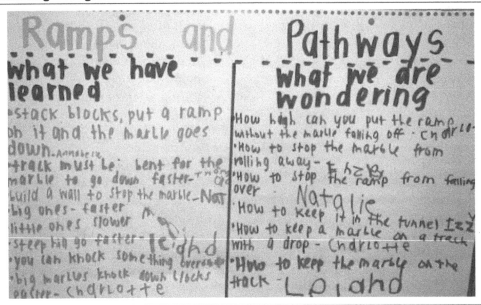

source of documentation for the monitoring of progress in science concepts (see Appendix E), engineering behaviors (see Appendix C), and engineering habits of mind (see Appendix A). To help you record the engineering of an individual or of a group when your attention must be split, set your cell phone or tablet to capture a time-lapse video of activity at the center. Viewing it will give you a

sense of how the space is being used and who is using it. When you can be available, in addition to or instead of video, you can take still photographs of various stages of a response to the challenge. Use the images as prompts for the children involved to describe their design decisions, their successes, and their failures, and to help them plan what to do next.

INTEGRATIVE STEM AND LITERACY IN KINDERGARTEN

Brandy Twedt

When I began teaching kindergarten, I identified with most early childhood educators in that I had little self-confidence in teaching science. In my undergraduate coursework, I had taken science courses designed to deepen my own understanding of science, but I still didn't feel comfortable in my understanding of science concepts. To add to this discomfort, I had minimal early childhood science teaching coursework in my teacher preparation program. Most of it centered on teaching upper elementary students. There was little direction for those of us who planned on teaching in kindergarten, 1st grade, or 2nd grade. Coursework on literacy learning was much more prevalent.

Attention to early science wasn't much better when I began my career as a kindergarten teacher. Only 15 minutes a day were reserved for either science or social studies instruction. There wasn't time for both. The district had not purchased any science curriculum for early childhood and encouraged us to use an online science program that advertised itself as aligning with standards and required minimal teacher preparation. This program told us what materials to have on hand, and then led me and my students through a lesson as we watched a video. The online program was a great tool, as it took full responsibility in teaching children science. I merely had to assist. However, the program supplied only about 4 units per grade level, with each unit being about 3 or 4 lessons, or about 16 science lessons out of 180 school days. Because the program was developed to serve teachers across the country, the lessons were broad and were not personally meaningful to me or my students. The lessons did not take into account my kindergartners' prior knowledge of local geology, flora, and fauna, and of course, they could not connect with my kindergartners' unique and current interests in the world and how it works.

Several years into my career, I decided to pursue a master's degree in literacy education. In one of the first courses, I was introduced to the idea of integrative STEM and literacy. In my review of literature, I noticed a trend in notable integrative STEM approaches such as Concept-Oriented Reading Instruction (CORI), In-Depth Expanded Application of Science (IDEAS), Seeds of Roots, the Science Writing Heuristic (SWH), and Argument-Based Strategies for STEM Infused Science Teaching (ASSIST). All expressed the need to engage in hands-on investigations, peer collaborations, and student discussions to clarify understandings. In addition, each of these models of integration urged the need for writing to incorporate literacy skills. However, all of these approaches addressed learning beginning in grade 3. My professor urged me to examine integrative STEM and literacy within the context of force and motion through an experience called Ramps and Pathways (Counsell et al., 2016). Intrigued, I launched an action research project with my kindergartners by incorporating a Ramps and Pathways center into our reading workshop. Drawing upon my review of literature of integrative experience in grades 3 and up, I made sure the students were actively engaged in the Ramps and Pathways station with peers to allow for rich collaboration and discussion. I incorporated the writing aspect by providing access to writing materials for students to record their discoveries. At times journal reflections were required, and at other times students were simply encouraged to interact with the materials. Upon completion of required entries, students were given direct feedback on the clarity of their writing and future applications to strengthen their writing.

Recalling the need to incorporate writing, I began by completing a KWL chart with my kindergartners to establish what they already knew about the purpose of ramps (see Figure 5.60). They shared some general ideas, such as the following:

- A ramp is for someone to go up.
- A ramp is for a truck, and a pathway is for a train.
- A ramp is for something to go by.
- A pathway is something to drive on.
- A ramp is for stairs.
- People can walk on a ramp.
- Skateboards can go up ramps.

As part of the KWL chart, I also documented what my students wondered about ramps and pathways. They offered these comments:

Figure 5.60. KWL Chart

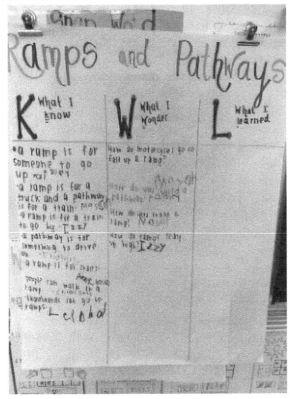

Figure 5.61. Brandy Twedt's Kindergartners' Ramp Rules

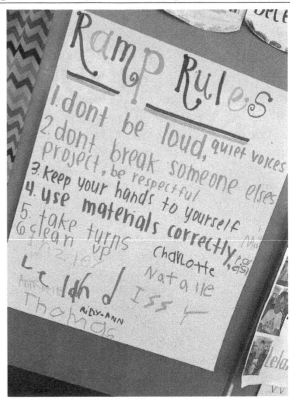

- How do motorcycles go so fast up a ramp?
- How do you build a pathway?
- How do you make a ramp?
- How do ramps stay up high?

I introduced the children to the area of the classroom where the ramps and pathways building would take place. My kindergarten classroom did not have any wooden unit blocks, so I borrowed them from the Iowa Regents' Center, along with a set of tracks. I placed the material on shelving that was easily accessible by the kindergartners. This center would operate alongside literacy centers, and we knew it would be an exciting place to work. The web-based science program we had experienced led us through the science lesson step by step. In stark contrast, with Ramps and Pathways my kindergarten students would be independently engaging in concepts in force and motion using unit blocks, tracks, and objects to move, all new materials to my kindergartners. To ensure the center ran smoothly, I invited them to help come up with an agreement with how the center would work. At

first, the children's contributions to the writing of the rules were expressed with negative language that mirrored the language of rules they had previously experienced, such as "Don't be loud," "Don't break someone else's project," and "Keep your hands to yourself" (see Figure 5.61). To help them focus more on how these behaviors would look in a more positive sense, I encouraged the addition of this positive language: for example, after "Don't be loud," we added "quiet voices."

We began our exploration in the center with a focus on building with unit blocks. Since ramps and pathways rely on structures to build ramps and keep track in place, it was important the children spend time exploring the part-part-whole relationship in wooden unit blocks, and how placement and position of blocks and attention to weight and balance affect the sturdiness of the entire structure (see Figure 5.62). After several days of building sturdy structures, I added track and standard-sized marbles to the block center. I wanted to keep the experience open-ended to allow the kindergartners to be creative and solve their own problems, and started with this

Figure 5.62. Building Sturdy Structures

Figure 5.63. Building Walls

Figure 5.64. Relationship Between Slope and Speed

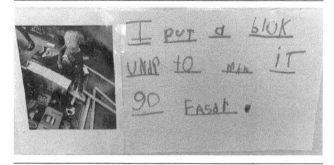

Figure 5.65. Interactive Writing

on this interest, I photographed children as they worked. After school, I selected photos to print out and left space to write beside each image. I shared the photo with the builder and asked them to explain what they were thinking about in the photo. Their explanations provided me with evidence of their current understandings of force and motion (see Figure 5.64), such as the relationship between the steepness of a slope and the speed of the marble, as well as their use of science and engineering practices. The lines drawn on the paper for each word in the sentence helped children make sense of the written word (see Textbox 5.6 and Figure 5.65).

simple open-ended question: "How can I make the marble move without touching it or blowing on it?"

As children built ramps and tested them, one of their first problems was keeping the marbles from rolling away. Some of them solved this problem by building walls around their work (see Figure 5.63). I soon found that their interest in their work was a catalyst for writing. They wanted to write about what they were doing and figuring out. To capitalize

TEXTBOX 5.6. INTERACTIVE WRITING AND DEVELOPING A SENSE OF WORD

Children's interest in their ramp and pathway systems provided rich opportunities to develop their understanding of the written word through interactive writing. After discussing what one student was doing in the photo (see Figure 5.66), I told him I wanted to post the photo on the wall for others to read and understand what he was working on. We worked together to make a one-sentence statement to describe the action in the photo. Then we counted on our fingers as we repeated the sentence to figure out how many words we would need to write.

Teacher: Let's count on our fingers how many words that is. I—made—a—wall—to—stop—the—marble (pointing to a finger for each word). I counted eight words. How many did you count?

Child: I counted eight too.

Teacher: Let's draw a line to write each one of those words. (Repeats the sentence, drawing a line for each word.)

Teacher: Now let's get your words written down on each of those lines. You know how to write the first word, *I*. (Child writes *I* on the first line.)

Teacher: Let's read from the beginning again. I made . . . What sounds do you hear in *made*?

Child: /m/—/a/—/d/. (Child writes down *m—a—d* on the next line.)

Teacher: Let's read from the beginning as we point to each word. I made a . . . You know how to write the word *a*.
(Child writes *a* on the next line.)

Teacher: Let's read from the beginning again. I made a wall. What sounds do you hear in *wall*?

Child: /w/ and /l/.

Teacher: Write down the letters that make those sounds.
(Child writes *w—l* for wall.)

Teacher: Let's read again from the beginning. I made a wall to . . . You know how to write *to*.

Child: Yeah! T—O! (Writes *to*.)

Teacher: Read it back now for us.

Child: I made a wall to stop. Stop is the next word. I know how to write stop. I see it on stop signs. (Writes *stop* on the next line.)

Child: I made a wall to stop the . . . (Writes *the*.)

Child: I made a wall to stop the marble. I don't know how to spell marble.

Teacher: What sounds do you hear in marble?
(Child whispers *marble* as he writes *M B L*.)

Child: I made a wall to stop the marble. I'm done!

Teacher: Do you want to see how close you came to the spellings?

Child: Yes!

Teacher: You have eight words in your sentence, and you already know how to spell five of them! You only need help with three. In the word *made* the only thing you are missing is the silent *e* at the end that makes the *a* say its name. I'll add it for you. (Teacher adds the *e* to complete the word *made*.) In the word *wall* you are very close! You have the *w* for the /w/ sound and the *l* for the /l/ sound at the end. I just need to add an *a* between the /w/ and /l/ sounds and another *l* at the end. (Teacher adds missing letters.) Only one more word.

Child: Marble!

Teacher: Yes. *Marble.* You have the *m* for the beginning sound of /m/. Now let's add *ar* to stand for the /ar/ sound. You already have the /b/ sound and the /l/ sound for the end of the word *marble*. The only thing left is an *e* at the end. M—a—r—b—l—e. Marble.

Child: (Points to each word while reading.) I made a wall to stop the marble. I'm going to put a period at the end.

Figure 5.66. How Will It Move?

Figure 5.67. Will It Roll?

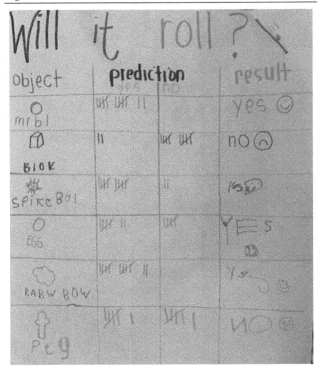

My kindergartners were curious to learn whether they could move other objects besides marbles on a ramp (see Figure 5.66). This was a meaningful context to introduce the idea of making a prediction and using a table to document their findings (see Figure 5.67). In the first column, I sketched a picture of each object. The children labeled each object, providing me yet another window into their understanding of print. For example, some children were writing in all capital letters. Others included lowercase letters. The child who labeled the block as *blok* let me know she was beginning to represent consonant blends.

As children made their predictions of whether the object would roll or not, I documented their prediction using tallies. Using tallies in a meaningful context helps children make sense of part-whole relationships as they count groups of five. Some children needed to point to every mark to count all. Some children could look at a tally of five and count by fives. Some could count by fives and then count on.

In the last column, we documented the results, using *yes* to represent objects that rolled, and *no* to represent objects that did not. After two rounds of

documenting, children asked to write either yes or no in the final column.

I found my kindergartners enjoyed making drawings of their work and explaining their drawings through writing. It was fascinating to see children's understanding of print revealed in their temporary spellings. All viewed themselves as writers, as they were able to communicate their ideas through temporary spellings. The kindergartners were comfortable with the process of learning to

Figure 5.68. Drawing, Labeling, and Writing

Figure 5.69. I Build a Ramp

write. They knew many of the words were not spelled correctly, but they also knew they would learn these spellings over time. Many began to experiment with the text feature of labeling in their drawings (see Figures 5.68, 5.69, and 5.70)

Children's interest in designing and building systems of ramps and pathways inspired the creation of a class sentence pattern book, *Look What We Can Make!* Charlotte drew an intricate drawing of herself and her friend, Riley Ann, engaged in moving a big blue marble, along with an orange marble rolling into a box of other marbles. Her sentence pattern states, "Look! I can make a bridge to make the marble go faster" (see Figure 5.71). Leland shared his design, which included a trap (see Figure 5.72).

After some time I asked the children to share what they had learned and what they were still wondering (see Figure 5.59). Documenting their ideas a second time illustrated their high engagement connected to their personal explorations. Morrow and Gambrell (2019) reported research that found children's growth in reading and writing was faster in classrooms with authentic reading and writing of science information. I noticed my kindergartners were writing longer pieces and including more details. They grew in their understanding of sound–symbol association, spacing between words, using punctuation, and writing to convey meaning. Not only did I see benefits in their writing, but also

Figure 5.70. Speech Bubbles

Figure 5.71. A Bridge to Move Marbles

students' communication skills appeared to become more complex through their discussions and elaborate explanations of what was working and what was not.

Barriers I faced in integrating STEM and literacy were actually minimal and did not interfere with student learning. It took some adjusting to balance the district literacy curriculum with the interactive writing and STEM writing. The student interest in mastering writing in STEM investigations took children's development far beyond Common Core mandates. Other barriers included a bit of frustration that I could not observe children's work in the STEM center as often as I would have liked to, as I was attending to small-group reading time. Clean up time can sometimes be a challenge, as the children want to keep working. And one warning I have for other teachers is the importance of including a rug for children to build on. The sound of blocks collapsing on a hard surface floor is loud.

There were significant benefits to integrating STEM and literacy. My kindergartners were engaged and on task in the STEM center. They were

Figure 5.72. A Trap for Marbles

never distracted as they worked. I found my kindergartners independently using new vocabulary such as *steep, motion, base, stable, sphere, rotate*—all learned through the work of Ramps and Pathways. When

problems arose, they were motivated and eager to solve them. They *always* picked the STEM center when it was a choice, and they wanted to share what they were learning every day.

Moving forward in my continuous development as a teacher, I will be able to help increase my students' motivation levels surrounding literacy and science learning with hands-on activities that deepen their understanding of both content areas. There was high interest in cocreating class books and in engaging in interactive writing. The collaborative nature of the STEM center led to more opportunities to develop skills in listening and speaking as the children shared ideas and findings and created plans. My hopes are to continue to find ways to integrate instruction to create meaningful connections and try to help reduce the shortage in STEM-related work fields by exposing students to science learning early on in their education. I can easily say that integrative instruction now has a place among my core values of teaching. After viewing the success of this action research, I want to continue to give my students access to rich learning environments that produce high levels of engagement.

This action research sparked a passion in me to provide more STEM opportunities. By integrating science inquiry and literacy instruction, educators can begin to bring more awareness to STEM careers by engaging in science and engineering phenomena and behaviors that have been lacking in schools.

CHAPTER 6

Family and Community Engagement With Ramps and Pathways

It is only when teachers make concerted and sustained efforts to learn about children's experiential knowledge and families' funds of knowledge that they can conceive new ways of engaging and partnering with families and of teaching that is relevant to children's daily lives. (McWayne et al., 2020)

Promoting family learning around science represents an important opportunity to reinforce science learning during out-of-school time. (Tuttle et al., 2017)

Just as in Chapter 2, where teachers were urged to forge partnerships with administrators, in this chapter we explore ways for early childhood educators to create productive relationships with the families who entrust their preschool through 2nd-grade classroom children to their care. Children are best served when all the adults who share them work together to provide environments that embrace inquiry and nurture STEM learning. In this chapter we refer to families rather than parents, acknowledging that a variety of adults and even older siblings might be more available than parents to serve as supports for out-of-school learning.

THE VALUE OF PARTNERING WITH FAMILIES

A family's participation in a child's academics enhances the child's success in school (Callanan et al., 1995; Crowley et al., 2001). Many decades of research on and implementation of family literacy programs, such as supporting parents to do shared reading with preschoolers in their home, have shown how children's literacy development can be improved (Fikrat-Wevers et al., 2021). Equivalent programs for engaging families in STEM learning are not as long established and tend to be aimed at middle-level grades, preadolescents and older,

rather than early childhood education. Sammet and Kekelis (2016) featured such programs in a white paper about engaging girls in STEM. Science success in school is related to the mentor role that parents exhibit; children who have high science success levels at their schools have relatively higher averages of science process skills (Es et al., 2019). However, parents who are not STEM professionals could well use support in being mentors. Having home conversations about STEM experiences like Ramps and Pathways deepens children's interest in science (Falk & Dierking, 2010; Ghate, 2016; Ho, 2010; Tenenbaum & Callanan, 2008; Tuttle et al., 2017; Vedder-Weiss & Fortus, 2013; Yanowitz & Hahs-Vaughn, 2016).

When teachers view families as their partners in education and strive to develop relationships built on trust and partnership, the adults work together to enhance the children's learning in Ramps and Pathways experiences at school and at home. By establishing a relationship that is grounded in mutual goals, children and parents may take more risks in their learning endeavors, such as with Ramps and Pathways. As Gonzalez-Mena (2017) explained,

In the case of educational programs, that means that parent involvement isn't something the teacher does in addition to the program for children, but that the program includes the family as an integral, inseparable part of the child's education and socialization. (p. 7)

Recent projects (Kekelis & Sammet, 2019; McWayne et al., 2020; Tuttle et al., 2017) have given us guidelines for moving from the typical school-dominated model for engaging families to more equal partnerships, where teachers share the driver's seat with families. Doing so helps educators get to know the families so they have the information needed to situate the curriculum to be culturally responsive and to meet individual child learning needs. Kekelis and Sammet's (2019) white paper, *Changing the Game in STEM With Family Engagement,* resulted from a review of the literature, interviews with leaders in family engagement, and observations of STEM programs for families. The authors (Kekelis & Sammet, 2019) found the following practices to hold promise for engaging families in STEM support for their children:

1. Listen, learn, and build relationships with families.
2. Empower parents with research and resources.
3. Prioritize access and inclusion.
4. Provide professional development for impactful family engagement.
5. Evaluate impact. (p. 9)

We will use these practices to organize this chapter, referring to other recent projects as well, and making direct applications to learning in the Ramps and Pathways context. Many times educators' contact with families can feel forced or foreign to them. Too often educators think only about family involvement in terms of volunteering in the classroom during school hours or fund-raising. Going beyond the typical family–school relationship to become true equal partners requires thinking of relationally situated and culturally situated engagement efforts as we plan activities with and for our families (Li et al., 2021).

LISTEN, LEARN, AND BUILD RELATIONSHIPS WITH FAMILIES

Educators build relationships with their children by getting to know their interests and abilities. In the same manner, educators can build relationships with the adults in their children's families and partner with them to provide a meaningful year of learning together. While many adults feel comfortable reading books to their children, STEM may not be a domain in which they are comfortable. Just as early childhood educators often feel intimidated by their lack of background in STEM and how to teach it, so do parents and other family caregivers. Even family members who are themselves STEM professionals, for instance, engineers, may be at a loss about how to engage their young children in STEM in age-appropriate ways. Whatever has been working for an educator engaged in professional learning for early childhood STEM can also work for children's family members. As an educator begins to think about building relationships with children and families regarding Ramps and Pathways, a good place to start is suggesting to families some activities that they are comfortable with and confident in doing with their child. Those ideas are most fruitful when they are informed by what the educator has learned about the uses of ramps and pathways in children's everyday lives. For example, some families have a ramp entrance to their homes, or a driveway that serves as a ramp on a hill or to a below-grade garage. Families may have a swing set in their yard with a sliding board, or they may spend time in a favorite neighborhood or community park that has a slide. They may even visit a water park with a variety of slides. Perhaps there are curb cuts on sidewalks the family uses frequently. Beyond just ramps, what are the textures of pathways the families use regularly, such as smooth or broken sidewalks, or trails on dirt, grass, gravel, or asphalt? Families can also visit community centers and museums that can offer more complex equipment than is available at home (see Figure 6.1). This also allows children to take the lead in explaining to their families how to investigate by demonstrating what they have learned in their classroom experiences.

A great beginning to showing respect for family culture is to have the families teach the teacher about who they are, what they value, and what their everyday lives are like. McWayne et al. (2020) described three ways teachers can learn about families:

- Listening to, talking with, and observing children, which give teachers important information about children's out of school lives. . . .

Figure 6.1. Investigating Ramps at a Community Science Center

- Indirectly learning what families know and do, such as during neighborhood walks. . . .
- Directly learning what families know and do . . . through joint activities . . . as equal partners; through family–teacher discussion groups, as a way to engage in conversations . . . ; and through observations during home visits. (p. 23)

Examples of how to apply each of these to Ramps and Pathways follow.

School to Home and Back to School

Without leaving the classroom, educators can hold a group meeting with children to generate a chart about what they already know about ramps and pathways in their everyday lives. Cocreating this chart is a strong start to integrating literacy with science. By asking questions about where they have ramps around their neighborhood, educators can attend to the vocabulary the children use to describe where they see different types of structures. A child on a farm may use a ramp to load their equipment onto a trailer, while a child in an apartment may use a ramp to walk to their front door. A child who may notice a ramp at the local park and a child with a skate park nearby bring different experiences with ramps.

An example of children investigating a ramp structure in their neighborhood is shown in Figure 6.2. The children compared the different textures on the two slides as they examined this ramp a bit more closely during their play at the park. To share what was documented on the chart with the family, a school-to-home form could be sent with each child that day, perhaps with a drawing the child had done in school depicting where they have seen ramps or different pathways in their neighborhoods (see Figure 6.3). To turn it into a two-way communication, that is, a school-to-home-to-school form, the educator could suggest that someone in the family ask the child to use everyday materials to create a ramp. In the example in Figure 6.4, a child in a primary grade used a book and a chair to create a ramp for their monster truck at home.

What kind of a return rate, from home back to school, can an early childhood educator expect? In

Figure 6.2. Comparing Textures

Figure 6.3. School-to-Home Activity: Drawing Pathways Back Home

Figure 6.4. School-to-Home-to-School Activity: Drawing of a Construction Made at Home

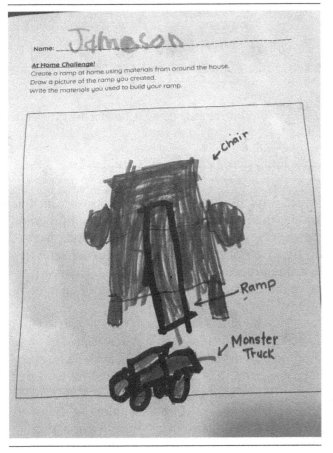

the example that McWayne et al. (2020) gave of an information sheet sent home for a water movement unit, the teacher "received three sheets back (two in English, one in Spanish). She used this information to begin the unit of study, starting with the class's morning meeting" (p. 23). Whatever returns busy families can make will be useful input, and over time, more or at least different families may be able to engage. Providing families with clear directions and developmentally appropriate expectations is key. It is also a good idea to provide to families who have younger children some options to complete the task, while always remembering its purpose: to provide communication between home and school. Some possible options could be that parents can email, text, comment on social media communication (such as Seesaw, or ClassDojo), or help the child complete the expected task. Sometimes, after a long day of learning, asking a child to sit and do more seat work can be overwhelming for parents and children. Such a demand can be met with exhaustion and frustration on both ends, and then nobody wins.

In the meantime, a form of regular communication can be established as families are invited to respond as they are able. Teachers who have gotten to know the families of the children in their classroom can use available media to reassure them that play-based learning is real learning. Preschool teacher Jessica Sass described one way of keeping families informed:

> We utilize an online photo and video sharing platform that allows parents to see what we are doing within centers each day. Many times people see this as just play, but when I am able to send a video along with a caption, it gives parents the opportunity to see just what we are doing when we are playing, that it's not just play but serious work! It is nice to be able to show parents the rich topic that is Ramps and Pathways.

Become Familiar With Families' Landscapes

One way of indirectly learning what is available to families in their surroundings might be for a teacher

Figure 6.5. Examining a Grass Pathway in the Community

Figure 6.6. Examining a Paved Pathway in the Community

different? What changed? Is it harder to ride your bike?

Partnering to Hold a Community Event

Direct ways of learning from families can include joining them in a community-sponsored program, such as one offered by a local company that focuses on making places more accessible for wheelchairs. Instead of meeting on teacher turf at school, teachers and families would be on equal footing in community spaces, conversing as peers.

McClain and Zimmerman (2019) carried out research in library settings, where families were supported to make connections between a local science issue and their life experiences. This provided opportunities for individual and group knowledge growth, contextualized understanding of the issue, and mutually supported science sense-making between parents and children. "When families learn as they participate within a science-rich learning

to drive through one or more neighborhoods of the school, and perhaps even take photographs of different structures, ramps, and pathways to use as prompts in class discussions and then to share with families to continue the conversations at home. For example, an educator could share about some of the pathways children could take on their bicycles and have them compare and contrast the different surfaces (see Figures 6.5 and 6.6). The educator could challenge the children to examine the different surfaces on which they walk or ride their bikes or scooters when they are at home. How does it feel

Figure 6.7. Using a Ramp to Move Food to a Bear

environment, we envision parents and children bringing their shared knowledge and experiences together to engage in informed discussions with each other and with scientists" (McClain & Zimmerman, 2019, p. 156). Educators can also challenge their families to look for ramps around their community in expected and unexpected places. Figure 6.7 demonstrates one a young learner found in an unexpected place: a ramp to feed a bear at a zoo.

Making Home Visits

While home visits from time to time are sponsored by elementary schools for kindergarten and primary grade teachers (Meyer et al., 2011), educators of children birth to age 5 are most familiar with meeting families on their own terms, at places of their choice, if not in the home. In the Readiness through Integrative Science and Engineering (RISE) project, teachers on home visits found that they could "take

notice of familiar objects and activities that might be relevant for planning classroom STE experiences" (McWayne et al., 2020, p. 23). In anticipation of a Ramps and Pathways project, the home visitor could casually observe such things as curb cuts on sidewalks near the home, ramp entrances to homes in the surrounding area if not the child's own home, or sliding boards in outdoor play areas. Home visitors could break down hierarchical barriers by sharing their own journeys, how they too were not confident about STEM. And they can invite the families to learn along with the children and the educators as they all explore ramps and pathways together, not needing professional expertise and not needing all the answers in advance.

EMPOWER PARENTS WITH RESEARCH AND RESOURCES

Empowering parents with research and resources may be the easiest of the promising family engagement practices around Ramps and Pathways for educators to implement after their own learning about this area of beginning physics. All the inquiry processes and activities in this book are research-based and grounded in practice. With adaptations as needed to fit the characteristics of families, discovered while building relationships with them, the same STEM ideas and approaches that an early childhood educator has been learning can be shared with the adults and older siblings in the children's families. More standard school-to-home practices, such as send-home newsletters, in-school conferences, and school-based family nights, can all be effective in letting families know what and how their children are learning about ramps and pathways.

Two-Way Communication

However, even more effective is two-way communication, such as the take-home–send-back activity shown in Figure 6.4. School-to-home-to-school communication not only is a way to get information about children's access to ramps and pathways outside of school; it can also give adults in the family a more concrete sense of what the topic is. "Access to engaging STEM curriculum may be hampered not only by language barriers but also by a lack of connection to children's prior knowledge and cultural and community context" (McWayne et al., 2020, p. 26). Child-friendly language is less likely to intimidate adults whose own understandings of science, of school language, and of child development are not strong. For instance, instead of using a science word like *momentum*, say "harder to start and stop." In turn, educators can use what children and families already do in their day-to-day lives to help inform and deepen learning about ramps and pathways in school by incorporating family-familiar language and objects into the classroom.

Partnering With Libraries to Provide Resources

Libraries can be a rich resource for families and educators alike, providing a more comfortable venue for some families than a school can be, making available on-site (as well as lending) books and even materials for under resourced preschool and school settings. Sometimes families can find it easier to follow models of librarians in story hours than to translate a classroom teacher's written directions for sharing books with children. If the thought of teaching children at home about beginning physics topics like ramps and pathways can be intimidating to families or make them feel that they need to directly teach facts, simply sharing a book from a library story hour and repeating some associated activities can instead be more playful and fun (see Figure 6.8).

Supporting Families in Crafting Questions

McClain and Zimmerman (2019) brought families and scientists together outside of school, in the public community setting of a library, to study how to use questions to engage families in local science issues. Just as the kinds of questions illustrated throughout this book engage children's interests, the researchers found that family-focused question prompts ("take a moment to discuss with your family . . .") were more effective than either scientist-focused questions (asking a question but immediately answering it themselves, like a rhetorical question) or closed-ended questions (picking one response from the audience, responding with an evaluation, like teacher-directed Inquiry–Response–Evaluation, and then moving on). And in the same way that educators and, indeed, scientists too, need support in

Figure 6.8. Father and Sons Share a Book About Ramps and Pathways

learning more effective questioning methods, Tuttle et al. (2017) recommended scaffolding parent–child interactions by giving parents a set of talking tips as a way for them to interact with their children in science activities. Such scaffolding motivates children to continue inquiring about their investigation and promotes parents to engage in science talk and listening with their children. In Figure 6.9, the recommendations from Tuttle et al. (2017) are in the left column (adapted quotations), with examples of applications to Ramps and Pathways in the right column (from the authors of this book).

As educators learn the best ways to build relationships with the families of the children that they share, resources like these questions can be used to support family members in a variety of situations. Some family members will be able to attend a more traditional school-based STEM night or family education event that includes children, or a community-based gathering where educators can provide science

Figure 6.9. Talking Tips From Tuttle et al. (2017) and Ramps and Pathways Examples

Talking Tips for parents to encourage productive science talk in an activity	Ramps and Pathways example while exploring with a ball and a piece of wood (or any flat or slightly curved surface)
1. Re-voicing what the child said	Oh, you said your ball changed direction when going down your ramp.
2. Asking child to restate someone else's reasoning	What was that your sister said about her ramp?
3. Asking child to apply their own reasoning to someone else's reasoning	You said you could make your ball roll down faster than before. Can you show your sister what else she could try so she could do that too?
4. Prompting child for further participation	Can you find a way to make your ball roll slowly?
5. Asking child to explicate their own reasoning	You said that the system you built is too fragile for the big marble. How can you create a system that is strong enough to move a big marble?
6. Using wait time	(That means to not be in a hurry to get an answer, and to watch for an answer that might be in an action rather than spoken.)
7. Encouraging your child to extend what they learn to other situations	What would happen if you used this small ball instead of the larger one?
8. Encouraging your child to observe	Oh look! What is happening there?
9. Encouraging your child to make predictions	What do you think would happen if you changed the incline of your ramp?
10. Encouraging your child to figure out how to solve a problem	How can you get the marble to change directions two times? Three times?

Note: Talking Tips adapted from Tuttle et al. (2017, p. 176). See Tuttle et al. for additional sources that informed their Talking Tips.

Figure 6.10. STEM Family Night

and perseverance in working through challenges" (see Figure 6.10).

At in-person events, the educator can provide a handout of questions to take home, while modeling their use with children and materials. Other families who prefer to learn via writing can be sent examples in a traditional class newsletter, or by email, text, or classroom-based social media. In addition to the examples given in Figure 6.9, all of the suggested questions throughout this book for educators to use with children could also be used by families. The educator could share the questions that are working best in their classroom, with the potential for use at home to reinforce the learning in the classroom.

activities at a booth or table. Educator Lisa Chizek has planned many STEM family nights with great success. She said, "The STEM festivals were a good way to engage families. As they were playing with their children (or just watching), it provided a good opportunity for families to see their children's excitement

PRIORITIZE ACCESS AND INCLUSION

Educators begin their relationship by trying many different ways to connect with families to learn about their children and their lives at home. When educators start with this type of approach it opens doors for communication and creates a space for all children to learn and be successful. Friedman and Mwenelupembe (2020) shared how creating a space for children with Different Experiences, Cultures, Abilities, and Languages (DECAL) allows the educators to fully include everyone in the learning experiences.

Successful educators strive for a space that works for each and every child. The key to making those appropriate adaptations and accommodations is finding out from families what their children's interests, strengths, and challenges are, information that can best be discovered by listening, learning, and building relationships with families. One family shared a photograph of an inclusive park in their neighborhood that accommodated children with mobility challenges on an adaptive slide, which all children could use (see Figure 6.11). Information from families can then be used in planning with universal design for learning in mind, as described in earlier chapters.

Figure 6.11. Adaptive Park and Ramps

While attention to integrating literacy with STEM has been increasing, the potential for integrating social studies with STEM grows as family engagement helps educators to situate the curriculum culturally. When analyzing the structures children create to build their ramps and pathways, children can look at structures of the past, such as structures and pathways from Egyptian, Mayan, Aztec, or Incan cultures (see Figures 6.12 and 6.13). These might serve as quality examples of what people of the past did to build sturdy pathways and structures to withstand the test of time. Perhaps have children peruse books to look for photographs or provide examples printed for children to examine the different pathways or structures different cultures provided.

PROVIDE PROFESSIONAL DEVELOPMENT FOR IMPACTFUL FAMILY ENGAGEMENT

Chapter 2 acknowledged the need to bring administrators along in understanding early STEM in the classroom so they could provide the proper supports; they may also need to be convinced to support more engagement with families. Professional learning for educators and administrators on how to nurture family engagement will enhance STEM learning as well as learning in all domains. Getting Head Start administrators to dedicate to STEM one or more regularly scheduled family program events might be a welcome suggestion. On the other hand, getting a school board to provide time and money to support home visits by kindergarten and primary-grade teachers might take a years-long campaign and possibly a grant funding source.

EVALUATE IMPACT

Creating a fun way to engage families in Ramps and Pathways exploration can provide educators a space to evaluate the impact of their Ramps and Pathways investigations. A STEM night or family education event with children would give educators the opportunity to take anecdotal notes or use a Ramps and Pathways checklist to be recording briefly while circulating as families try out what they are learning (see Tuttle et al., 2017, for a rubric they used when observing parent–child interaction in nonformal

Figure 6.12. Example of an Inca Pathway

STEM activities). If there is a funding source for the professional development or for family engagement, the funder's requirements for outcomes can be built into the assessment and evaluation to be able to report to the funder about family engagement. Based on their preferred communication channels, families can be given an easy way to share what they are seeing at home related to the phenomena of ramps and pathways and how their child is displaying their connections with what they are learning in their educational space.

Best evaluation practice occurs directly after collecting assessment data, deciding what worked or didn't work as a function of the event. Especially important is to judge the value of the connections made with families. The same learning outcomes can be applied to families by using the Ramps and Pathways assessments being used in the classroom for children. Such an evaluation process provides opportunities for educators to change, lift up, or improve Ramps and Pathways experiences and try again, both improving on classroom practices with information from interacting with the families, and improving the next family event.

SUMMARY

Figure 6.13 Example of an Inca Ramp

In this chapter, we shared a multitude of ways to create productive relationships with families while engaging in Ramps and Pathways exploration. As educators evolved in their learning and exploration of ramps themselves, they found they naturally began to take on the role of early childhood STEM ambassadors, bringing Ramps and Pathways to family night events, after-school functions, and even to other public settings, such as county conservation buildings open to families on weekends. Informal institutions are key settings that provide family sensemaking opportunities related to science and other topics (Bell et al., 2009; McClain & Zimmerman, 2019; Zimmerman & McClain, 2016). When families and educators work together to embrace inquiry and nurture STEM learning, everyone wins.

Engineering Habits of Mind in Ramps and Pathways

Term	Katehi et al. (2009) Description of Engineering Habits of Mind	How Engineering Habits of Mind May Look in Young Learners (adapted from Chalufour & Worth, 2004)
Systems Thinking	Systems thinking equips students to recognize essential interconnections in the technological world and to appreciate that systems may have unexpected effects that cannot be predicted from the behavior of individual subsystems.	• Adjusts both ends of a track • After adjusting one component, coordinates positions of other components before testing
Creativity	Creativity is inherent in the engineering design process.	• Generates own design • Flips, rotates, or repurposes materials • Considers different ways of arranging supports, tracks, barriers • Resists premature closure by continuing to add to complexity even after a successful test
Optimism	Optimism reflects a worldview in which possibilities and opportunities can be found in every challenge, and every technology can be improved.	• Does not abandon structure after a failed test • Uses failed tests as opportunities to find solutions • Tries again after multiple failed tests
Collaboration	Engineering is a team sport; collaboration leverages the perspectives, knowledge, and capabilities of team members to address design challenge.	• Asks for help from a peer • Considers suggestions of a peer • Asks to test a peer's system • Uses peer's system as a model • Provides encouragement and/or advice to a peer
Communication	Communication is essential to effective collaboration, to understanding the particular wants and needs of a "customer," and to explaining and justifying the final design solution.	• Shares success of structure with a peer • Explains success of structure with a peer • Asks for help and discusses problem with a peer • Offers advice to a peer • Volunteers to build for another and asks what the peer wants in a design • Writes or draws about system
Ethical Considerations	Ethical considerations draw attention to the impacts of engineering on people and the environment, including possible unintended consequences of a technology, the potential disproportionate advantages or disadvantages for certain groups or individuals, and other issues.	• Coordinates use of space with peers • Coordinates use of materials with peers • Takes responsibility for knockdowns • Considers safety

Progress Monitoring of Young Students' Engineering Habits of Mind

Student:_____ Birth Date: _____
Date Exploration Begun:_____ Completed: _____

Habit of mind	Student growth	Evidence
Systems Thinking	☐ Emerging ☐ Sometimes ☐ Consistently	
Creativity	☐ Emerging ☐ Sometimes ☐ Consistently	
Optimism	☐ Emerging ☐ Sometimes ☐ Consistently	
Collaboration	☐ Emerging ☐ Sometimes ☐ Consistently	
Communication	☐ Emerging ☐ Sometimes ☐ Consistently	
Attention to Ethical Considerations	☐ Emerging ☐ Sometimes ☐ Consistently	

Engineering Behaviors in Ramps and Pathways

NGSS K–2 Engineering Design	Engineering design behaviors in Ramps and Pathways

Asking Questions and Defining Problems
 	
Asking questions and defining problems in K–2 builds on prior experiences and progresses to simple descriptive questions.
 	
• Ask questions based on observations to find more information about the natural and/or designed world. (K-2-ETS1-1)
• Define a simple problem that can be solved through the development of a new or improved object or tool. (K-2-ETS1-1)
	Has ideas what features to include in the ramp structure and poses own design problems.
	
	Locates and gathers materials; uses materials in a variety of ways, resulting in
	
	• Straight pathways
	• Making objects move on single-section ramps of any length
	• Making objects continue to move on a series of tracks on a straight pathway
	• Making objects continue to move on a series of tracks on a straight pathway with target at end
	• Making objects continue to move on a pathway with hills
	• Making objects continue to move on a pathway with a drop
	• Making objects continue to move on a pathway with a jump
	• Changing directions:
	  » Making objects turn a corner
	  » Making objects continue to move on a pathway with angles not requiring a banking system
	  » Making objects continue to move on a pathway with angles requiring a banking system
	  » Making objects reverse direction (switchbacks)
	• More that one moving part to get an object to continue on a pathway with fulcrums
	• Targets:
	  » Making objects move (roll, fall, fly, etc.) into a container
	  » Making objects knock down or crash into a target (blocks, domino, animals, cars, etc.)
	• Begins with materials that support design idea
	• Asks for or locates materials that assist in building design
	• Rotates or reconfigures materials to create design

Developing and Using Models Modeling in K–2 builds on prior experiences and progresses to include using and developing models (i.e., diagram, drawing, physical replica, diorama, dramatization, or storyboard) that represent concrete events or design solutions. • Develop a simple model based on evidence to represent a proposed object or tool. (K-2-ETS1-2)	**Elects to represent their system in a model** • Selects when to draw their system after success • Selects when to draw a plan before building • Uses photographs to explain how the system works • Uses marks on photographs or drawings to indicate motion and direction of an object on a system

(continued)

NGSS K–2 Engineering Design	Engineering design behaviors in Ramps and Pathways
Analyzing and Interpreting Data Analyzing data in K–2 builds on prior experiences and progresses to collecting, recording, and sharing observations. • Analyze data from tests of an object or tool to determine if it works as intended. (K-2-ETS1-3)	**Notices, observes, and analyzes areas of failure** • Pinpoints where a problem occurs • Observes problem area closely to decide what changes need to be made (subtle adjustments or major redesign) **Views failures as an opportunity to problem-solve and perseveres. Does not give up, but engages in problem solving until a solution is found** • Does not give up when it is found the design is not in agreement with laws of physics and perseveres by engaging in redesign **Tests in an iterative fashion to make sure sections or whole system works** • Tests effectiveness of whole system or parts of system several times to determine the design works • Uses tests to make subtle changes in design **Consults others** • Asks others for help in problem solving • Asks others for opinion • Asks others to give them a design challenge **Offers and/or provides assistance to others in their design problems** • Notices a problem in another young student's design and offers assistance or provides a solution • Encourages others • Observes a problem area for another to allow two perspectives on what is happening **Explains design and communicates through oral or written documentation** • Shares experience with whole group • Asks class for additional ideas on problems • Draws or writes explanations of problems • Assists in creating documentation for documentation wall

Progress Monitoring of Young Students' Engineering Behaviors

Student:_____ Birth Date: _____

Date Exploration Begun:_____ Completed: _____

Engineering Behaviors	Student Growth	Evidence
Poses own design problems	☐ Emerging ☐ Sometimes ☐ Consistently	
Locates and gathers materials; uses materials in a variety of ways	☐ Emerging ☐ Sometimes ☐ Consistently	
Elects to represent their system in a model	☐ Emerging ☐ Sometimes ☐ Consistently	
Notices, observes, and analyzes areas of failure	☐ Emerging ☐ Sometimes ☐ Consistently	
Views failures as an opportunity to problem-solve and perseveres	☐ Emerging ☐ Sometimes ☐ Consistently	
Tests in an iterative fashion to make sure sections or whole system works	☐ Emerging ☐ Sometimes ☐ Consistently	
Consults others	☐ Emerging ☐ Sometimes ☐ Consistently	
Offers and/or provides assistance to others in their design problems	☐ Emerging ☐ Sometimes ☐ Consistently	
Explains design and communicates through oral or written documentation	☐ Emerging ☐ Sometimes ☐ Consistently	

Science Concepts Outcome Chart

Science Concepts	Young Student Behaviors
Forces: A force is a "push" or "pull" acting on an object. A force requires two objects to interact.	• Pushes an object to get it to move • Blows on an object to get it to move • Creates an incline to get the object to move • Releases an object from a height to get it to move Works with slope to: • Get a marble to move or stay • Move objects farther • Move objects faster and slower
Notices properties of objects and how the properties affect movement	Notices: • Symmetrical objects move more predictably than asymmetrical objects • Objects with flat sides slide • Objects with rough sides tumble • Cone-shaped objects move in a circle • Solids are heavier than hollow • Some objects tend to bounce Categorizes objects according to: • How they move on an incline • How far they move • According to their speed or how fast they move • According to difficulty in changing their direction
Notices and describes different types of movement	In explanations and descriptions, uses language such as: • Moves quickly or fast • Moves slowly • Moves straight • Moves in a curved path • Moves in a wobbly fashion • Speeds up • Slows down • Rolls, tumbles, wobbles, rotates, spins, floats, . . .
Grappling with Newton's 1st Law: An object at rest remains at rest and an object in motion will continue to move steadily in a straight line unless acted upon by an outside force. An object has "inertia": a tendency to resist changes in its state of motion or nonmotion. The more "inertia" an object has, the more resistance.	• Puts an object on an incline to get it to move • Puts a block at the end of a track to get the marble to turn a corner • Notices heavier objects are harder to change direction or stop • Slows a marble by adding a hill or decreasing an incline

(continued)

Science Concepts	Young Student Behaviors
Grappling with Newton's 2nd Law: An unbalanced or net force acting on an object will result in the object to speed up, slow down, and/or change direction.	• Speeds up a marble by starting with a higher incline or adding a steep incline to the system • Places a block at the end of a track to change the direction of a marble
Grappling with Newton's 3rd Law: For every action, there is an equal but opposite reaction.	• Builds a system where they are having the object strike another object such as a block, or another marble, or a lineup of marbles

Progress Monitoring of Young Students' Understanding of Science Concepts

Student:_____ Birth Date: _____
Date Exploration Begun:_____ Completed: _____

Science Concepts	Student Growth	Evidence

Forces: A force is a "push" or "pull" acting on an object.
 	
A force requires two objects to interact.
 	
  • A student pushing on a marble with her finger.
  • A marble dropped from some height.
  • A marble rolling down a ramp.
	☐ Emerging
	☐ Sometimes
	☐ Consistently	

Notices properties of objects and how the properties affect movement	☐ Emerging ☐ Sometimes ☐ Consistently	
Notices and describes different types of movement	☐ Emerging ☐ Sometimes ☐ Consistently	
Grappling with Newton's 1st Law: An object at rest remains at rest and an object in motion will continue to move steadily in a straight line unless acted upon by an outside force. An object has "inertia": a tendency to resist changes in its state of motion or nonmotion. The more "inertia" an object has, the more resistance.	☐ Emerging ☐ Sometimes ☐ Consistently	
Grappling with Newton's 2nd Law: An unbalanced or net force acting on an object will result in the object to speed up, slow down, and/or change direction.	☐ Emerging ☐ Sometimes ☐ Consistently	
Grappling with Newton's 3rd Law: For every action, there is an equal but opposite reaction.	☐ Emerging ☐ Sometimes ☐ Consistently	

References

Abel, M. B., Talan, T. N., Pollitt, K. D., & Bronfreund, L. (2016). *National principals' survey on early childhood instructional leadership.* McCormick Center for Early Childhood Leadership Publications. Paper 1. http://digitalcommons.nl.edu/mccormickcenter-pubs/1

Akerson, V., & Donnelly, L. A. (2010). Teaching nature of science to K–2 students: What understandings can they attain? *International Journal of Science Education, 32*(1), 97–124.

Andersson, K., & Gullberg, A. (2014). What is science in preschool and what do teachers have to know to empower children? *Cultural Studies of Science Education, 9*(2), 275–296. https://doi.org/10.1007/s11422-012-9439-6

Au, W. (2011). Teaching under the new Taylorism: High-stakes testing and the standardization of the 21st century curriculum. *Journal of Curriculum Studies, 43*(1), 25–45.

Banilower, E. R., Smith, P. S., Malzahn, K. A., Plumley, C. L., Gordon, E. M., & Hayes, M. L. (2018). *Report of the 2018 NSSME+.* Horizon Research.

Beck, I. L., & McKeown, M. G. (2007). Increasing young low-income children's vocabulary repertoires through rich and focused instruction. *The Elementary School Journal, 107*(3), 251–271.

Bell, P., Lewenstein, B., Shouse, A. W., & Feder, M. A. (2009). *Learning science in informal environments: People, places, and pursuits.* National Academies Press.

Berliner, D. (2006). Our impoverished view of educational reform. *Teachers College Record, 108,* 949–995.

Bilyeu, T. (2020, June 16). *Legendary psychologist Adam Grant on why leadership is all about humility, integrity, and adaptation* [Video]. YouTube. https://www.youtube.com/watch?v=31vFw4pipTA

Blanton, L. P., & Pugach, M. C. (2011). Using a classification system to probe the meaning of dual licensure in general and special education. *Teacher Education and Special Education, 34,* 219–234.

Bornfreund, L. (2012). Preparing teachers for the early grades. *Educational Leadership, 69*(8), 36–40.

Brophy, S., & Evangelou, D. (2007, June). Precursors to engineering thinking (PET). In *2007 Annual Conference & Exposition* (pp. 12.1169.1–12.1169.11).

Brown, K. C., Squires, J., Connors-Tadros, L., & Horowitz, M. (2014). What do we know about principal preparation, licensure requirements, and professional development for school leaders. *CEELO Policy Report.*

Buchanan, T. K., Burts, D. C., Bidner, J., White, V. F., & Charlesworth, R. (1998). Predictors of the developmental appropriateness of the beliefs and practices of first, second, and third grade teachers. *Early Childhood Research Quarterly, 13*(3), 459–483.

Bybee, R. W. (2013). *The case for STEM education: Challenges and opportunities.* NSTA Press.

Callanan, M. A., Shrager, J., & Moore, J. L. (1995). Parent–child collaborative explanations: Methods of identification and analysis. *The Journal of the Learning Sciences, 4*(1), 105–129.

Cambourne, B. (1988). Toward an educationally relevant theory of literacy learning: Twenty years of inquiry. *The Reading Teacher, 49*(3), 182.

Campbell, C., Speldewinde, C., Howitt, C., & MacDonald, A. (2018). STEM practice in the early years. *Creative Education, 9*(1), 11.

Casey, B. M., Andrews, N., Schindler, H., Kersh, J. E., Samper, A., & Copley, J. (2008). The development of spatial skills through interventions involving block building activities. *Cognition and Instruction, 26*(3), 269–309.

Center for Applied Special Technology. (2011). *Universal Design for Learning guidelines* (version 2.0).

Chalufour, I., & Worth, K. (2004). *Building structures with young children—Trainer's guide.* Redleaf Press.

Copple, C., & Bredekamp, S. (2009). *Developmentally appropriate practice in early childhood programs serving children from birth to age eight.* National Association for the Education of Young Children.

Counsell, S., Escalada, L., Geiken, R., Sander, M., Uhlenberg, J., Van Meeteren, B., Yoshizawa, S., & Zan, B.

(2016). *STEM learning with young children: Inquiry teaching with Ramps and Pathways.* Teachers College Press.

Crowley, K., Callanan, M. A., Tenenbaum, H. R., & Allen, E. (2001). Parents explain more often to boys than to girls during shared scientific thinking. *Psychological Science, 12*(3), 258–261.

Curwin, R. (2012). How to beat "teacher proof" programs. *Edutopia.* https://www.edutopia.org/blog/beating-teacher-proof-programs-richard-curwin

Developmental Studies Center. (1996). *Ways we want our class to be: Class meetings that build commitment to kindness and learning.* Author.

DeVries, R., & Sales, C. (2011). *Ramps & Pathways: A constructivist approach to physics with young children.* National Association for the Education of Young Children.

DeVries, R., & Zan, B. (2012). *Moral classrooms, moral children: Creating a constructivist classroom in early education.* Teachers College Press.

Dewey, J. (2001). *Democracy and education.* The Pennsylvania State University (Original work published 1916).

Dewey, J. (2009). Education as engineering. *Journal of Curriculum Studies, 41*(1), 1–5. https://www.doi.org/10.1080/00220270802169345 (Original work published 1922).

Diamond, A. (2016). Why improving and assessing executive functions early in life is critical. In J. A. Griffin, P. McCardle, & L. S. Freund (Eds.), *Executive function in preschool-age children: Integrating measurement, neurodevelopment, and translational research* (pp. 11–43). American Psychological Association. https://doi.org/10.1037/14797-002

Diamond, A., Barnett, S., Thomas, J., & Munro, S. (2007). Executive function can be improved in preschoolers by regular classroom teachers. *Science, 318*(5855), 1387–1388.

Diamond, A., & Lee, K. (2011). Interventions shown to aid executive function development in children 4 to 12 years old. *Science, 333*(6045), 959–964.

Diamond, A., & Ling, D. S. (2020). Review of the evidence on, and fundamental questions about, efforts to improve executive functions, including working memory. In J. M. Novick, M. F. Bunting, M. R. Dougherty, & R. W. Engle (Eds.), *Cognitive and working memory training: Perspectives from psychology, neuroscience, and human development* (pp. 143–431). Oxford University Press.

Dodge, D. T., Colker, L. J., Heroman, C., Berke, K., & Baker, H. (2016). *The creative curriculum for preschool: Vol. 2. Interest areas.* Teaching Strategies.

Donegan-Ritter, M., & Fitzgerald, L. M. (2017). Inquiry in inclusive preschools with tomorrow's teachers. *Science and Children, 55*(2), 76–80.

Durkin, K., Lipsey, M. W., Farran, D. C., & Wiesen, S. (2022). Effects of a statewide pre-kindergarten program on children's achievement and behavior through sixth grade. *Developmental Psychology, 58*(3), 470–484. https://doi.org/10.1037/dev0001301

Engel, S. (2011). Children's need to know: Curiosity in schools. *Harvard Educational Review, 81*(4), 625–645.

Engel, S., & Randall, K. (2009). How teachers respond to children's inquiry. *American Educational Research Journal, 46*(1), 183–202.

Es, H., Bozkurt Altan, E., & Gümüs, I. (2019). Examination of students' and their parents' experiences of out-of-school science experimentation within the context of parents' roles. *Acta Didactica Napocensia, 12*(1), 201–211.

Evanshen P., & Faulk, J. (2019). *Room to learn: Elementary classrooms designed for interactive explorations.* Gryphon House.

Falk, J. H., & Dierking, L. D. (2010). School is not where most Americans learn most of their science. *American Scientist, 98*(6), 486.

Farran, D. C. (2022, February 12). Early developmental competencies: Or why pre-K does not have lasting effects. *Defending the Early Years blog.* https://dey.org/early-developmental-competencies-or-why-pre-k-does-not-have-lasting-effects/

Feynman, R. P. (1969). What is science? *The Physics Teacher, 7*(6), 313–320.

Fikrat-Wevers, S., van Steensel, R., & Arends, L. (2021). Effects of family literacy programs on the emergent literacy skills of children from low-SES families: A meta-analysis. *Review of Educational Research, 91*(4), 577–613. https://doi.org/10.3102/0034654321998075

File, N., & Gullo, D. F. (2002). A comparison of early childhood and elementary education students' beliefs about primary classroom teaching practices. *Early Childhood Research Quarterly, 17*(1), 126–137.

Fitzgerald, L. M., & Dengler, R. (2010, May 4). *Use of productive questions by preservice teachers in early childhood classrooms.* Paper presented at annual meeting of the American Educational Research Association, Denver, CO.

Friedman, S., & Mwenelupembe, A. (2020). *Each & every child: Teaching preschool with an equity lens.* National Association for the Education of Young Children.

Froebel, F. (1974). *The education of man* (Rev. ed.). Augustus M. Kelley (Original work published 1887).

Gandini, L. (2011). Play and the hundred languages of children. *American Journal of Play, 4*(1), 1–18.

Gartrell, D. (2004). *The power of guidance: Teaching social–emotional skills in early childhood classrooms.* National Association for the Education of Young Children.

Geary, D. C., Hamson, C. O., & Hoard, M. K. (2000). Numerical and arithmetical cognition: A longitudinal study of process and concept deficits in children with learning disability. *Journal of Experimental Child Psychology, 77*(3), 236–263.

Geiken, R., Van Meeteren, B. D., & Kato, T. (2009). Teaching strategies: Putting the cart before the horse: The role of a socio-moral atmosphere in an inquiry-based curriculum. *Childhood Education, 85*(4), 260–263.

Ghate, D. (2016). From programs to systems: Deploying implementation science and practice for sustained real world effectiveness in services for children and families. *Journal of Clinical Child & Adolescent Psychology, 45*(6), 812–826. https://doi.org/10.1080/15374416 .2015.1077449

Gilliam, W. S. (2005). *Prekindergarteners left behind: Expulsion rates in state prekindergarten systems*. Foundation for Child Development.

Giordano, K., Interra, V. L., Stillo, G. C., Mims, A. T., & Block-Lerner, J. (2020). Associations between child and administrator race and suspension and expulsion rates in community childcare programs. *Early Childhood Education Journal, 39*(1), 125–133. https:// doi.org/10.1007/s10643-020-01049-1

Goddard, R., Goddard, Y., Kim, E. S., & Miller, R. (2015). A theoretical and empirical analysis of the roles of instructional leadership, teacher collaboration, and collective efficacy beliefs in support of student learning. *American Journal of Education, 121*(4), 501–530.

Gonzalez-Mena, J. (2017). *Child, family, and community: Family-centered early care and education*. Merrill Pearson.

Gopnik, A. (2012). Scientific thinking in young children: Theoretical advances, empirical research, and policy implications. *Science, 337*(6102), 1623–1627.

Greenfield, D. B., Jirout, J., Dominguez, X., Greenberg, A., Maier, M., & Fuccillo, J. (2009). Science in the preschool classroom: A programmatic research agenda to improve science readiness. *Early Education and Development, 20*(2), 238–264. https://doi.org/10.1080 /10409280802595441

Hackmann, H., & Engel, S. (2002). *Curiosity in context: The classroom environment examined*. Unpublished honors thesis, Williams College.

Harris, P. L. (2012). *Trusting what you're told: How children learn from others*. Harvard University Press.

Hawkins, D. (1965). Messing about in science. *Science and Children, 2*(5), 5–9.

Hawkins, D. (1974). *The informed vision and other essays*. Agathon Press.

Hefty, L. J. (2015). STEM gives meaning to mathematics. *Teaching Children Mathematics, 21*(7), 422–429.

Henderson, B., & Moore, S. G. (1980). Children's responses to objects differing in novelty in relation to level of curiosity and adult behavior. *Child Development, 51*(2), 457–465.

Heroman, C., Burts, D. C., Berke, K., & Bickart, T. S. (2010). *The creative curriculum for preschool: Vol. 5. Objectives for development & learning: Birth through kindergarten*. Teaching Strategies.

HighScope Educational Research Foundation. (2015). *Infant-toddler COR Advantage*. HighScope.

Hilton, E. C., Smith, S. F., Nagel, R. L., Linsey, J. S., & Talley, K. G. (2018, August). University makerspaces: More than just toys. In *International Design Engineering Technical Conferences and Computers and Information in Engineering Conference* (Vol. 51784, p. V003T04A010). American Society of Mechanical Engineers.

Ho, E. S. C. (2010). Family influences on science learning among Hong Kong adolescents: What we learned from PISA. *International Journal of Mathematics Education, 8*, 409–428.

Hong, S. Y., & Diamond, K. E. (2012). Two approaches to teaching young children science concepts, vocabulary, and scientific problem-solving skills. *Early Childhood Research Quarterly, 27*(2), 295–305.

Hooper, A., & Schweiker, C. (2020). Prevalence and predictors of expulsion in home-based child care settings. *Infant Mental Health Journal, 41*(3), 411–425. https://doi.org/10.1002/imhj.21845

Iowa Department of Education. (2018). *Iowa early learning standards* (3rd ed.). https://educateiowa.gov/docu ments/early-childhood-standards/2019/01/iowa -early-learning-standards-3rd-edition

Johnson, S. (2010). *Where good ideas come from*. Penguin.

Kamii, C., & DeVries, R. (1993). *Physical knowledge in preschool education: Implications of Piaget's theory*. Teachers College Press.

Katehi, L., Pearson, G., & Feder, M. (Eds.). (2009). *Engineering in K–12 education: Understanding the status and improving the prospects*. National Academies Press. http://www.nap.edu/catalog/12635.html

Katz, L. (2015). Lively minds: Distinctions between academic versus intellectual goals for young children. *Clearinghouse on Early Education and Parenting*. https:// dey.org/lively-minds-distinctions-between-academic -versus-intellectual-goals-for-young-children/

Kekelis, L., & Sammet, K. (2019). *Changing the game in STEM with family engagement*. https://stemnext.org /wp-content/uploads/2019/10/Changing-the-Game -in-STEM-with-Family-Engagement_Final_.pdf

Kersh, J. E., Casey, B. M., & Young, J. M. (2008). Research on spatial skills and block building in girls and boys. In *Contemporary Perspectives on Mathematics in Early Childhood Education* (pp. 233–251). Information Age Publishing.

Krajcik, J., & Czerniak, C. M. (2014). *Teaching science to children: A project-based science approach*. Routledge.

Krechevsky, M., Mardell, B., Rivard, M., & Wilson, D. (2013). *Visible learners: Promoting Reggio-inspired approaches in all schools*. John Wiley & Sons.

Li, L.-W., Ochoa, W., McWayne, C. M., Priebe Rocha, L., & Hyun, S. (2021). "Talk to me": Parent–teacher background similarity, communication quality, and barriers to school-based engagement among ethnoculturally diverse Head Start families. *Cultural Diversity and Ethnic Minority Psychology*. Advance online publication. https://doi.org/10.1037/cdp0000497

Luke, A. (2004). Teaching after the market: From commodity to cosmopolitan. *Teachers College Record, 106*(7), 1422–1443.

Margot, K. C., & Kettler, T. (2019). Teachers' perception of STEM integration and education: A systematic literature review. *International Journal of STEM Education, 6*(2). https://doi-org.proxy.lib.uni.edu/10.1186/s40594-018-0151-2

Martens, M. L. (1999). Productive questions: Tools for supporting constructivist learning. *Science and Children, 53*, 24–27.

Mattera, S., Rojas, N. M., Morris, P. A., & Bierman, K. (2021). Promoting EF with preschool interventions: Lessons learned from 15 years of conducting large-scale studies. *Frontiers in Psychology, 12*, 640–702.

McClain, L. R., & Zimmerman, H. T. (2019). Family connections to local science issues: How scientists use questions to engage families in personally relevant learning during science-themed workshops. *International Journal of Science Education, Part B, 9*(2), 154–170. https://doi.org/10.1080/21548455.2019.1584419

McClure, E. R., Guernsey, L., Clements, D. H., Bales, S. N., Nichols, J., Kendall-Taylor, N., & Levine, M. H. (2017). *STEM starts early: Grounding science, technology, engineering, and math education in early childhood*. Joan Ganz Cooney Center at Sesame Workshop (ED574402). ERIC. https://eric.ed.gov/?id=ED574402

McHugh, K., Abramowitz, K., Liu-Constant, Y., & Gardner, H. (2022). *Project Zero—The first fifty-five years*. https://pz.harvard.edu/resources/project-zero-the-first-fifty-five-years

McMurrer, J., & Kober, N. (2007). *Choices, changes and challenges: Curriculum and instruction in the NCLB era*. Center on Educational Policy.

McWayne, C. M., Mistry, J., Hyun, S., Diez, V., Parker, C., Zan, B., Greenfield, D., & Brenneman, K. (2020). Incorporating knowledge from children's homes and communities: A home-to-school approach for teaching STEM in preschool. *Young Children, 75*(5), 20–26. https://www.naeyc.org/resources/pubs/yc/dec2020/incorporating-knowledge-communities

Merriam-Webster. (n.d.). Inquiry. In *Merriam-Webster.com dictionary*. https://merriam-webster.com/dictionary/inquiry

Metz, K. E. (2008). Narrowing the gulf between the practices of science and the elementary school science classroom. *The Elementary School Journal, 109*(2), 138–161.

Meyer, J. A., Mann, M. B., & Becker, J. (2011). A five-year follow-up: Teachers' perceptions of the benefits of home visits for early elementary children. *Early Childhood Education Journal, 39*, 191–196. https://doi.org/10.1007/s10643-011-0461-1

Mitchell, S., Foulger, T. S., Wetzel, K., & Rathkey, C. (2009). The negotiated project approach: Project-based learning without leaving the standards behind. *Early Childhood Education Journal, 36*(4), 339.

Miyake, A., Friedman, N. P., Emerson, M. J., Witzki, A. H., Howerter, A., & Wager, T. D. (2000). The unity and diversity of executive functions and their contributions to complex "frontal lobe" tasks: A latent variable analysis. *Cognitive Psychology, 41*(1), 49–100.

Mooney, C. G. (2013). *Theories of childhood: An introduction to Dewey, Montessori, Erikson, Piaget and Vygotsky*. Redleaf Press.

Morrow, L. M. (2012). *Literacy development in the early years: Helping children read and write*. Rutgers.

Morrow, L. M., & Gambrell, L. B. (Eds.). (2019). *Best practices in literacy instruction* (6th ed.). Guilford Press.

National Center for Quality Teaching and Learning. (2022). *Preschool curriculum consumer report*. U.S. Department of Health and Human Services, Administration for Children and Families, Office of Head Start. https://eclkc.ohs.acf.hhs.gov/curriculum/consumer-report/preschool/curricula

National Research Council. (2004). *On evaluating curricular effectiveness: Judging the quality of K–12 mathematics evaluations*. National Academies Press.

National Research Council. (2007). *Taking science to school: Learning and teaching science in grades K–8*. National Academies Press.

National Research Council. (2009). *Engineering in K–12 education: Understanding the status and improving the prospects*. National Academies Press.

National Research Council. (2012). *A framework for K–12 science education: Practices, crosscutting concepts, and core ideas*. National Academies Press.

National Research Council. (2015). *Guide to implementing the Next Generation Science Standards*. Committee on Guidance on Implementing the Next Generation Science Standards, Board on Science Education, Division of Behavioral and Social Sciences and Education, The National Academies Press.

National Science Teachers Association. (2014). *NSTA position statement: Early childhood science education.* https://www.naeyc.org/sites/default/files/globally-shared/downloads/PDFs/resources/position-statements/Early%20Childhood%20FINAL%20FINAL%201-30-14%20%281%29%20%281%29.pdf

Navy, S. L., Kaya, F., Boone, B., Brewster, C., Calvelage, K., Ferdous, T., Hood, E., Sass, L., & Zimmerman, M. (2020). "Beyond an acronym, STEM is . . .": Perceptions of STEM. *School Science and Mathematics, 121*(1), 36–45.

Neuman, S. B., & Wright, T. S. (2014). The magic of words: Teaching vocabulary in the early childhood classroom. *American Educator, 38*(2), 4–13.

NGSS Lead States. (2013a). *Next Generation Science Standards: For states, by states.* National Academies Press.

NGSS Lead States. (2013b). *Next Generation Science Standards: For states, by states. Appendix F—Science and engineering practices in the NGSS.* National Academies Press. https://www.nextgenscience.org/sites/default/files/resource/files/Appendix%20F%20%20Science%20and%20Engineering%20Practices%20in%20the%20NGSS%20-%20FINAL%20060513.pdf

NGSS Lead States. (2013c). *Next Generation Science Standards: For states, by states. Appendix G—Crosscutting concepts.* National Academies Press. https://www.nextgenscience.org/sites/default/files/resource/files/Appendix%20G%20-%20Crosscutting%20Concepts%20FINAL%20edited%204.10.13.pdf

Nichols, S. L., & Berliner, D. C. (2008). Why has high-stakes testing so easily slipped into contemporary American life? *Phi Delta Kappan, 89*(9), 672–676.

Office of Head Start. (2015). *Head Start early learning outcomes framework: Ages birth to five.* U.S. Department of Health and Human Services, Administration for Families. https://eclkc.ohs.acf.hhs.gov/interactive-head-start-early-learning-outcomes-framework-ages-birth-five

Park, M., Dimitrov, D. M., Patterson, L. G., & Park, D. (2017). Early childhood teachers' beliefs about readiness for teaching science, technology, engineering, and mathematics. *Journal of Early Childhood Research, 15*(3), 275–291.

Parsons, R. D., & Brown, K. S. (2002). *Teacher as reflective practitioner and action researcher.* Wadsworth/Thomson Learning.

Partnership for 21st Century Learning. (2007). *Framework for 21st century learning.* http://www.p21.org/storage/documents/docs/P21_framework_0116.pdf

Partnership for 21st Century Skills. (2009). *Framework for 21st century learning.* https://www.battelleforkids.org/networks/p21/frameworks-resources

Pendergast, E., Lieberman-Betz, R. G., & Vail, C. O. (2017). Attitudes and beliefs of prekindergarten teachers toward teaching science to young children. *Early Childhood Education Journal, 45,* 43–52. https://doi.org/10.1007/s10643-015-0761-y

Petroski, H. (2003). Engineering: Early education. *American Scientist, 91*(3), 206–209.

Piaget, J. (1965). *The moral judgment of the child* (M. Gabain, Trans). Routledge & K. Paul. (Original work published 1932).

Piaget, J. (1971). *The construction of reality in the child.* Ballantine Books.

Piaget, J., & Duckworth, E. (1973). Piaget takes a teacher's look. *Learning, 2*(2), 22–27.

Piaget, J., & Inhelder, B. (1969). Intellectual operations and their development. *Experimental Psychology: ItsSscope and Method, 7,* 147–203.

Portsmore, M., & Milto, E. (2018). Novel engineering in early elementary classrooms. In L. English & T. Moore (Eds.), *Early engineering learning.* Springer.

Prinsley, R., & Baranyai, K. (2015). STEM-trained and job-ready. *Office of the Chief Scientist, 12,* 1–4.

Ramanathan, G., Carter, D., & Wenner, J. (2022). A framework for scientific inquiry in preschool. *Early Childhood Education Journal, 50,* 1263–1277. https://doi.org/10.1007/s10643-021-01259-1

Redmond, A., Thomas, J., High, K., Scott, M., Jordan, P., & Dockers, J. (2011). Enriching science and math through engineering. *School Science and Mathematics, 111*(8), 399–408.

Reiser, B. J., Novak, M., & McGill, T. A. W. (2017). Coherence from the students' perspective: Why the vision of the framework for K–12 science requires more than simply "combining" three dimensions of science learning. *Board on Science Education workshop: Instructional materials for the Next Generation Science Standards.* https://sites.nationalacademies.org/cs/groups/dbassesite/documents/webpage/dbasse_180270.pdf

Sammet, K., & Kekelis, L. (2016). *Changing the game for girls in STEM: Findings on high impact programs and system-building strategies.* https://www.techbridgegirls.org/what-we-do/advocacy-awareness/data-research/

Sarama, J., & Clements, D. H. (2009). Building blocks and cognitive building blocks: Playing to know the world mathematically. *American Journal of Play, 1*(3), 313–337.

Saul, W., & Reardon, J. (Eds.) (1996). *Beyond the science kit: Inquiry in action.* Heinemann.

Serafini, F. (2010). *Classroom reading assessments: More efficient ways to view and evaluate your readers.* Heinemann.

Shouse, A. W., Schweingruber, H. A., & Duschl, R. A. (Eds.). (2007). *Taking science to school: Learning and teaching science in grades K–8.* National Academies Press.

Silver, H. C., & Zinsser, K. M. (2020). The interplay among early childhood teachers' social and emotional well-being, mental health consultation, and preschool expulsion. *Early Education and Development, 31*(7), 1133–1150. https://doi.org/10.1080/10409289.2020.1785267

Spaepen, E., Bowman, B., Day, C. B., Chen, J., Cunningham, C., Donohue, C., Espinosa, L., Gartzman, M., Greenfield, D., Leslie, D., Levine, S., McCray, J., Schauble, L., & Worth, K. (2017). *Early STEM matters: Providing high-quality STEM experiences for all young learners.* Early Childhood STEM Working Group. http://ecstem.uchicago.edu

Tank, K. M., Moore, T. J., Dorie, B. L., Gajdzik, E., Sanger, M. T., Rynearson, A. M., & Mann, E. F. (2018). Engineering in early elementary classrooms through the integration of high-quality literature, design, and STEM + C content. In L. English & T. Moore (Eds.), *Early engineering learning* (pp. 175–201). Springer.

Taylor, M. W. (2013). Replacing the 'teacher-proof' curriculum with the 'curriculum-proof' teacher: Toward more effective interactions with mathematics textbooks. *Journal of Curriculum Studies, 45*(3), 295–321. https://doi.org/10.1080/00220272.2012.710253

Tenenbaum, H. R., & Callanan, M. A. (2008). Parents' science talk to their children in Mexican-descent families residing in the USA. *International Journal of Behavioral Development, 32*(1), 1–12. https://doi.org/10.1177/0165025407084046

Thornburg, D. (2009). Hands and minds: Why engineering is the glue holding STEM together. *Thornburg Center for Space Exploration.* http://www.tcse-k12.org/pages/hands.pdf

Tomlinson, C. A., & Germundson, A. (2007). Teaching as jazz. *Educational Leadership, 64*, 27–31.

Trautmann, N., MaKinster, J., & Avery, L. (2004, April). *What makes inquiry so hard? (and why is it worth it?).* Paper presented at the annual meeting of the National Association for Research in Science Teaching, Vancouver, BC, Canada.

Tu, T. (2006). Preschool science environment: What is available in a preschool classroom? *Early Childhood Education Journal, 33*, 245–251. https://doi.org/10.1007/s10643-005-0049-8

Turkle, S. (Ed.). (2008). *Falling for science: Objects in mind.* MIT Press.

Tuttle, N., Mentzer, G. A., Strickler, L., Bloomquist, D., Hapgood, S., Molitor, S., Kaderavek, J., & Czerniak, C. M. (2017). Exploring how families do science together: Adult–child interactions at community science events.

School Science and Mathematics, 117(5), 175–182. https://doi.org/10.1111/ssm.12221

U.S. Department of Education, Office for Civil Rights. (2016). *Key data highlights on equity and opportunity gaps in our nation's public schools.* https://www2.ed.gov/about/offices/list/ocr/docs/2013-14-first-look.pdf

Van Meeteren, B. (2016, December). *Literacy through science: Literacy activities observed during K–1 science activities.* Paper presented at the conference of Literacy Research Association, Nashville, TN.

Vartuli, S. (1999). How early childhood teacher beliefs vary across grade level. *Early Childhood Research Quarterly, 14*(4), 489–514.

Vedder-Weiss, D., & Fortus, D. (2013). School, teacher, peers, and parents' goals emphases and adolescents' motivation to learn science in and out of school. *Journal of Research in Science Teaching, 50*(8), 952–988.

Venville, G., Wallace, J., Rennie, L. J., & Malone, J. (1998). The integration of science, mathematics, and technology in a discipline-based culture. *School Science and Mathematics, 98*(6), 294–302.

Wan, Z. H., Jiang, Y., & Zhan, Y. (2020). STEM education in early childhood: A review of empirical studies. *Early Education and Development, 32*(7), 672–692.

Warden, C. (2021). *Inquiries: A guide to planning with and for children, Issue 1.* https://www.facebook.com/ClaireWardenLtd/videos/inquiries-issue-1/696987307888329/

Watson, S., Williams-Duncan, O. M., & Peters, M. L. (2022). School administrators' awareness of parental STEM knowledge, strategies to promote STEM knowledge, and student STEM preparation. *Research in Science & Technological Education, 40*(1), 1–20. https://doi.org/10.1080/02635143.2020.1774747

Wheatley, G. H. (1990). Spatial sense and mathematics learning. *Arithmetic Teacher, 37*, 10–11.

Wolfgang, C. H., Stannard, L. L., & Jones, I. (2001). Block play performance among preschoolers as a predictor of later school achievement in mathematics. *Journal of Research in Childhood Education, 15*(2), 173–180.

Wulf, W. (1998). The urgency of engineering education reform. *The Bridge, 28*(1). https://www.nae.edu/7580/TheUrgencyofEngineeringEducationReform

Yanowitz, K. L., & Hahs-Vaughn, D. L. (2016). Adults' perceptions of children's science abilities and interest after participating in a family science night. *School Science and Mathematics, 116*(1), 55–64.

Zimmerman, H. T., & McClain, L. R. (2016). Family learning outdoors: Guided participation on a nature walk. *Journal of Research in Science Teaching, 53*(6), 919–942. https://doi.org/10.1002/tea.21254

Index

The letter *f* after a page number refers to a figure.

About the Editor and the Authors

Allison J. Barness is an assistant professor in the Department of Teaching at the University of Northern Iowa. Her areas of research include professional learning, STEM and literacy connections, and social–emotional learning.

Shelly L. Counsell is a retired associate professor of early childhood education. She is an early childhood consultant and Early Years Columnist with NSTA's *Science & Children*. Her areas of research include early STEM, inclusion, disability studies, diversity, democratic learning communities, and reflective practice.

Mary Donegan-Ritter is an emerita professor of early childhood education at the University of Northern Iowa. Her areas of research include coaching for professional development and STEM curriculum in inclusive early education.

Lawrence Escalada is a professor of physics and science education and director of science education at the University of Northern Iowa. He engages in physics and science education research with a focus on curriculum and professional development and its impact on student learning and teaching practices.

Linda May Fitzgerald is an emerita professor of early childhood education at the University of Northern Iowa. She has coedited and contributed to a variety of books and other publications, primarily with a focus on improving teacher education.

Sherri Peterson is the program coordinator at the Iowa Regents' Center for Early Developmental Education. She has worked as an early childhood special education teacher, Early ACCESS coordinator, consultant, coach, and adult educator for over 4 decades in both rural and urban settings. She is an advocate for equitable learning environments for all children.

Brandy Smith is an early childhood special education consultant with Central Rivers Area Education Agency in Iowa. Her areas of research include social–emotional learning, early childhood outdoor learning environments, and professional development for early childhood educators.

Jill Uhlenberg is an emerita professor of early childhood education. Her primary foci have been on infant and toddler learning, problem solving, and curriculum development, and their relationship to teacher education.

Sarah Vander Zanden is an associate professor of literacy education at the University of Northern Iowa. Her areas of research include critical literacy and literacy teacher education.

Beth Dykstra Van Meeteren is director of the Iowa Regents' Center for Early Developmental Education at the University of Northern Iowa. Her areas of research include early STEM, early engineering, and integrative STEM and literacy.